Progressive Rock Reconsidered

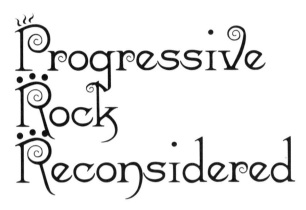

Progressive Rock Reconsidered

Edited by
Kevin Holm-Hudson

Routledge

New York & London

Published in 2002 by
Routledge
29 West 35th Street
New York, NY 10001

Published in Great Britain by
Routledge
11 New Fetter Lane
London EC4P 4EE

Routledge is an imprint of the Taylor & Francis Group.

Printed in the United States of America on acid-free paper.
Design and typography: Jack Donner

10 9 8 7 6 5 4 3 2 1

Library of Congress Cataloging-in-Publication Data

Progressive rock reconsidered / edited by Kevin Holm-Hudson
        p. cm.
    Includes bibliographical references and index.
    ISBN 0–8153–3714–0 (alk. paper)—ISBN 0–8153–3715–9 (pbk.: alk.
paper)
        1. Progressive rock music—History and criticism. I. Holm-Hudson, Kevin.

    ML3534.P76 2001
    781.66—dc21

                                                    2001019231

Contents

Acknowledgments

This book would have never happened without the contributions of many people.

Soo Mee Kwon at Routledge got the ball rolling. Richard Carlin, my editor at Routledge, offered consistently patient, professional, and exacting comments that helped immeasurably to make the manuscript more coherent. Lisa Vecchione, my production editor at Routledge, nurtured the book along through its final stages.

Fred Maus of the University of Virginia led me to some scholars, including Dirk von der Horst and Jennifer Rycenga. The scope of this book was greatly enhanced by his suggestions.

Chuck Lord, at the University of Kentucky, and Virginia Gorlinski, at Northwestern University, made important contributions and helpful comments in reviewing different parts of the manuscript. John Buccheri and Paul Aliapoulios, both of Northwestern University, encouraged the development of a sophomore-level theory class on progressive rock, which shared a symbiotic relationship with the development of this book. I particularly wish to thank my students of that class for their open-mindedness in engaging with a style of rock music that was largely unknown to them.

Paul Whitehead, who designed the covers for a number of vintage progressive rock albums in the 1970s (including Genesis's *Nursery Cryme* and *Foxtrot*) provided our cover art, which was supported in part by funds from the Office of Research and Graduate Studies at the University of Kentucky. I would like to thank them for their support.

Joseph Byrd and Dorothy Moskowitz Falarski of the band United States of America, Ian Williams of Don Caballero, and David Cross of the 1972–74 incarnation of King Crimson graciously answered many questions and provided valuable insights regarding their work with their respective groups.

On a more personal note, I wish to thank my mother for allowing my unfettered collection of progressive rock albums by Emerson Lake and Palmer, King Crimson, and Pink Floyd at an early, impressionable age. My wife Karen tolerated my many visits to used-CD stores and Ebay in the name of "research" and shared my ups and downs at seeing this book through to completion. My children Miranda and Toby offered constant inspiration and humor as they wondered about their dad's taste in "thunky alien music." For these reasons, this book is dedicated to my family.

Introduction

Kevin Holm-Hudson

At this writing, rock music has had a history of nearly half a century—longer if one considers the roots of rock and roll to extend farther back into the work of certain rhythm and blues or country artists. Over the last twenty years, rock's history has become a part of academic study, attracting the attention of researchers in musicology, music theory, gender studies, communications, and social sciences, among other fields. While such diverse perspectives have enriched the study of most genres of popular music, progressive rock has until now been explored primarily by music theorists, musicologists, and fans (who have often lacked a necessary critical perspective). Notable earlier studies of progressive rock—including Bill Martin's *Listening to the Future* and Edward Macan's *Rocking the Classics*—have been written from a largely musicological perspective, and—in the case of Macan's study—have focused exclusively on British progressive rock bands. This book brings together—for comparison and contrast—the work of a variety of authors from a wide range of academic disciplines, to reconsider progressive rock in a way that transcends commonly held stereotypes of the genre. The authors in *Progressive Rock Reconsidered* assume a broader view, one that incorporates textual analysis, sociology, journalism, gender studies, and religious studies as well as hermeneutic study of "the music itself."

From 1969 to about 1977, progressive rock—a style of self-consciously complex rock often associated with prominent keyboards, complex metric shifts, fantastic (often mythological or metaphysical) lyrics, and an emphasis on flashy virtuosity—dominated FM radio and rock album charts. When punk became an ascendant force in popular culture in 1976–77, the excesses and high-cultural pretensions of progressive rock made it an easy target, hastening its demise. Today progressive rock is relegated to a footnote in most rock histories and considered a symptom of 1970s excess rather than a genre worthy of closer examination.

Progressive rock as a *genre* has remained largely unstudied because of its complexity and diversity of styles; this eclecticism also makes it much more difficult to categorize than more homogeneous styles such as reggae or country rock. Indeed, *progressive rock,* as the term was used in the late 1960s, had an even broader meaning than it does today. The phrase was first used by critics such as Lester Bangs to collectively describe a number of emerging styles in the late 1960s, from the "jazz-rock" of bands such as Blood, Sweat and Tears to the Southern rock of the Allman Brothers Band. Each of these styles eventually became established genres, symptomatic of the general fragmentation of the rock audience in the early 1970s. *Progressive rock* came to describe those bands that aimed at incorporating some degree of cultivated musical influence (whether that of nineteenth-century European art music or American jazz) into a rock context.

Progressive rock has also been labeled "art rock," "symphonic rock," or "classical rock." Katherine Charlton, in her book *Rock Music Styles: A History,* prefers the term art rock, noting that "much jazz rock is also progressive rock."[1] Other writers, however, have reserved the term *art rock* for bands that appropriated an image in a cool, ironic fashion reminiscent of 1960s pop artists (Roxy Music, for example) or those that were inspired by trends in avant-garde art (such as the Velvet Underground or Talking Heads). While these bands are not progressive rock groups, these styles do occasionally converge. For example, Roxy Music's first album was produced by erstwhile King Crimson lyricist Peter Sinfield, and former Roxy synthesizer player Brian Eno has not only collaborated with King Crimson guitarist Robert Fripp but also with the Talking Heads. Moreover, some of Fripp's 1970s solo work has revealed him to be as influenced by minimalism as were bands such as the Velvet Underground.

Jerry Lucky, in his book *The Progressive Rock Files,* has come up with what is perhaps the best definition of progressive rock, if only to highlight the diversity within the genre:

> Progressive Rock is music that incorporates:
> * Songs predominantly on the longish side, but structured, rarely improvised.
> * A mixture of loud passages, soft passages, and musical crescendos to add to the dynamics of the arrangements.
> * The use of a Mellotron or string synth[esizer] to simulate an orchestra backing.[2]
> * The possible inclusion of a live symphony orchestra backing.
> * Extended instrumental solos, perhaps involving some improvisation.
> * The inclusion of musical styles from other than a rock format.
> * A blending of acoustic, electric and electronic instruments where each plays a vital role in translating the emotion of compositions which typically contain more than one mood.
> * Multi-movement compositions that may or may not return to a musical theme. In some cases the end section may bear little resemblance to the first part of the song.
> * Compositions created from unrelated parts. . . .[3]

Unfortunately, the potential for any balanced critical appraisal of progressive rock has been tainted by faulty generalizations caused by a lack of familiarity with progressive rock as a whole. Note that Lucky's definition makes no direct mention of classical-rock fusion or of virtuosity, two factors that are often brought up as evidence of "pretension" in progressive rock. Progressive rock has suffered from the misperception that it was a (failed) attempt to merge "classical" music with rock, thereby enabling rock to "progress" beyond its blues-based roots by emphasizing sophistication of structure and virtuosity. Admittedly, that stereotype does apply fairly well to progressive rock's most commercially successful groups such as Yes, Genesis, and Emerson Lake and Palmer (ELP). All three of these bands shared an emphasis on virtuosity and a tendency to explore extended suite-like song structures. All three of these groups also reached their critical zeniths between 1972 and 1974 (Yes with 1972's *Close to the Edge,* Genesis with *The Lamb Lies Down on Broadway* in 1974, and ELP with *Brain Salad Surgery* in 1973), roughly the midpoint of progressive rock's most visible period.

It is hoped that this book will serve to expand the accepted definitions of progressive rock. The chapters on Rush and Pink Floyd, for example—bands whose "progressive" status is sometimes hotly debated, not least by progressive rock's fans—invite the reader to consider whether it is more important to think of progressive rock in terms of its *groups* or in terms of its *musical style(s).* Focusing on the musical aspects of a particular group's output (style) rather than a historical/categorical approach (groups) shows that while the number of enormously successful progressive rock groups was perhaps small, the influence of progressive rock style in the 1970s was significant. A number of 1970s groups—Rush, Kansas, and Jethro Tull—went through a "progressive phase." Even Boston, a group that would hardly be considered "progressive" today, included on their first album the instrumental "Foreplay" (a play on the German word for "prelude," *Vorspiel*), which is a clear nod to the organ style of Keith Emerson of ELP. The influence of progressive rock style on these and other examples of "prog lite" in the 1970s is perhaps an area for further study.

About This Book

This book is divided into three parts. The bulk of the essays, in part 2, focus primarily on some of the major progressive rock groups to make an impact on 1970s rock (Yes, King Crimson, and so on). In some instances there are two contrasting essays on each band, inviting cross-disciplinary comparisons of groups in the progressive rock "canon."

Parts 1 and 3 invite a wider consideration of progressive rock beyond its conventionally assumed historical boundaries. Contrary to some accounts, progressive rock did not spring full-grown, as from the head of a rock Medusa, in 1969; nor did it vanish in 1977. The essay on the United States of America (USA) in part 1 shows that some of the characteristics of progressive rock are found in so-called "experimental-psychedelic" groups of the 1960s. While other authors (Macan, for example) have previously stated that progressive rock was an outgrowth of psychedelia, USA provides compelling evidence for the roots of not only the eclecticism of progressive rock, but also for its highbrow ambitions (some might say pretensions). John Sheinbaum's essay establishes an important context for all of the essays in this book; as he notes, the aesthetics of progressive rock—colored by its educated, avant-garde influences—amount to a virtual negation of conventional rock values. Before rock turned "progressive" it had been characterized by its African-American or "blues" derivation, Dionysian values, and working-class socioeconomic status. As a result of "betraying" these root values, progressive rock was widely condemned by most rock critics even in the face of its popular acceptance and consequent commercial success. The essays in part 2, therefore, reconsider—from various analytical perspectives—the merits of this music that had been so subject to critical vilification.

Part 3 focuses on progressive rock's lingering influence. Although progressive rock no longer dominates the airwaves or the stadium circuit today, its legacy can be found in the countless "neoprogressive" bands that can be found on the Internet and through specialty dealers such as Wayside Music. Progressive rock's influence has also circumspectly manifested itself through the "postrock" of Tortoise and Jessamine, the art-thrash of bands such as Sonic Youth, and the highbrow pastiche of Radiohead. While these bands may protest being labeled "progressive" owing to that term's 1970s connotations, without the precedent of progressive rock those bands would have very different styles. Theo Cateforis's essay on "math rock" at the end of this book explores one of the startling turnarounds of rock history: how progressive rock, formerly blasted into irrelevance by punk, resurfaced in a new guise through the work of certain 1990s alternative bands. The channel between 1970s progressive rock and 1990s alternative has chiefly been through King Crimson, one of the few vintage progressive rock bands to continue "progressing" into the new millennium. The irony is that most "progressive" bands that wear the label have ceased to progress beyond the stylistic conventions established in the 1970s, whereas those bands that continue to progress refuse to accept the progressive label. Even Robert Fripp has sought to revise King Crimson's history by distancing the group from the very genre it helped create.[4]

In short, to situate progressive rock in its proper musical *and* historical context, we must recognize that its story begins well before 1969 and hasn't ended yet (if bands such as Radiohead are any indication). By reconsidering progressive rock not as a monolith but as a "family tree" of various related styles (with a variety and number of bands far exceeding the few stadium-filling "dinosaur" bands of the 1970s), we can come away with a broader sense of the critical value of the genre.

Progressive Rock's Historical Context

Virtuosity in rock was nothing new at the end of the 1960s, but many progressive rock musicians extended the instrumental skills of earlier musicians such as Jimi Hendrix or Eric Clapton to a new level of expertise. In fact, the stage histrionics of Keith Emerson's organ playing with the Nice, and later with ELP—which included stabbing the keyboard with knives and coaxing feedback from the instrument—offer compelling parallels with Hendrix's theatrics. However, the blues-based background of Hendrix or Clapton was supplanted with (but not entirely replaced by) classical ambitions, including literal classical training in the case of Emerson or Yes's Rick Wakeman.

The addition of elements of art music (once considered to be rock's antithesis) to the stylistic melange of rock has its roots, along with so many other innovations, in the music of the Beatles. "In My Life" (from 1965's *Rubber Soul*) features a sped-up "classical" piano solo played by George Martin. At nearly the same time, the Byrds released "She Don't Care About Time," the B-side of their "Turn! Turn! Turn!" single, which incorporated part of Johann Sebastian Bach's "Jesu, Joy of Man's Desiring" in its twelve-string guitar solo. While these isolated art-music references (melodic or stylistic) are of course not progressive rock, they do offer a glimpse of the ripe conditions for experimentation in rock that ultimately led to the progressive genre.

Two more direct predecessors of progressive rock, however, were Procol Harum's "A Whiter Shade of Pale" and the Moody Blues' album *Days of Future Passed,* released in 1967 and 1968, respectively. Procol

Harum's song juxtaposed a Dylanesque lyric (and a piano-and-organ dual keyboard instrumentation that also seemed inspired by Bob Dylan) with an organ line paraphrased from two Bach compositions.[5] *Days of Future Passed* followed in the path blazed by the Beatles' *Sgt. Pepper's Lonely Hearts Club Band* with a concept album exploring the metaphysical implications of a day from dawn to nightfall; it also fed the pseudoclassical ambitions of many a progressive rock band to come by employing a symphonic orchestra. Although the orchestrations appeared to owe more to 1940s Hollywood film scores than to Beethoven, the symphonic qualities of *Days of Future Passed* were further strengthened by making heavy use of the mellotron.

Both "A Whiter Shade of Pale" and *Days of Future Passed* are transitional recordings, coming out of the psychedelic trends that were in vogue in 1967 and also pointing the way toward the emergence of progressive rock. Procol Harum's classical borrowings were but one element in a style that drew more heavily on blues, folk, and music-hall pop; and the Moody Blues' second album, 1968's *In Search of the Lost Chord* (which includes the tribute to Timothy Leary, "Legend of a Mind"), shows their psychedelic allegiances more explicitly.

Nonetheless, the critical adulation given *Sgt. Pepper*—including accolades from the art-music establishment (classical-music critic Joan Peyser, for example, wrote that *Sgt. Pepper* "is an extraordinary work, not just comparable to a new sonata or opera, but far more important. It is a work of art that has sprung from unexpected, nonart roots"[6])—encouraged many rock musicians to think that their music might indeed be "art," and that their recordings were capable of attaining lasting status. As John Covach described it:

> What was distinctive about the progressive-rock movement that arose out of the British-invasion scene . . . was an attitude of art-music "seriousness"—critics often called it pretentiousness—that many of these musicians brought to their music making. Among the most ardent fans of progressive rock at the time, there was the perception that these musicians were attempting to shape a new kind of classical music—a body of music that would not disappear after a few weeks or months on the pop charts, but would instead be listened to (and perhaps even studied), like the music

of Mozart, Beethoven, and Brahms, for years to come. In their sometimes uncompromising adherence to what they took to be lofty art-music standards, progressive-rock musicians often seemed to be more interested in standing shoulder to shoulder with Richard Wagner or Igor Stravinsky than with Elvis Presley or Little Richard.[7]

Progressive Rock and Critical Opinion

Ironically, the "serious" experimental impulses that seemed so right to critics in the psychedelic flowering circa 1967 were declared to have gone horribly wrong by 1977. The words of Paul Morley, assessing the conditions that led to the rise of punk rock, are typical:

> Look back to 1967, and the rich stream of precocious British rock musicians produced some extraordinary music over the next few months: Pink Floyd, Family, Traffic, Nice, Cream, Audience, Fairport Convention, Who etc. Achieving too much too soon, probably unprepared to accept and adapt to the pressure, the musicians of this beginning soon obliviously caused all the problems (and failed to react to them) that helped create the eventual smugness and complacency. Their adventure and neatly applied musical accomplishment ran into a brick wall; the musicians continued, caring little about their indulgence and isolation. . . . The musicians' smugness about their early, often accidental successes erupted into intolerable narrow-mindedness about their newer music and its effects. The music became slicker, the morals slacker. "Progressive rock" emerged out of the little, fascinating, psychedelic-oriented burst of the late sixties, a music of horrible hybrid and clinical, cynical technical superiority. Listeners lapped up its empty complexity. . . . The music drifted further and further away from even the vaguest abstractions of what rock & roll is all about. It became, more and more, music to consume.[8]

The long-standing critical antipathy toward progressive rock has led to a dearth of serious discussion of this genre and its cultural context. For example, the only mention of progressive rock in Clinton

Heylin's 670-page anthology *The Penguin Book of Rock and Roll Writing* is the previous paragraph from Paul Morley. Such a parenthetical inclusion, typical of the majority of rock-history texts, implies that the genre had little impact on the rock soundscape of the 1970s; however, the commercial successes of Yes, Emerson Lake and Palmer, and other progressive rock groups during this period certainly indicate otherwise. ELP, for example, earned five million pounds through live appearances in 1974, surpassed in tour grosses only by the Rolling Stones, the Who, and Led Zeppelin.[9] Album sales are even better documented; for example, Yes had five Top 10 albums between 1972 and 1977, with *Close To The Edge* (1972) peaking highest at number 3.[10] Similar chart success can be found for ELP, Jethro Tull, and Pink Floyd (whose *Dark Side of the Moon* was on *Billboard*'s charts for a record 741 weeks). Although progressive rock was never a genre known for its "singles"— with the notable exception of Pink Floyd's "Money" (number 13 in 1973) and Yes's "Roundabout" (number 13 in 1972)—the success of progressive rock albums, bolstered by airplay of album tracks on FM radio, ensured the continued presence of progressive rock groups on the American arena circuit.

The preoccupation of some progressive rock artists with aspects of serious "art music" was condemned by many mainstream critics as abandonment of rock's roots in the blues; as Morley writes, "the music drifted further and further away from even the vaguest abstractions of what rock & roll is all about." While it is true that progressive rock tended to downplay the explicit blues style (and blues covers) of groups such as Cream or the Rolling Stones, the blues was not ignored altogether. In fact, among the mainstream progressive rock groups, only Genesis seemed to ignore blues influences entirely. Emerson Lake and Palmer frequently used twelve-bar-blues structures in their songs; King Crimson frequently incorporated passages derived from the twelve-bar-blues harmonic progression (from the "Mirrors" section of "21st Century Schizoid Man" in 1969 to the metrically distorted blues progression in the middle of 1974's "Starless"); and even Yes made the Beatles' "I'm Down" a staple of their mid-seventies live shows.

Morley's assertion that progressive rock "became . . . music to consume" also does not hold up under scrutiny. The music of the 1970s *in general* could be described as "music to consume," in large part due to the rapid merging of record labels during this period into multinational conglomerates such as WEA (Warner-Elektra-Atlantic). Disco—with an impact extending to songs such as Rod Stewart's "Do Ya Think I'm Sexy" and the Rolling Stones' "Miss You"—and radio-ready harmonized soft rock by bands such as the Eagles and Fleetwood Mac are perhaps more apt examples of "music to consume," and arguably contributed as much to the general musical stagnation that led to punk's abrasive corrective. The number of comparably successful progressive rock bands of this period could be numbered in the single digits (Yes, ELP, Genesis, Pink Floyd, Jethro Tull, and perhaps, sporadically, King Crimson); others remained "cult" bands with little commercial impact. Clearly most progressive rock bands weren't simply doing it for the money.

It is also a misconception to equate all (or even most) progressive rock with attempts to integrate aspects of art music into the rock medium. This oft-cited merging of the highbrow and lowbrow is the "horrible hybrid" to which Morley refers; as Lester Bangs memorably put it, "Everybody knows Classical-Rock (alternating with -Jazz) Fusions never really work."[11] In fact, only Emerson Lake and Palmer (and, to a lesser extent, Renaissance) incorporated literal classical themes into their work to any great degree; Emerson's solos with ELP frequently quoted from a variety of nonclassical sources as well, from jazz standards (such as "Salt Peanuts") to "Turkey in the Straw."[12] While some groups did experiment with extended suite structures that developed material in a manner reminiscent of classical music, this tendency may also be traced to the Beatles, who connected several previously unrelated songs in a suite-like fashion on 1969's *Abbey Road*. On the other hand, a lesser-known progressive rock scene associated with the Canterbury region of England (exemplified by bands such as Soft Machine and National Health) eschewed the classics in exchange for a jazz-rock orientation.

A Network of Styles

When progressive rock is considered in terms of more than the handful of superstar bands that toured U.S. arenas in the mid-1970s, it is revealed to be an extraordinarily fluid style, bringing together influences as diverse as John Coltrane (Magma), Japanese koto music (Jade Warrior), early music (Gryphon), Béla Bartók (King Crimson), British and Celtic folk music (Jethro Tull), and free improvisation with real-time electronics (early Pink Floyd). Given these many distinct styles, a picture of progressive rock emerges that is somewhat less well defined than the prevailing critical view of it (i.e., "classical" influences, long songs, virtuosity, pretentiousness, British-based), but is richer for it. There is not much common ground between ELP and Jade Warrior, but there is room for both within the genre of progressive rock (and within Jerry Lucky's definition of the genre). Similarly, while groups such as Pink Floyd or Tangerine Dream might not share all of the commonly accepted attributes of progressive rock (virtuosity, for example), they certainly shared overlapping audiences and exhibited the same progressive tendencies toward experimentation and breaking out of traditional rock music song forms.

In fact, Pink Floyd's distinctive contribution to progressive rock is what John Cotner describes as the "quasi-instrumental fantasy" in his essay discussing Pink Floyd's "Careful With That Axe, Eugene." Although Cotner maintains that the "fantasy" is unique to Pink Floyd's work, Gregory Karl independently arrives at a similar conclusion in his examination of the "narrative form" of King Crimson's *Larks' Tongues in Aspic* compositions. Similarly, Emerson Lake and Palmer's "Trilogy," which I analyze in this collection, follows a psychodramatic pattern not unlike the nineteenth-century tone poem, with its emphasis on narrative established through thematic development. The emphasis on suggesting a narrative or merely fantastic imagery through sound alone is another vestige of psychedelia, with the added awareness of nineteenth-century programmatic art music.

In general, it may be more accurate to describe progressive rock as an attempt to merge rock's beat with certain aspects of art music's style, in terms of harmony, metric complexity, or extended form (a "classical influence" in all three of these areas need not be present). The presence of classical elements in this style has until now invited more traditional theoretical analysis, particularly of harmony and form. Dirk von der Horst's essay in this book, therefore, contributes a new approach. In his look at a disputed sonata form in Yes's "Close to the Edge," von der Horst avoids the traditional theoretical examination of "the music itself," instead examining the song from a "reader-response" perspective influenced by scholars in gender studies and feminist criticism. His analysis of the song comes down somewhat closer to traditional negative assessments of progressive rock's "classical aspirations," because he sees such aspirations as contributing to progressive rock's constructions of masculinity.

But Is It Art?

Progressive rock's "art" posturing also would appear to militate against its status as a "music to consume." Bill Martin negotiates this paradox by claiming that progressive rock functioned as a "popular avant-garde":

> In its time, progressive rock represented something unique in the entire history of art: a "popular avant-garde." For most aestheticians and social theoreticians, the very idea is oxymoronic. Supposedly, an avant-garde can only be appreciated by an elite; supposedly, this elite appreciation is part of the very definition of the concept of avant-garde. But we might take a page from Marx, and argue that "once the inner connections are grasped, theory becomes a material force". . . . The point is that the motive forces of society are grasped when a significant part of society is compelled to expand its understanding of these forces. Then this understanding becomes a real force in the lives of many people. As the late sixties gave way to the seventies, many people were prepared by their social experience to be open to experimental, visionary, and utopian music that was brilliantly crafted and performed.[13]

Durrell Bowman makes a similar point in this collection. His argument is that certain rock music following in the wake of early-'70s British progressive rock served as an "alternative classical music" for young, white, suburban and working-class North American and British males. This included the late-'70s "progressive hard rock" of the Canadian band Rush, the music of which inscribed a peculiar, experimental individualism (which itself contradicts the countercultural/Marxist utopian thesis espoused by Macan and Martin), but one that made use of various musical elements common to progressive rock, including extended formal constructions, instrumental virtuosity, and complex metrical patterns.

Gregory Karl, in one of the Internet discussions that took place during this book's formative stages, concurred with this view of progressive rock as an "alternative classical music," noting that

> [progressive rock was] created or intended as art and was, not uncommonly, received in that spirit as well. Moreover, some of it . . . was, apparently, consciously created under the same aesthetic premises as much western art music of the nineteenth and twentieth centuries—that music captures important aspects of internal life, that it invites deep spiritual involvement, etc. Of course, such ambitious intentions are apt to come off as pretensions when reach exceeds grasp. But on its own terms . . . [progressive rock] captures some aspects of the '70s Zeitgeist extraordinarily well, particularly, in its portraits of terror. I suspect that some of this music will be of interest to future generations who want to broaden their understanding of what life was like for the first generation growing up under the shadow of mutual assured destruction.[14]

Thus, while progressive rock may not always explicitly draw from nineteenth-century art-music models, its "popular avant-garde" orientation as argued by Martin certainly seems logical. In fact, Joseph Byrd of the American band The United States of America claims today that the group aimed to introduce the techniques of the avant-garde into a rock context. Their sole album (which predated the 1969 release of King Crimson's *In The Court of The Crimson King*, considered by most writers to be the first true progressive rock album) can be regarded as an early experiment with many of the same techniques and ideals that came to distinguish progressive rock (see "The 'American Metaphysical Circus' of Joseph Byrd's United States of America" in this volume).

Expanding beyond the high-culture positioning of the musical "text" in progressive rock, one can observe a similar influence in progressive rock's lyrics. Classic works of literature influenced a number of progressive rock songs. While this is certainly not true of all such songs, and although there are again psychedelic-era precursors (for example, Jefferson Airplane's "White Rabbit," based on Lewis Carroll's *Adventures of Alice in Wonderland*, or Cream's "Tales of Brave Ulysses," inspired by Homer's *Odyssey*), an unusual number of progressive rock songs are inspired by ambitious, occasionally even obscure literary sources. Genesis's "The Fountain of Samalcis," for example, is an adaptation of the myth of the first hermaphrodite found in the *Metamorphoses* of Ovid (4.285–388). Yes's vocalist/lyricist Jon Anderson has related that the lyrics to "The Gates of Delirium" were inspired by a reading of Leo Tolstoy's *War and Peace.*[15] Samuel Taylor Coleridge's poem *The Rime of The Ancient Mariner* not only inspired Rush's "Xanadu" (discussed by Durrell Bowman in this volume), but also an entire concept album by David Bedford. Homer's *Odyssey* was the inspiration for King Crimson's "Formentera Lady" and "The Sailor's Tale" on their *Islands* album (1971).

A more unusual literary source led to the making of Yes's *Tales from Topographic Oceans* in 1973; the entire eighty-minute, two-album composition is based on a single footnote found in Paramahansa Yogananda's *Autobiography of a Yogi.* The obscurity of this reference— and the length of the album it generated—added fuel to critics' charges that progressive rock was self-indulgent and pretentious; indeed, *Tales* has retained a special notoriety as emblematic of all that was critically "wrong" with progressive rock. Jennifer Rycenga examines the literary and religious symbolism in Yes's work of this period, both on *Tales* and *Relayer.* Her findings regarding Jon Anderson's familiarity with Hinduism are perhaps not surprising, but what is surprising is that this aspect of *Tales* has not been previously considered.

Sometimes the literary connection has to do more with a general style than an individual work. The lyrics of Pink Floyd's Roger Waters espouse a remarkably consistent existentialist worldview; it is this consistency of vision, according to Deena Weinstein, that raises Waters's lyrics to transcend their genre and become "art." Weinstein also situates Waters's lyrics within other prevailing social and literary trends of the late 1960s, including the antiwar movement and naturalistic romanticism.

The "serious" subject matter of progressive rock songs did not escape the ironic commentary of its own practitioners. Jethro Tull, for example, took the literary preoccupations of their peers to satirical extremes by conceiving *Thick As A Brick* (1972) as a setting of an epic poem by the (fictitious) writer Gerald "Little Milton" Bostock. More recently, King Crimson's "Dinosaur" (from 1995's *THRAK*) is, according to lyricist Adrian Belew, literally about a dinosaur; yet, with its guitar-synthesizer timbres that evoke the sound of mellotrons and Robert Fripp's famous remarks in 1974 about progressive "dinosaur bands," a more ironic interpretation is hard to resist. Brian Robison discusses the factors contributing to widespread fan misinterpretation of "Dinosaur" in this volume; his essay also raises pertinent questions about how progressive rock has become "fossilized" as a historical category rather than a musical one.

At the root of progressive rock's so-called highbrow positioning, both musically and lyrically, is the sociology of its audience, which was markedly different from that of other contemporary rock styles. Class distinctions are particularly important in Britain, a rock culture that "prefers its heroes, if not genuinely working-class, at least superficially so."[16] Edward Macan, in his excellent study *Rocking the Classics: English Progressive Rock and the Counterculture,* has pointed out that British progressive rock groups virtually without exception were formed and nurtured in universities or the British equivalent of private schools. Their members made no effort to conceal their upper-middle-class background, an attitude critics condemned as elitist.[17] Furthermore, the British progressive rock scene has its roots in the south of Britain, an area more upper-class and white-collar than areas farther north. Macan writes, "Obviously, a style like progressive rock, with its references not only to classical music but also to the art and literature of high culture, was not going to spring from a working-class environ. Its emergence depended on a subculture of highly educated young people."[18] Conversely, the emergence of punk is linked to its roots among the large numbers of disenfranchised, working-class youth who were marginalized from this elite demographic that had been at the core of the progressive rock audience. When one considers the allegiance of most mainstream rock critics to the ideal of rock as a working-class form of cultural expression, it is easy to understand why progressive rock was so vilified by critics in its day, and airbrushed from latter-day rock histories as an anomaly.

Battle lines need not be drawn, however. Rock has always been shamelessly eclectic, even parasitic in its appropriation of musical styles and extramusical references; at its peripheries, the distinctions truly become sloppy. More recent progressive groups such as Ozric Tentacles add reggae to their mix of styles, and the Orb self-consciously draw on progressive rock's legacy even as they continue to be categorized as an "ambient techno" band. "Chamber progressive" or "avant-prog" groups such as Thinking Plague are perhaps better described as contemporary classical ensembles with a rhythm section. (Some of the members of Thinking Plague even perform live using scores and music stands—as did, for that matter, The United States of America.) "Post-progressive" groups such as Don Caballero and Radiohead also draw upon selective aspects of vintage progressive rock, even as they actively seek to distance themselves from associations with the genre. Given these examples, one may indeed wonder where progressive rock "ends" and becomes psychedelia, free jazz, experimental art music, or heavy metal.

Progressive rock is a style far more diverse than what is heard from its mainstream groups and what is implied by unsympathetic critics. In fact, CD stores with a separate "progressive" section often continue to file ELP, Rush, Yes, and the other more popular progressive groups in their mainstream "rock/pop" section. It is this rich complexity of styles—not just its intricacy of arrangements or the virtuosity of some of its musicians—that enables progressive rock to maintain a devoted and growing "taste public" years after being consigned to the ash bin of irrelevance by rock critics. In this sense, perhaps progressive rock has indeed become the "alternative classical" music suggested by Covach and Bowman, even as traditional art music repertories find themselves forced by declining and aging audiences to market themselves in ever more innovative ways.

Notes

1. Katherine Charlton, *Rock Music Styles: A History* (Boston: McGraw-Hill, 1998), 164.
2. A mellotron is a keyboard instrument that functions somewhat like an analog version of today's digital samplers. The keyboards generally came with several factory-preset sounds, including a choir, strings, and flutes.

Pushing down a key would trigger a tape of, for example, strings playing the desired pitch.

3. Jerry Lucky, *The Progressive Rock Files* (Burlington, ON: Collector's Guide Publishing, 1998), 120–21.

4. Robert Fripp, "Afterword One: Prog Rock and Its Criminals." Booklet notes to King Crimson, *Epitaph* (Discipline Global Mobile compact disc DGM9607, 1997), 43.

5. The two Bach pieces alluded to in "A Whiter Shade of Pale" are the "Air on a G String" from the *Orchestral Suite No. 3 in D Major,* BWV 1068, and the fourth movement (chorale) from the cantata *Wachet Auf, Ruft Uns die Stimme,* BWV 140.

6. Joan Peyser, "The Beatles and The Beatless," in Jonathan Eisen, ed. *The Age of Rock, vol. 1* (New York: Vintage Books, 1969), 131.

7. John Covach, "Progressive Rock, 'Close to the Edge,' and the Boundaries of Style." In John Covach and Graeme M. Boone, eds. *Understanding Rock: Essays in Musical Analysis* (New York: Oxford University Press, 1997), 4.

8. Paul Morley, "New Pop UK." In Clinton Heylin, ed. *The Penguin Book of Rock and Roll Writing* (New York: Viking, 1992), 201–2.

9. Paul Stump, *The Music's All That Matters: A History of Progressive Rock* (London: Quartet Books, 1998), 184.

10. Joel Whitburn, *The Billboard Book of Top 40 Albums* (New York: Billboard Books, 1995), 340–41.

11. Lester Bangs, "Exposed! The Brutal Energy Atrocities of Emerson Lake and Palmer." *Creem,* March 1974: 43.

12. In this respect, Emerson's performance practice may be regarded as descending from the soloing of Jimi Hendrix. See, for example, Hendrix's "Strangers in the Night" quotation in the middle of his performance of "Wild Thing" at the 1967 Monterey Pop Festival, or his quick reference to the Beatles' "I Feel Fine" in his often-bootlegged performance of "Hey Joe/Sunshine Of Your Love" on Lulu's January 1969 TV special.

13. Bill Martin, *Listening to the Future: The Time of Progressive Rock* (Chicago: Open Court Press, 1998), 2.

14. Gregory Karl, personal communication with the editor, July 28, 1999.

15. Martin, *Listening,* 233.

16. Nick Logan and Bob Woffinden, "Genesis." In *The Illustrated Encyclopedia of Rock* (New York: Harmony Books, 1977), 91.

17. Edward Macan, *Rocking the Classics: English Progressive Rock and the Counterculture* (New York: Oxford University Press, 1997). See especially chapter 7, "A Sociology of Progressive Rock," 144–66, and chapter 8, "The Critical Reception of Progressive Rock," 167–78.

18. Macan, *Rocking,* 147.

References

Bangs, Lester. "Exposed! The Brutal Energy Atrocities of Emerson Lake & Palmer." *Creem*, March 1974, 40–44, 76–78.

————. "The Progressives: Rock Stylizations from Brahms to the Auto-Destruct Guitar." In Richard Robinson and the editors of *Creem*, eds. *Rock Revolution: From Elvis to Alice: The Whole Story of Rock and Roll.* New York: Curtis Books, 1973.

Charlton, Katherine. *Rock Music Styles: A History.* Boston: McGraw Hill, 1998.

Covach, John, and Graeme M. Boone, eds. *Understanding Rock: Essays in Musical Analysis.* New York: Oxford University Press, 1997.

Eisen, Jonathan, ed. *The Age of Rock, vol. 1.* New York: Vintage Books, 1969.

Heylin, Clinton, ed. *The Penguin Book of Rock and Roll Writing.* New York: Viking, 1992.

Logan, Nick, and Bob Woffinden. *The Illustrated Encyclopedia of Rock.* New York: Harmony Books, 1977.

Lucky, Jerry. *The Progressive Rock Files.* Burlington, ON: Collector's Guide Publishing, 1998.

Macan, Edward. *Rocking the Classics: English Progressive Rock and the Counter-culture.* New York: Oxford University Press, 1997.

Martin, Bill. *Listening to the Future: The Time of Progressive Rock.* Chicago: Open Court Press, 1998.

Rees, Dafydd, and Luke Crampton. *Dorling Kindersley Encyclopedia of Rock Stars.* New York: Dorling Kindersley, 1996.

Stump, Paul. *The Music's All That Matters: A History of Progressive Rock.* London: Quartet Books, 1998.

Whitburn, Joel. *The Billboard Book of Top 40 Albums.* New York: Billboard Books, 1995.

part 1

History Context

1

Progressive Rock and the Inversion of Musical Values

John J. Sheinbaum

Critical response to 1970s progressive rock was often brutal. Critics decried the genre's virtuosity, complexity, and indebtedness to "classical," or "art" music as a betrayal of rock's origins. At its core, rock journalists' reaction against the style stemmed from a countercultural political agenda: rock is supposed to be a rebellious music, a music that shocks the "establishment" and challenges its conventions. A style of rock so influenced by the music of the establishment—which seemed to aspire to the privileged status held by that music—could only be met with derision; indeed, progressive rock musicians were seen as no less than "war criminals."[1] Critics did not assert their program baldly in reviews, however; these were, after all, supposedly well-reasoned considerations of a given album. Writers hunted for a mode of criticism that would seem to attack the "music itself" to justify their preformed final judgment. "Authenticity" was characteristically the key weapon: the farther a progressive rock album was from rock's rhythm-and-blues roots, from the ideals of a "natural" unstudied simplicity, the more seditious and treasonous the result.[2]

In John Koegel's *Rolling Stone* review of *The Yes Album* (1971),[3] for example, the simplicity represented by brief radio-friendly singles is missed: "The material consists of fewer short songs and more lengthy pieces. The only three-minute tracks on this record are 'The

Clap,' Steve Howe's acoustic guitar quickie recorded at one of Yes' concerts in London, and 'A Venture,' a straightforward rocker sandwiched between a pair of longer compositions on the second side." Songs of the desired length are not very important—they come across like "quickies" and "straightforward" tunes—while the focus is on the long pieces, characteristically described as "compositions." The musical complexities are seen as unfortunate: Richard Cromelin's review of *Fragile* (1972) asserts that "they're good and they know it, so they tend to succumb to the show-off syndrome."[4] Self-consciousness is at issue here; "authentic" artists engage their music intuitively, while these musicians highlight surface virtuosity simply because they can. Their music is always mediated by technical display, which stands between artist and audience, and distances listeners from the music. The opening words of the Yes entry in *The Rolling Stone Album Guide* neatly summarize critical opinion: "Pointlessly intricate guitar and bass solos, caterwauling keyboards, quasi-mystical lyrics proclaimed in an alien falsetto, acid-dipped album-cover illustrations: this British group wrote the book on art-rock excess."[5] From the perspective of rock journalists, the displays of technique don't communicate deep feelings and important messages; the strange and excessive tone colors stand in the way of natural expression; and the difficult-to-understand lyrics and visuals are not aimed at the common listener. All of the things that rock music *should* be doing, in their view, are not accomplished—or even attempted—in the progressive rock style.

Thus, when considering progressive rock within a more general history of rock music, the style and its chief progenitors appear as little more than a blip on the radar screen. In Robert Palmer's *Rock and Roll: An Unruly History*, the longtime contributing editor to *Rolling Stone* includes no discussion at all of the progressive rock phenomenon during the early 1970s, nor are there even references to most of the major bands.[6] Even more telling is John Rockwell's "Art Rock" essay in the *Rolling Stone Illustrated History of Rock and Roll*.[7] His portrait of rock history, from the perspective of the mid-1970s, takes the shape of an "organic" narrative chronicling a rise, maturity, and decline.[8] While the *progressive* label would seem to imply forward movement, Rockwell instead sees the style as a clear sign of rock's decadence and decay: "[T]here is a morphology to artistic movements. They begin with a rude and innocent vigor, pass into a healthy adulthood and finally decline into an overwrought, feeble old age. Something of this process can be observed in the passage of rock and roll from the three-chord primitivism of the Fifties through the burgeoning vitality and experimentation of the Sixties to the hollow emptiness of much of the so-called progressive or 'art' rock of the Seventies."[9] Authenticity is once again the key. Rock's roots are wrapped up in notions of the natural and simple, and a second stage of "vital" maturity occurs in the 1960s rock of the politically conscious counterculture. But progressive rock, which supposedly eschews those roots in favor of "artistic" complexities, results in a "hollow emptiness," in a degeneration of rock's former glory.

These considerations tie together the very different examples included in Jimmy Guterman and Owen O'Donnell's humorous book *The Worst Rock 'n' Roll Records of All Time.*[10] The entries on their list are almost always one of two types: either crass commercial product—think Milli Vanilli—or pretentious, self-indulgent progressive rock. The poles come together with respect to the hallowed concept of authenticity, for both "slick product" and "incomprehensible complexities" are seen as avoiding the natural and simple, the province of "real rock." Given progressive rock's supposedly small role in rock history, the style warrants more than its fair share of attention in the book. Over 20 percent of the "33 1/3 Rules of Rock and Roll" are addressed to the style: "Rock-and-roll songs with an orchestral choir are bound to be horrible. . . . Rock lyrics are not poetry. . . . The quality of a rock-and-roll song is inversely proportional to the number of instruments on it." Subtlety is not exactly the order of the day; rule 22 states that "formidable technical proficiency is never sufficient. This rule explains why art rock is always bad."[11] Signs associated with the art music tradition—whether the sound of a choir, poetic texts, the grandiosity of thick instrumentation, or even polished technique itself—are all seen as masking an inherent emptiness at the core.

Taken as a whole, the conventional criticisms of progressive rock highlight a special sort of value problem for the style. What is notable is not the critical disdain itself, but the *mode* of criticism, because it draws upon a value system diametrically opposed to the one most often used to evaluate music in Western society. Consider table 1.1, which outlines many of the ways genres, styles, repertories, or even individual pieces are often split into "high" and "low" categories. The parameters considered here cover "the music itself," as well as aspects of context and reception. Of course, the list does not represent any sort of "truth"; rather, these are common strategies used to argue that a given piece of music is worthy (a "high" piece) or not (a "low" piece).

Although these notions often masquerade as objective evaluations,

Table 1.1. Conventional "High"/"Low" Dichotomies.

	"High"	"Low"
Label:	"Classical"	"Pop," "Rock," etc.
Forces:	Orchestra	Electric/electronic instruments
Coherence:	"Unified," with "development"— material repeated, but with important differences	"Repetitive"
Historical force:	Traditional	Trendy, momentary in importance
Site:	Mind (intellectual)	Body (sexual)
Difficulty:	Complicated	Simple, common
Response:	Moving	Uninteresting
Background:	Professional training	Rough, casual, natural
Audience:	Fancy dress; silent attention	Comfortable; talking and applause
Class and Education:	Upper class, elite, well educated	Middle and low social strata, not highly educated
Purpose:	Abstract contemplation	Entertainment, background
"Author":	Composer	Performer
Originality:	Innovative	Derivative
Skill:	Genius	Craftsperson

we can more properly recognize them as windows to certain biases and agendas. Indeed, the dichotomies listed are all familiar ones. "High" music in the Western tradition uses the tone colors and forces of the art-music tradition, while "low" music is filled with the trendiest sounds of artificial electric and electronic instruments. "High" music is said to be unified through organic processes of thematic development, distinct from the mere machine-like repetitions of "low" music. "High" music is complicated and innovative, stemming from people with high degrees of professional training, while "low" music is simple and derivative, the product of natural, casual craftspeople. "High" music is created by a composer, ideally a genius, who fixes the piece in a score, while "low" music is reproduced by performers who take liberties with the "music itself" at each playing. A related notion, then, is that "high" music is timeless, removed from its context and only about its internal structures; "low" music is instead a part of its context, which is inherently fleeting. The audience for "high" music is a well-educated elite who allow the music to work on their intellect as they sit, well-dressed, at silent attention; their "low" counterparts come from lower social strata, and allow music to entertain them and to affect their bodies as they dance, talk, and respond with applause when so moved. These qualities don't really tell us much about the music at all, but they speak volumes on what we conventionally value.[12]

What is fascinating about the critical reception of progressive rock, however, is that the very signs commonly held as sources of value in the reception of Western music in general have become signs of the very opposite within the context of rock criticism. Table 1.2 lists many characteristics associated with progressive rock, and as can easily be seen, on its face the style appears to strive toward the realm of "high" music. The treatment of thematic material, rhythm and meter, harmony, and formal shape all tend toward the complex, at least from the point of view of standard rock music. Long compositions, multimovement structures, a focus on virtuosic instrumental sections, and an evocation of "orchestral" timbres all signal parallels to the symphonic repertory. And the audience, especially in the original context for the style (late 1960s–early 1970s southern England), is drawn from the white, educated, male, upper middle class—a privileged socioeconomic stratum, to be sure.

Table 1.2. Stylistic Characteristics of Progressive Rock (Derived from Edward Macan).

Soundscape:	Reaching "beyond" conventional rock instrumentation; explorations of sound; focus on keyboards; acoustic versus electric sections
Thematic material:	Use of riffs (short repeating ideas); potential for "development" reminiscent of classical music
Rhythm & meter:	Syncopations, tricky rhythms; less reliance on 4/4 time signature
Harmonic progression:	Less reliance on "three-chord" songs, and the simplest chords
Lyrical material:	Mythology, nature, utopia versus technology, modernism; surrealism
Visual material:	Elaborate surrealistic album covers; elaborate stage shows
Influences:	Use of blues, jazz, classical, folk, the Anglican Church, "exotic" musics
Length:	Longer songs; toward whole album (concept album) structures
Deployment of band:	Long instrumental sections; less focus on singer (tenor); virtuoso playing; "choral" vocal arrangements
Form:	Embellishment of traditional shapes (AABA, verse-chorus); less reliance on traditional shapes; unconventional forms
Site:	Toward the mind; less focus on the (dancing) body
Historical period:	Considered "flourishing" in the early- to mid-1970s
Historical setting:	Originally southern England, especially the London area; then, in the United States
Cultural influences:	Psychedelia, late-1960s counterculture (against "establishment," largely metaphorical)
Audience:	White, educated, upper middle class; slight differences in the United States.
Gender:	Primarily male musicians; primarily male audience

However, from the point of view of the large majority of rock critics, the trappings of "high" music were not signals of value at all, or—perhaps more sharply stated—were merely signals of *conventional* value. The dreaded "establishment" and its institutions had a great stake in continuing to assert the value of "high" culture. Rock music, meanwhile, potentially possessed great societal power in its embodiment of a countercultural program, in its ability to challenge conventions of value with shocking efficacy. Removed from its historical context, it would seem that rock, a "low" genre, had led to the advent of progressive rock, a style of rock that could be considered "high" music. But at a time when such intimations of value were being called into question, those very signs of prestige left progressive rock with the overwhelmingly negative critical opinion it received.[13] This reception represented no less than a *complete inversion of musical values*: striving for the conventionally "high," as progressive rock was said to do, was devalued, and aspects conventionally ascribed to "low" music were prized.

A corollary point must be made: progressive rock's defenders, the musicologists and music theorists who are in an institutional position to answer these widespread criticisms, largely agree that progressive rock displays strong connections to "high" music. Analytic tools and language derived from the study of Western art music, and the implicit value judgments associated with them, are employed in such a way that analyses of progressive rock parallel analyses of "classical" music. Edward Macan's *Rocking the Classics*, the most complete, and in many ways effective, study of progressive rock thus far published is a case in point. Macan is sympathetic to the concerns of the "new musicologists" whose program is to deconstruct the conventional value systems: he is ready to "challenge virtually every assumption that my academic training had imbued in me"; and he resists "the musicologist's temptation to make this book primarily an analytical study of progressive rock. I believe that rock . . . is as much a cultural practice as a musical style, and that the sonic element—the music itself—is not necessarily the 'primary' text."[14] The centerpiece of the book, however, is an analysis of four different progressive rock pieces, and Macan's concerns do not result in a different sort of analytical technique. The discussion of Emerson Lake and Palmer's "Tarkus" focuses on the tonal plan, without questioning the meaning that overall tonic-to-dominant-to-tonic motion might have in a work like this; Yes's "Close to the Edge" is explained with (often questionable) analogies to sonata form, yet the assumptions behind why such a model might lend value to this piece go unexplored; the piano introduction to Genesis's "Firth of Fifth," filled with pop-derived and ragtime-like figuration, is described as an "overture" that utilizes "*fortspinnung*" as in a "Baroque toccata."[15]

A slightly earlier and less self-conscious example can be found in Nors S. Josephson's 1992 *Musical Quarterly* article on progressive rock.[16] "Classical" terminology is used to describe just about everything: bubblegum pop "la la" refrains are considered a use of "Renaissance madrigal idioms"; repeating riffs are described as "Baroque passacaglia" patterns or "Classical/Romantic variation structures"; vocal techniques range from "recitative-like" to emphatically "operatic"; and so on. It is not that there are no factual connections between these aspects of rock music and stylistic or formal tendencies in the art-music tradition, but that describing rock with the terminology of "high" music often seems to be an end in itself. The implicit message is that this music can be understood as *good* music because it can be written about in a similar manner to the music of the "great tradition."[17] Although progressive rock's critics and defenders draw very different conclusions about the style's value, there is widespread agreement on the level of observation: progressive rock is a musical style shot through with both surface and structural affinities for and connections to "classical" music.

A result of strictly adhering to these value systems, whether the conventional sort applied to "high" music or the negative image used for evaluating rock music, is that critics and scholars alike seem to value stylistic purity. A "pure" music would transparently reflect a given system of value; indeed, a piece's value would seem to be derived from the degree to which it matched expectations. Thus in many cases, a lack of purity by itself is cause for criticism. For example, Robert Christgau, the influential, longtime record reviewer for the *Village Voice*, has written critically about Yes: "They segue effortlessly from Bach to harpsichord to bluesy rock and roll and don't mean to be funny."[18] Rockwell denigrates progressive rock as "pastiche," as "the free and often febrile switching among different styles within the same piece."[19] The best example comes from Lester Bangs, who describes Emerson Lake and Palmer's music as "the insidious befoulment of all that was gutter pure in rock."[20] The inversion of musical values is perfectly captured: rock, while a "gutter" music, is still best when it is "pure," and to add influences of and references to the establishment's "high" music is to "befoul" it in an "insidious" manner. Both classical and rock musics are supposed to be pure; to mix the two results in something "funny," in a mongrel "pastiche" of styles.

The problem with this view is that little in the world exhibits a true purity, least of all a musical style like progressive rock. Notions of purity are more properly recognized as the product of abstract critical systems, not deep understandings of real examples. To value purity is, in a sense, to put the cart before the horse: instead of drawing a critical method from the music, the music is instead held up to a standard that it cannot hope to meet, except perhaps in the most stereotypical examples. As table 1.2 shows, progressive rock is doomed along these lines, because a hallmark of the style is precisely its widespread eclecticism. The rock critic treats the music as conventionally "high"—a clear signal that this is "bad" rock music—or as a stylistically impure music, resulting in the same conclusion. The university music professor treats it as conventionally "high" music as well—though here it's simply a sign of value in and of itself—and through the use of traditional analytical language, leaves eclecticism off the table, because "impurities" would be a problem.

Neither of the equal-but-opposite value systems constructed around classical and rock musics illuminate progressive rock convincingly. As obvious as it sounds, progressive rock, for all its "classical" leanings, is still a subgenre of rock music; any value system that relies on notions of stylistic purity will either find the style lacking or do violence to it by explaining so-called impurities away. Instead, a more fruitful approach can be developed by relocating these strict systems, using them as opposite ends of a spectrum that defines the wide range of possibilities available within the style's inherent eclecticism.[21] Thus, instead of leaving the "low" aspects of progressive rock off the table (whether by taking them for granted or pretending that they don't exist), or considering progressive rock as a successful "fusion [of] rock and art-music practices,"[22] I believe we should highlight the tensions, frictions, and incompatibilities among these very different musical value systems. The progressive rock repertory does not construct a synthesis at all, but instead occupies the spaces *between* these value systems. Often, the same song—sometimes the very same passage—can be read in contradictory ways, and the dialectic itself can be the focus of discussion.

To demonstrate that progressive rock conforms to no single musical value system, I will present a close reading of Yes's "Roundabout," one of the first progressive rock singles to achieve commercial success. These observations are not meant to represent an exhaustive analysis of "Roundabout"; rather, they are fragmentary discussions that accentuate the ways very different modes of understanding music can be juxtaposed and simultaneously evoked.

Dialectical Tensions in "Roundabout"

"Roundabout," and the album *Fragile*, from which it was drawn, represent strong examples of commercially viable progressive rock. Yes's previous effort, *The Yes Album* (1971), while performing much more strongly than their first two records in America, barely cracked the Top 40. *Fragile*, on the other hand, shot up the charts: by the end of February 1972 the album reached as high as number 4 in *Billboard*, and before the end of April the album had been certified as gold, selling over half a million copies. "Roundabout" did quite well as the album's single, peaking at number 13. In addition, *Fragile* began an extended period of success in the marketplace for Yes; all of their remaining studio albums during the 1970s reached the Top 10.

My focus here on "Roundabout" makes no claim that the song is one of the best, or even most representative, examples of the repertory we call progressive rock, although it is an exceptionally strong song that remains a staple in the Yes canon even decades later. Indeed, the importance of "Roundabout" is best seen from the point of view of its reception. The popular understanding of the progressive rock style is best shown by studying a hit single by one of the most successful progressive rock outfits.

An exploration of "Roundabout," therefore, can help us to gain a deeper understanding of how progressive rock is interpreted against the background of different musical value systems. I will focus on three general areas, each of which suggests how this song thematizes tensions between, in gross terms, conventional "classical" and "rock" (or more broadly, "vernacular music") values: tensions between "high" and "low"; between traditions of musical fixity and improvisation; and between modes of understanding music primarily as sonic structure or as cultural product.

"High" versus "Low"

The introduction to "Roundabout" (0:00–0:43) is, in many ways, the locus of the song's stylistic references to the art-music tradition. The first sound heard, simple as it may be, strikes against the background of rock conventions: a crescendo. Regardless of the actual volume at which a rock song is played, it is almost always interpreted as loud. Fine gradations of dynamic level, while an essential part of the mixing process in the studio, are used to address relative balances among the different elements on the recording, but the overall dynamic level is quite static, save for an occasional explicit contrast between a "soft" section and the rest of the song. Yet one of the defining stylistic characteristics of the art-music tradition, at least from the middle of the eighteenth century onward, was an ensemble's ability to effect large-scale continuous gradations of volume. Thus the "orchestral" timbre of the backward-taped piano chord rising from inaudible to strikingly loud that opens "Roundabout" is not a neutral event. It is heard as a reference to, and an intimation of, the sonic qualities of "classical" music. Within just the first few seconds, the song seems to announce that what will follow is decidedly *not* going to be your standard rock-and-roll fare.

Immediately following the opening crescendo, the sound of Steve Howe's nylon-string classical guitar continues to construct the network of "classical" associations. The harmonics and brief phrases around E minor are out of time, cadenza-like, and the hushed and intimate atmosphere invites one to settle in and listen closely. The classical guitar reference, however, is in certain ways out of historical sync with the crescendo reference, because much of the guitar's repertory stems from lute music of the seventeenth century and earlier. At the return of the introduction in the middle of the song (4:57–5:49), the classical guitar timbre is joined by another reference to "high" music, an organ played with virtuosic figuration. The final use of the introduction music occurs at the very end of the song, during the "outro" (7:52–8:29). Here, a harmonic twist provides another art-music reference. At the end of the introduction, with classical guitar simultaneously playing bass line and melody, a descending sequence arrives on the tonic E minor to begin the first verse section. However, when that descending idea returns to conclude the entire song, the arrival on the expected tonic is changed to an E major sonority, and this final chord is held until the sound fades naturally. The use of the "Picardy third" to end the song, a formula first widespread in the sixteenth century and most characteristic of minor-key pieces of the Baroque era, is the last in the chain of "high" references that characterizes the introduction and its related sections. Though the allusions are somewhat haphazard from a historical point of view, they collectively create an atmosphere in which "Roundabout" can be heard in light of art-music practices.[23]

Yet that is only the beginning of the story; the introduction and its related passages can also be interpreted outside the "classical" orbit. The second guitar phrase concludes on a held low C, the sixth scale degree in the key of E minor. A second "backwards-piano" crescendo occurs at this point, on C, and at its peak is immediately followed by the reentry of the guitar, once again on E minor. But this harmonic motion, from VI to i in E minor, is decidedly not the harmonic syntax characteristic of strict common practice period music; one would expect the submediant to descend a half step to the dominant, and then proceed unproblematically to the tonic. Here, though, even through the web of art-music references, a less formal motion derived from modal practice—one much more characteristic of rock music—is used.

The organ figuration during the internal statement of the introduction is worth revisiting as well. One can talk about the technique necessary to perform these quick arpeggiations, and even, perhaps, about the "development" from the introduction to this moment, because the organ fleshes out the harmonic background only implied in the song's opening passages. But above all, Rick Wakeman's organ here creates an "effect": as a way of setting the lyric's intimations of nature, specifically "the lake," at this point, the undulating passagework and round timbre create the sonic equivalent of a peacefully burbling

stream.[24] There are, of course, many art-music precedents of construct-
ing similar textures; but from the perspective of values, how music is
conventionally *supposed* to be understood, such an extramusical
description would be considered a surface phenomenon at best, one
that does little to plumb the depths of meaning in the artwork's structure. This middle moment in "Roundabout," though, seemingly *asks* to
be heard as a coloristic effect; to do so is not to argue that the music is
lacking depth, but to argue that the "high" system of musical value is
not the only, or most important, arbiter of what is essential in this song.

The "high"/"low" tensions become even clearer when considering
the introduction alongside the two main sections of the song, the verse
and chorus (see figs. 1.1a and 1.1b; the first verse is 0:43–1:17; the first
chorus is 1:45–2:14). While the introduction is largely out of metered
time and invites quiet contemplation, both of these sections are based
on hard-rocking, multilayered grooves that engage the body in sensu-
ous movement. The verses are powered by Chris Squire's virtuosic bass
playing, but to use "virtuosity" as code for "high" music here is to miss
the way that his prominent line creates a sense of rhythmic drive by
articulating syncopations and then emphasizing the downbeats. The
guitar riff and rhythm-section stomp of the major-key chorus sections
work similarly, further highlighting the degree to which this song
breathes the air of the rock repertory. To be sure, there is a fair degree of
complex metrical and hypermetrical planning through these sections.
The second and third phrases of each verse shorten their second bar by
two beats, resulting in a 2/4 measure in the midst of the expected 4/4
framework. Thus these phrases last for "three-and-a-half" bars, not the
conventional four. In addition, it is notable that the verses comprise a
total of three phrases, not the two or four that would be expected in a
straightforward hypermetrical scheme. The chorus, too, is based on the
"three-and-a-half-bar" phrase, but here it is the fourth and final measure of each phrase that is shortened to a 2/4 bar. The chorus is hyper-
metrically tricky as well: before the E minor chord held on the word
"you" that ends each chorus section, *five* of these altered phrases sound.
Now, these structures are fairly intricate, especially compared to rock
music in general. But the marvel of these sections, to my ears, is that the
groove remains paramount throughout. The complexities are there to
be counted, they are part of the "facts" of the song, but most listening

experiences of "Roundabout" focus instead on the effect of the groove, on how smoothly the song moves along. The difficulties are not meant to be heard as such; they are subsumed within, as Cromelin puts it, the "thick, chugging texture."[25]

Two further aspects of "Roundabout" help to bring these dialectical tensions between "high" and "low" qualities to the fore. First, consider the tricky keyboard-led moment that occurs before the third verse (2:25–2:29), and again after the following chorus, just before the contrasting bridge section (3:21–3:25). This can easily be heard as a brief "developmental" passage: there is a descent toward the E-minor tonic reminiscent of the end of the introduction, and it is placed within a framework of shifting meters. Compared to the smooth effect of the meter changes during the verse and chorus, this moment is filled with striking activity: the introduction-derived motive first sounds in 4/8, and is followed by four related motives in 3/8 (they are one eighth-note shorter because they do not repeat the final note). But at the same time, the passage functions within the equally audible hypermetrical groove. Preceding the moment before the third verse are six bars of 4/4: a four-bar phrase concluded with a synthesizer lick, and then two further measures. The verse groove serves as the background pattern for the entire six measures. The tricky moment itself lasts for sixteen eighth-notes, or the equivalent of two measures in the background 4/4 meter. These two measures, added to the previous two measures of unproblematic 4/4, make up a four-measure phrase that perfectly balances the initial four-bar phrase. Thus, while the surface is momentarily broken with this passage, it also functions as part of a straightforward 4 + 4, eight-measure introduction to the third verse.

The second aspect concerns another intimation of "development" in the song. Figure 1.1a sketches the guitar riff used during the E-minor verses, while figure 1.1b sketches the riff used in the G-major choruses. Clearly the verse riff is transformed, through a transposition to the relative major, into the main guitar idea of the chorus; such large-scale processes could easily be seen as lending "Roundabout" something of a thematic "unity."[26] What shouldn't be lost in this description, however, is the nature of the material being described: these are not "themes" or "motives" but riffs, short emblematic repeating ideas that, through their repetitions and roles within the texture,

Figure 1.1a. Verse riff (sketch).

Figure 1.1a. Chorus riff (sketch).

Figures 1.1a and 1.1b. Riffs from "Roundabout."

help to create the grooves of these two sections. To point out their relations is not the same as describing their function. The riffs move up and down by step within their local tonic areas, round and round again, and keep time flowing forward with well-placed syncopated accents interacting with other emphases on the beat.

Interpreting "Roundabout" *solely* as a rock song misses much of the detail that invites consideration alongside the art-music tradition, but at the same time, to describe the song as if it were merely a piece *of* that tradition also misses much of the detail essential for understanding the song in terms of its background as rock music. The tensions between the systems provide a more complete framework from which to consider the song.

Fixity versus Improvisation

We tend to view the written score as the ideal form of a piece of "classical" music; on the other hand, we tend to value popular music as performance, specifically in the extent to which musicians can improvise new ornaments, figurations, and solos at each playing. Even considering only the studio recording of a song, something of these opposing approaches can be heard. Some aspects of the music are constructed such that we hear them as planned, fixed for all imagined performances, while others can be interpreted as singular events that we would expect to hear differently each time we attended a concert.

In "Roundabout," the extended solo section of the song (5:49–7:04) illustrates this marriage of these two different approaches. Judging from live performances and live albums, the "Roundabout"

solos were either largely composed in the first place, or if originally
improvised, were then "fixed" on the recording and treated as set solos
thereafter. But the *effect* of the solo section is an interplay of fixed and
improvised elements; neither perspective can adequately describe the
section. An organ solo begins this part of the song, and it is constructed
like an improvised display. The band lays down the groove from the
chorus and repeats this clearly structured theme four times. This provides a musical backbone on top of which the soloist may improvise.
Wakeman's solo has the sound of improvisation; there are numerous
references to the G-major tonic sonority, brief ideas seem happened
upon by chance and are then repeated and varied, and scalar runs and
passagework connect one arrival with the next. But at the same time,
the solo section is meticulously planned. The background chorus
groove is not made up of easy four-bar phrases; the last bar of each
phrase contains only two beats. Wakeman must keep the composed
structure in mind to keep the phrases of his solo in sync with the four-
teen-beat repeating pattern played by the rest of the band.

More to the point, the four organ solo phrases are immediately followed by a passage that doesn't sound improvised at all, but gives the
distinct impression of being composed (see fig. 1.2). The melody
instruments suddenly come together for a virtuosic unison idea that is
stated over four bars of 4/4. The figure rises and falls, with a syncopation at the apex; it is then repeated down a whole step, back at the original pitch level, and then back down with a rhythmic variation
emphasizing the strong beats instead of the syncopated spaces between.
The underlying changes of this new material now function as a background groove in and of itself, and Howe takes an improvisatory electric guitar solo over the next four bars. Then, as two improvising
musicians trading phrases might do, the solo passes back to the organ.

Figure 1.2. Unison lick during solo section, "Roundabout" (sketch).

But the two organ phrases here are the trickier "three-and-a-half bar" variety derived from the chorus. Following the organ the composed licks return, now with the melodic material moved up a fifth. When the guitar solo reenters for the final phrases of the solo section, there might be an expectation that freer improvisation would return. But compared to the spiky activity of the first guitar break, at this point Howe uses a great deal of sustain to present a soaring melody that seems composed. And for the last five bars of the section, the entire band comes together to play a planned, motivically based conclusion. Thus both soloing instruments display effective improvisatory rock soloing within the section, and there is even an air of the excitement of live performance amid the trading of phrases from one soloist to the other. Yet, at the same time, the structures within the section are invariably carefully worked out, and even the improvisatory style of soloing is challenged because it is continually juxtaposed with fixed, developmental passages for the whole band.

Structural versus Cultural Understanding

Something of a values-laden split exists between approaching music primarily as sonic structure or as the product of culture. Insights gleaned from an exploration of "the music itself" seem to implicitly claim that these methods are the best path to a direct understanding of a given work. At the same time, writers who ground their analyses in culturally derived readings continue to argue for the importance and relevance of their approach, pointing out the range of ideological content inherently contained in seemingly "objective" structural analyses.

The differing views of progressive rock exhibit this dichotomy. Structural analyses show—and implicitly prize—the complexity of this music and its affinities with the art-music tradition. Meanwhile, culturally based critiques of the style argue that those very tendencies, in light of the social/cultural/political agenda ascribed to rock music as a whole, leave progressive rock lacking. And as I have argued, even though Macan's study on the whole is concerned with both sorts of paradigmatic approaches, the analyses of "the music itself" show little connection with the countercultural concerns present on a metaphorical level.[27]

More provocative, however, is the extent to which progressive rock songs can simultaneously suggest these different sorts of hearings. On the one hand, a close reading of "Roundabout" invites a structural approach. In addition to the "three-and-a-half bar" phrases, other rhythmic, metrical, and hypermetrical issues abound. The bridge section sticks to four-bar phrases in a consistent 4/4, but the instrumental groupings of two phrases alternate with vocal groupings of three phrases. To cite one other example, the bulk of the "outro" oscillates between measures of three and four beats. Temporal parameters are not the only structures of note; tonality is at issue, because against the background of most rock songs, "Roundabout" alternates between E minor and its relative major, and concludes with a move to the parallel major. Form is notable as well, because the verse and chorus are full of interconnections, and those conventional sections are joined by the addition of numerous others, which serve to expand the song past the boundaries of most rock music.

Yet at the same time, the lyrics of "Roundabout" invite readings beyond internal musical structures, to the concerns of the counterculture played out on a metaphorical level. The nature imagery throughout the song, with its references to mountains, lakes, and valleys, suggests (as in much progressive rock) the pastoral utopia of a time long ago, which stands in contrast to the dehumanizing technology of modern society.[28] Nature is not at peace during the bridge section, though: amid the musical storm of minor-key unison licks and active Latin-tinged percussion, the lyrics present the "swirling wind . . . as weather spins out of hand." The full nature/technology dialectic is not explicitly present in this song, but the storm may represent the effects of current corruptions against the eternal natural world; the last new line of text in this section states that "next to your deeper fears we stand surrounded by a million years." Thus, "Roundabout" revels in the glory of timeless pristine nature both as an idealized past and as a utopian vision of the future, able to resist and withstand the bleak effects of modern society.

The lyrics evoke not only the "countercultural ideology [of] resistance and protest," as Macan puts it, but also the progressive rock phenomenon itself. This reading of the lyrics is by no means a full-fledged interpretation; indeed, the lyrics as a whole may have no clear coherent meaning, reveling instead in ambiguity, suggestion, and free association. The surrealist leanings here have wide connections to the uses of surrealism in progressive rock's lyrics and visuals in general. Listeners would surely approach this song with the same expectations of seemingly hidden or shadowy meanings that they would bring to other examples of the style.[29] The fact that most progressive rock of the time was specifically a British phenomenon is evoked as well: as a noun, "roundabout" is chiefly a British term, referring to a traffic circle or a merry-go-round. Both meanings are evoked in the lyrics, through the "morning driving" described at the end of the verses, and the "ring" of dancing, singing children in the second verse. And on a more general level, references to circular motion abound throughout the lyrics, from the movement "in and around the lake" to the weather "spinning" out of control, and more generally to the cyclic rise and fall of the seasons through "ten true summers."

In fact, the "purely musical" devices and structures are anything but pure. A perspective that focuses on "the music itself" is most effective when "Roundabout" is placed *in context*, when it is seen against the background of rock music and as a part of the historically situated progressive rock style. Observations about temporal parameters outside the foursquare mold—multiple tonal areas, expansions of song forms, and so on—are important for our interpretations of "Roundabout" because these factors interact with our expectations for rock music as a whole. The norms of progressive rock, where we expect a fair degree of complexity, and where evocation and subversion of those rock structural traits are considered normal, are also essential baselines for our understanding. As with any piece of music, the "facts" worth incorporating into an analysis and interpretation function against the background expectations of a style, and that musical background can be more fully understood as interacting with its time and place.

Real pieces of music rarely prove philosophical points; they are rich structures that can be heard and understood from a variety of perspectives. The different systems of musical value that are commonly used to evaluate "high" and "low" music may describe a sort of musical purity, but such descriptions are ultimately thin ones, for they either fail to capture the multiple currents in much of the music around us or lead us to conclude that this music is somehow lacking. Part of why progressive rock is intriguing and exciting is because the style brings these contradictions, inconsistencies, and tensions among multiple value systems to the fore. Rather than view the style as a value problem, though, we can reorient our perspective to see how progressive rock is about such value problems, is about the narrowly constructed conventional systems of value themselves. Our understanding of progressive rock as a culturally situated musical phenomenon can only be enhanced by embracing the spaces—uncomfortable as it may be—between these differing notions of musical purity.

Notes

I would like to thank the students in my classes " 'High' and 'Low': The Valuing of Music in Western Society" (Cornell University, 1997-1998), and "Gates of Delirium: The Context, Analysis, and Reception of Progressive Rock" (University of Rochester, Spring 2000), for contributing to many of the ideas and perspectives presented in this paper.

1. See Edward Macan, *Rocking the Classics: English Progressive Rock and the Counterculture* (New York: Oxford University Press, 1997), 167–78. As Macan puts it, more important than any musical factor was the notion that progressive rock was "not a style of the oppressed" (177). The epithet is from Lester Bangs, with reference to Emerson Lake and Palmer, in "Exposed! The Brutal Energy Atrocities of Emerson Lake and Palmer," *Creem*, March, 1974, 40; quoted in Macan, 167.
2. As Macan rightly points out, to disdain progressive rock because of a seeming lack of black influence is dangerous territory indeed, because it implies that blacks are inherently more "natural," and by extension more "primitive." See Macan, *Rocking*, 171.
3. See *Rolling Stone*, July 22, 1971, 40, 42.
4. See *Rolling Stone*, March 16, 1972, 56.
5. *The Rolling Stone Album Guide*, ed. Anthony DeCurtis and James Henke, with Holly George-Warren (New York: Random House, 1992), 793. The Yes essay is written by Mark Coleman.
6. Robert Palmer, *Rock and Roll: An Unruly History* (New York: Harmony Books, 1995). This volume is a companion to the PBS documentary series on the history of rock. Pink Floyd is the only major progressive rock band discussed, but the focus is on the earliest stages of the group's career and their connection to 1960s psychedelia.
7. John Rockwell, "Art Rock," in *The Rolling Stone Illustrated History of Rock and Roll*, ed. Jim Miller (New York: Rolling Stone Press/Random House, 1976), 322–26.
8. For an explication of how linear narratives have been adapted in the con-

struction of many music histories, see James Webster, "The Concept of Beethoven's 'Early' Period in the Context of Periodizations in General," *Beethoven Forum* 3 (1994): 1–27.

9. Rockwell, "Art Rock," 322.

10. Jimmy Guterman and Owen O'Donnell, *The Worst Rock 'n' Roll Records of All Time* (New York: Citadel Press, 1991).

11. Ibid., 13–15.

12. One important sign is the extent to which such labels are applied to almost any level of critical inquiry. We often make value judgments along "high"/"low" lines when discussing whole styles of music, but we also recapitulate the split within a given style, within an artist's or composer's work, and sometimes even within an individual work. The process of comparative valuing is something we *do* rather than a process by which we objectively describe the musical world external to us.

13. Indeed, Macan's thesis, that progressive rock played out the concerns of the counterculture on a metaphorical level, can be seen as an attempt to recapture value for the style on the very terms used by its critics.

14. Macan, *Rocking*, vii, 4.

15. See Macan, *Rocking*, 85–125. The fourth example Macan treats, the entirety of Pink Floyd's *Wish You Were Here* (1975), shows less recourse to art music analogies; on the other hand, without these tools, the discussion resembles more of a beginning-to-end description of the album than a well-reasoned analysis.

16. Nors S. Josephson, "Bach Meets Liszt: Traditional Formal Structures and Performance Practices in Progressive Rock," *Musical Quarterly* 76 (1992): 67–92.

17. It is a strange phenomenon that at this point, when "new musicological" perspectives are questioning these conventional value systems and rethinking how art music can and should be analyzed, the very same codes should be used, unquestioningly, as a means for validating vernacular musics. Recent writing on progressive rock is by no means the only area where this takes place; indeed, the most egregious examples are often found in scholarship on jazz.

18. Robert Christgau, *Rock Albums of the '70s: A Critical Guide* (New York: Da Capo Press, 1990), 435. Yes's *Close to the Edge* is given a grade of "C+," a step up from the grade of "C" awarded in the original edition of the book (*Christgau's Record Guide: Rock Albums of the '70s*, 1981).

19. Rockwell, "Art Rock," 323, 324.

20. Bangs, "Exposed!," 44; quoted in Macan, *Rocking*, 169.

21. This approach generally agrees with John Covach's perspective, that what drives the style is a "fascination with engaging art-music practices in a rock context." See John Covach, "Progressive Rock, 'Close to the Edge,' and the Boundaries of Style, in *Understanding Rock: Essays in Musical*

Analysis, ed. John Covach and Graeme M. Boone (New York: Oxford University Press, 1997), 6. However, it is notable that the specifics of Covach's analysis of "Close to the Edge" take the "rock context" for granted, resulting in a discussion often indistinguishable from that which would be applied to a symphonic work: for example, a half-step motive is utilized at foreground, middle-ground, and background levels, unifying the piece.

22. Ibid., 7.

23. Covach makes this point convincingly, that the art-music references in progressive rock are "drawn freely from . . . very different styles. . . . One gets the sense that for these rock musicians, as well as for the audience for whom they compose, record, and perform their music, all of these borrowings are of the same kind: 'classical.'" Ibid., 8.

24. Cromelin's *Rolling Stone* review explicitly describes Rick Wakeman's work here as "liquid organ trills."

25. The same could be said for many examples of metrical play in progressive rock. The frequent use of 7/8 time in Rush's music, for example, is fascinating not because such a meter is "complex," but because the admittedly complex meter is used as the backdrop for grooves that sound so smooth, balanced, and straightforwardly regular.

26. This isn't the only aspect of the song that suggests "unity" across different sections. Lyrics are notably repeated and subtly blurred as well. The first two verses share their last three lines (the CD liner notes contain a misprint as compared to the recording), the final line of those verses is clearly evoked in the final line of the third verse, the uptempo bridge section ends by repeating the first two lines of the first verse, and the fourth and final verse repeats all of the first verse's lyrics, with the substitution of "You spend the day" for the original "I spend." In addition, the middle repetition of the introduction includes a quiet version of the chorus's first two lines, and a telescoped version of that section's final line.

27. Bill Martin argues similarly in his recent book on progressive rock; he writes that "to *integrate* the two levels of analysis, formal and historical, that is of course the great difficulty — and I do not know that Macan has completely pulled this off." See Martin, *Listening to the Future: The Time of Progressive Rock 1968–1978* (Chicago: Open Court, 1998), 132.

28. See Macan, *Rocking*, esp. 69–84, on characteristic themes in the lyrics of progressive rock, and their implicit connections to the agenda of the counterculture. My reading of the lyrics of "Roundabout" follows Macan's model.

29. Ibid., 70–72.

2 The "American Metaphysical Circus" of Joseph Byrd's United States of America

Kevin Holm-Hudson

In surveys of the history of popular music, the short-lived Los Angeles group the United States of America is rarely mentioned. Although the group enjoyed a fair amount of critical attention and media notoriety surrounding the release of its only album in 1968—Lilian Roxon gave the band a nearly one-and-a-half page entry in her seminal *Rock Encyclopedia* and composer Elliot Schwartz praised the group's music for its "enormous creative vitality" in his *Electronic Music: A Listener's Guide*[1]—the band has received only parenthetical mentions in later rock history accounts.[2] Interest in the United States of America has increased in recent years, however: Richie Unterberger's 1998 book *Unknown Legends of Rock 'n' Roll* contains a chapter devoted to the band, and its album was reissued on CD in 1997 by Britain's Edsel label.

The United States of America is usually considered to be a "psychedelic-experimental" group by rock historians. Given the group's cultural context (California, on the heels of the famous "Summer of Love" said to be initiated by the Beatles' *Sgt. Pepper*), this is an easy although perhaps inaccurate description of the band. The lyrics of even its more "psychedelic" songs—such as "The Garden of Earthly Delights" (its title borrowed from the famous nightmarish painting by Hieronymus Bosch)—hint at a chemical experience more threatening than benign, in the spirit of the Velvet Underground rather than the

Grateful Dead. Other songs, such as "The American Way of Love" and "I Won't Leave My Wooden Wife for You, Sugar," contain ironically pointed social commentary analogous to Frank Zappa's Mothers of Invention, a group that used the term "psychedelic" only as an epithet of derision. More significantly, the United States of America's musical ambitions—largely the vision of composer Joseph Byrd—suggest that the group was an isolated, homegrown predecessor of the "progressive" or "art rock" style that became prominent, chiefly among British bands, in the early 1970s.

What distinguishes the United States of America from some of its contemporaries (such as the Byrds at the time of *The Notorious Byrd Brothers*, or Zappa's Mothers of Invention) is the seriousness and skill with which they incorporated avant-garde and other influences into their music. The Byrds, for example, brought to their experimentation a wide-eyed enthusiasm that at times bordered on naïveté (this is demonstrated by the bonus track "Moog Raga" on Columbia's CD reissue of *The Notorious Byrd Brothers*). Zappa's skill as a composer and musician is undeniable, but his lyrics and titles often introduced a comical and at times scatological element that is at odds with progressive rock in general. The mission of the United States of America, on the other hand, was eminently serious. As Joseph Byrd has put it, "the idea was that we were going to bring the avant-garde into rock."[3]

Origin and Influences

Edward Macan, in his study of British progressive rock *Rocking the Classics*, writes that progressive rock was "never a working-class style"; rather, it was "the vital expression of a bohemian, middle-class intelligentsia."[4] College and university campuses proved to be fertile environments for fostering English progressive rock; Macan notes that the members of Van der Graaf Generator, Henry Cow, Pink Floyd, and Genesis, to name a few, all met in colleges or the English equivalent of private schools.[5] Similarly, the United States of America was formed at UCLA in 1967, its members actively studying new music composition or ethnomusicology. While other contemporary groups certainly may have formed under similar circumstances, the United States of America's academic pedigree was particularly impressive among rock bands.

Much of the band's musical vision can be traced to composer Joseph Byrd, who played keyboards, contributed electronic music effects, and wrote or cowrote eight of the ten songs on the album. Byrd was classically trained in music composition, receiving his B.A. from the University of Arizona, where he studied with Barney Childs. A Columbia Records biography of Byrd, found on the liner notes of his 1969 solo release *The American Metaphysical Circus*, describes his background succinctly:

> After graduation, Byrd received Stanford University's Sollnit Fellowship for graduate study in composition. But Byrd chose to split for New York, where he had already begun listening to electronic music and meeting young, far-out Berkeley experimental composers. During his years on the New York modern music scene, Byrd worked as conductor, arranger, teacher, Associate Producer for a record company, and assistant to critic-composer Virgil Thomson. He was also gaining recognition as one of the leading young experimentalists, and his works were being performed from Paris to Tokyo. Then Joe Byrd came out to U.C.L.A. and ended up living in one of the early Ocean Park beachfront communes with a group of Indian musicians, artist and graduate students.[6] While serving as a teaching assistant at U.C.L.A., he studied acoustics, psychology, and Indian music, but his interest inevitably returned to experimental and environmental music. By the summer of 1967, Byrd had dropped out of U.C.L.A. to become once more a full-time experimental composer and happening-producer.[7]

Indeed, none of the musicians in the United States of America had any rock background to speak of. Violinist Gordon Marron was, according to Byrd, "by no means a rock musician,"[8] but was instead classically trained and an expert interpreter of avant-garde music, particularly the work of composer Morton Feldman. Drummer Craig Woodson had studied African drumming extensively, and bassist Rand Forbes was a virtuoso string bass player (he brought to the United States of America one of the first fretless electric basses in rock). The musicians were therefore playing as "outsiders" adopting a rock style.

Byrd recalls, "We all improvised, of course, but in a 'contemporary music' style, because we all came with that baggage. Nearly all the 'solos' I wrote, because, although I was not a good instrumentalist, I was an arranger with a vast array of styles."[9] In fact, the band's live performances often incorporated experimental free improvisation such as was in fashion in the avant-garde at the time (and which would also be an element of King Crimson's live shows in 1973–74); the band also often performed from written scores.[10] Byrd claims today that the scores were "a virtue born of necessity" because the musicians were more comfortable using score notation, not fully comfortable with playing in a rock style.[11] The scores also proved to be a distinctive visual aspect of the group's performance; Byrd recalls how the stand lights provided "a kind of other-worldly lit-from-below effect."[12]

Byrd thus came to playing rock through his work in staging avant-garde performance art "happenings," and the Dadaist atmosphere of those events influenced his later live work with the United States of America. During Byrd's early 1960s visit to New York, he became loosely affiliated with the Fluxus movement, the group of conceptual composers, poets, and artists that included Yoko Ono, La Monte Young, and Dick Higgins; he also met John Cage and David Tudor. In the spring of 1963 he met Dorothy Moskowitz, later to become the singer for the United States of America.

Moskowitz received a degree in government from Barnard College, and also spent some time at Columbia University, where she received informal composition advice from Otto Luening. She describes herself as having been "a collegiate songwriter" upon graduation;[13] this changed when she attended a Karlheinz Stockhausen concert at the MacMillan Theater at Columbia. As she now describes it, "It probably changed my life because I suddenly became a devotee of 'new music.'"[14]

When Byrd and Moskowitz met in New York, she was a production secretary for RCA Victor and he was a production manager at Capitol Records; together, they worked on a Time/Life record series that was a narrative history of America with musical examples. Byrd produced and arranged many of the recordings, while Moskowitz helped with production, research, and liner notes. Moskowitz remembers unearthing scores to songs such as "Greenwood Mountain," "Tyler and Tippecanoe," and "Rally Round the Flag," which were "arranged by Byrd with a keen sense of style and fidelity to the period. I don't know how he learned all about the craft or whether it was instinct."[15] Byrd was passionately interested in earlier American vernacular music—nineteenth-century hymns, marches, and popular songs—and was consequently drawn to the music of Charles Ives. It was Ives's music that best united Byrd's twin interests in nineteenth-century music and the avant-garde.

In the summer of 1963, Byrd and Moskowitz left New York for California. It was at UCLA's Institute for Ethnomusicology, studying with scholars such as Charles Seeger, that Moskowitz learned about vocal styles of different cultures, most notably those of Indian classical music;[16] in 1965, Moskowitz and Byrd contributed to a Folkways LP of Indian music by Gayathri Rajapur and Harihar Rao.[17] Moskowitz's vibrato-less style of singing, which some rock writers compared to that of Jefferson Airplane's Grace Slick, was actually more likely inspired by these classes; she has also cited the cool jazz vocal stylings of Chet Baker as one of her influences.[18]

From 1964 to early 1966 Byrd directed The New Music Workshop of Los Angeles, a group that performed the music of Cage, Stockhausen, Feldman, and others. Among the ensemble's performers were violinist Gordon Marron, bassist Rand Forbes, and percussionist Craig Woodson, students at UCLA who were later to join the United States of America. During this period Byrd also traveled to the San Francisco Tape Center and saw what was being done there in studio tape composition.[19]

Byrd and Moskowitz parted company at the end of 1966; she returned to New York while he remained in Los Angeles, forming the United States of America with a fellow composer named Michael Agnello. By the early summer of 1967 Moskowitz had returned to join the new group; Agnello left soon afterward over struggles with Byrd over the group's direction. At the core of the dispute between Byrd and Agnello was whether the group should compromise its ideals by recording for a major label such as Columbia.[20] According to Byrd, Agnello was a "genuinely working-class guy" with philosophical beliefs similar to the anarchist "diggers" movement;[21] Byrd, on the other hand, supported the aims of the American communists, particularly regarding use of the tools of capitalist production to advance revolutionary ideas from within the status quo.[22] Byrd was drawn to this group because, among the many leftist groups working for social change, the Communist Party was "the one group that had discipline, an agenda, and was willing to work within the existing institutions to educate and radicalize American society. The surprise is that I lasted as long as I did (about 10 years). I left the party in the early 70s because of my view that women constituted an exploited economic class, a position so unorthodox it could not be tolerated."[23]

During this period Byrd was active politically as well as musically. He worked with the nascent free speech student movement at UCLA; organized a band to play labor and freedom songs at rallies for activist Dorothy Healey, then campaigning for Los Angeles tax assessor; and created the New Left School, which lasted from 1965 to 1969 (Dorothy Moskowitz taught a course at the school called "Feminism 1," and Byrd taught a course in Hegelian dialectics).[24]

The influence of leftist political thought on the United States of America should not be minimized. It was not merely a trendy label in keeping with the times; in fact, the group eschewed association with any of the popular styles of the day (according to Byrd, "the best way to present our political message . . . was to give the audience no easy hook to hang us on").[25] Everything from the intentionally generic original package design (a plain white cover with the group's name in stenciled letters, within a brown manila envelope), to songs such as "Love Song for the Dead Ché," to the group's name, which Byrd suggested changing to "Julius and Ethel Rosenberg" when Columbia initially balked at the name's political implications,[26] were intended to further the concept of introducing revolutionary ideas using the tools of capitalist economy. It was the artistic equivalent of guerrilla warfare.

"The Most Spectacularly Electronic Group Around"

Byrd detailed his aesthetic aims for the United States of America in a 1993 letter to writer/critic Richard Kostelanetz. It amounts to a manifesto for his vision of the group: "I started the band as an avant-garde political/musical rock group, with the idea of combining: (1) Electronic sound (not 'electronic music'!) . . . (2) Musical/political radicalism . . . (3) Performance art."[27]

In their efforts to bring the avant-garde into rock, the United States of America also drew upon popular rock styles of the time. Byrd recalls, "[F]or me, Country Joe and the Fish, Jefferson Airplane, the Paul Butterfield Blues Band, and Blue Cheer were all useful ingredients. I certainly was aware of the Beatles, probably too much so, and I was an early fan of an unknown songwriter named Randy Newman. . . . But you should realize that I was probably the most eclectic person on the planet."[28]

The group was signed to Columbia Records by David Rubinson, whom Byrd and Moskowitz knew from their Time/Life days. Rubinson had become a staff producer for Columbia, and would later produce albums for Herbie Hancock; Peter, Paul and Mary, and Santana. The album was not a notable commercial success. It spent nine weeks on the charts in the United States, peaking at number 181 on the *Billboard* album chart in May 1968; the album failed to chart in Britain.[29] It did, however, attract a fair amount of critical attention, chiefly because of the then startling use of Byrd's "electronic sound" on the album. Creating these sounds was a laborious process because of technical limitations; according to Byrd, "the only available functioning keyable synthesizers were Robert Moog's at twenty thousand dollars plus. We were left with whatever sounds I could squeeze from three variable wave-shape generators, modulating one another."[30]

These oscillators were built for the group by Richard Durrett, credited on the album as creator of the "DURRETT Electronic Music Synthesizer and Ring Modulator." Electronic devices were also used on the album, and in live performance, to process other instruments and Moskowitz's voice. Lilian Roxon describes, for example, how Marron played an electric violin supplemented by an octave divider, which could supplement the violin's sound with electronic "doublings" of the note at an octave above or below; the band also used fuzzboxes, ring modulators, and tape echo machines such as the Echoplex.[31] This primitive but intricate setup proved to be surprisingly versatile.

According to Moskowitz,

> Synthesizers in those days were so unpredictable—that was part of their appeal. You didn't know what was going to happen! So you'd turn on the volume—you'd get a "squawk," or you might

> get a "blep." It really didn't matter, so long as you were playing in rhythm. And that was very exciting. So you'd go "bling, bling," and that became part of the rhythm track. . . .
>
> In the mid-'60s, a synthesizer was considered an instrument on its own terms, not a means of duplicating the sound of something else. It expanded the palette and gave the music a dangerous edge. It certainly did lend a richness.[32]

The prominence of electronic sound on the album is indeed striking for a 1968 recording, particularly considering that the Beatles made their first tentative use of the Moog synthesizer on *Abbey Road* the following year.[33] Throughout the album Marron's violin is rarely left untreated and is often modified by octave dividers, tape delay, wah-wah pedals, and so on. Moskowitz's voice is sometimes slightly filtered for an ethereal effect ("Cloud Song") or processed with a ring modulator for a sinister edge ("The American Metaphysical Circus").[34]

According to Roxon, the result was "an abundance of riches" that was met with mixed critical response: "Unbelieving enthusiasm on one hand, and boredom on the other."[35] One high-profile performance at New York's Fillmore East on March 29, 1968, received a lukewarm commentary from writer Richard Kostelanetz, who wrote, "Byrd himself plays an ersatz synthesizer that produces a familiar array of electronic sounds, all of them far too loud, in a kind of obvious way (though rock listeners may find them surprising). Dorothy Moskowitz has a voice distinguished only for its imitation of the South Indian drone; but every time Byrd activated his machines, everything else was drowned out. The drummer [Craig Woodson] reportedly had all sorts of electronic supplements available to him, but the solos he took sounded to my ear undistinguished. At the end of their set, Byrd walked off the stage looking disgusted. If the group develops, they could be extraordinary; for now they are just strikingly original."[36]

Quotation and Psychosis: "The American Metaphysical Circus"

The opening selection on the album, "The American Metaphysical Circus," shows something of the group's electronic experimentation, as well as the influence of nineteenth-century vernacular music and the multiple-ensemble overlays of Charles Ives. No fewer than five layers of sound are heard in the opening minutes of the record: a calliope playing the march "National Emblem,"[37] a ragtime piano playing "At A Georgia Camp Meeting,"[38] two marching bands, playing "Marching Through Georgia" and "The Red, White and Blue" (switching left and right channels in tribute to one of Ives's father's most famous musical experiments), and two tracks of electronic sounds.

The lyrics portray a series of images in a circus setting:

> At precisely eight-o-five
> Doctor Frederick von Meir
> Will attempt his famous dive
> Through a solid sheet of luminescent fire.[39]

One is reminded not only of the Beatles' famous psychedelic circus ("Being for the Benefit of Mr. Kite") but also, as the song progresses, of the darker imagery in progressive rock songs such as King Crimson's "Cirkus," Renaissance's "Trip To The Fair," and Emerson Lake and Palmer's "Karn Evil 9." Interestingly, this song predates them all; Byrd wrote the lyrics around 1964–65 in reference to Dr. Kurt von Meier, an art history professor at UCLA who supported Byrd's performance art activities.[40] The distortion of (or separation from) reality associated with psychosis is also conveyed musically. For example, Moskowitz's voice is progressively distorted using a ring modulator, so that by the end of the song her words are nearly unintelligible.

Disassociation is also conveyed musically through chromatic mediant harmonic progressions. While such progressions are occasionally found in late-nineteenth-century and early-twentieth-century art music,[41] in this song such progressions are the norm, ruling out any semblance of conventional harmonic progression. Figure 2.1 shows the harmonic progressions of the verse and chorus.

The second half of each phrase is virtually a sequence of the first half, transposed down a major third, making the chromatic mediant relationship active at the phrase level as well as from chord to chord. The harmony of the chorus, while not of a chromatic-mediant nature, is no more functional than the verse: here the chromatic mediant movement is replaced by root motion of either a major or minor second.

Fig. 2.1. Harmonic Progression in "The American Metaphysical Circus."

The coda resumes the Ivesian overlay, made all the more explicit by its inclusion of two of Ives's favorite melodic quotes: "Marching Through Georgia" (in the left channel) and "Columbia! the Gem of the Ocean" (the last music heard in the right channel). This song, then, embodies the techniques of quotation collage associated with Ives, electronic processing of natural sound (the voice) in the manner of Stockhausen,[42] and chromatic mediant relationships characteristic of nineteenth-century art music.

Stylistic Irony: "I Won't Leave My Wooden Wife for You, Sugar"

Compared with "The American Metaphysical Circus," "I Won't Leave My Wooden Wife for You, Sugar" might sound superficially as though it were done by a different group. The fuzz bass and frying-pan-like electronic "clank" (again, a ring-modulated tone) punctuating each measure suggest the lowbrow musical revelry of Spike Jones, while the lyrics skewer sexual mores and suburban hypocrisy in a manner reminiscent of Frank Zappa's Mothers of Invention.[43] Moreover, the verse and chorus collectively fit the harmonic progression of that most time-honored lowbrow form, the twelve-bar blues.

The song's middle solo uses ring-modulated oscillator glissandi to suggest a slide whistle over a busily improvised accompaniment evocative of Dixieland jazz—another reference to Byrd's fascination with old-time American music, as is the gramophone-like filtering of the voice and violin in the second verse. The song incongruously ends with a quiet Salvation Army–style hymn tune played by a brass band; Moskowitz remembers the song's working title as "The Electric God" ("or maybe I called it that just to annoy [Byrd]," she adds) and notes that the late jazz trumpet player Don Ellis played in the arrangement.[44] The tune was evidently important to Byrd at this time; a different version of the song, arranged as a theme and stylistic variations, appears on his post-USA album with the Field Hippies. Ironically, Byrd now recalls that this tune, thought to be original at the time, was also a quote: "The little Sunday-School tune that I composed turned out to be (to my chagrin) a Japanese Methodist hymn, recalled presumably from my tenure as choir director for a West LA Japanese congregation."[45]

Collage and Recapitulation: "The American Way of Love"

The album's prevailing techniques of quotation, collage, and parody reach an apotheosis in the album's closing song, "The American Way of Love," a triptych consisting of "Metaphor for an Older Man," "California Good-Time Music," and "Love is All." The first part is musically simple but lyrically unusual for its time, addressing the activities of homosexual prostitutes on New York's 42nd Street. "California Good-Time Music" parodies the pop culture of California, with breezy harmonies reminiscent of the Beach Boys or the Mamas and the Papas. The transition into "California Good-Time Music" is achieved by a modal improvisation featuring a solo on the electric violin, complete with guitar-like note bends. "California Good-Time Music" is a subverted pop song with wah-wah violin, abnormally extended phrase lengths, and an unusual direct modulation into the chorus. Most strik-ing, however, is "Love is All." This concluding section juxtaposes a Jimi Hendrix–like, whole-tone, fuzz-bass ostinato with a collage of themes from every other song in the album in a grand recapitulation, itself a bow to the polytextural layerings of the album's opening.

The idea of recapitulation by collage is not uncommon to later progressive rock albums; similar collages of previously heard material can be found in Pink Floyd's *Atom Heart Mother* (1970), Rick Wake-man's *No Earthly Connection* (1976), and Pink Floyd's *Dark Side of the Moon* (1973), in which the opening track "Speak to Me" functions as a sort of collage overture. In the case of the United States of America, however, both the technique of collage and the group's ironic stylistic eclecticism are derived from Byrd's fascination with Ives. Dorothy Moskowitz says, "a strong case can be made for Byrd's being Ives' [*sic*] spiritual heir. Consider Ives' incorporation of popular band music and Byrd's use of Cream, Hendrix and Beach Boys elements in his col-lages."[46]

Rock, or New Music?

Even by the extravagant standards of late-1960s rock, the album was an intricate product of the studio; if Byrd was not a virtuoso instrumen-talist, he was a virtuoso arranger. Even "Love is All" is hardly a haphaz-ard collage; the song ends with vocal fragments of the album's other songs newly "harmonized" to a composed string-orchestra coda. Fur-thermore, the group replicated these dense textures in live perfor-mance, an unusual accomplishment given the state of live electronic music in the 1960s. Byrd's letter to Kostelanetz provides some detail regarding the group's use of electronic effects in concert and its sense of performance art theater. He writes, "Our set closed with a 'Farewell Symphony' treatment of 'The American Way of Love.' On the record, we ended side 2 with a collage of electronic sound and tape loops from the album. In live performance, we did the same thing, the musicians leaving one by one, until I was alone, apparently singing repeatedly 'how much fun it's been' (actually, a tape loop); then I left too, and the loop continued to the end."[47]

Byrd's description, with its reference to Franz Joseph Haydn's "Farewell Symphony" and tape loops, sounds uncannily highbrow for a Fillmore East performance and hints at the aesthetic tensions that soon dissolved the group. Unterberger notes that Byrd and Marron even got into a backstage fistfight at this particular performance.[48] Part of the problem seems to have been conflicting agendas within a band that was formed with the best of democratic intentions; Byrd later wrote, "I had assembled too many personalities; every rehearsal became group therapy. A band that wants to succeed needs a single, mutually acceptable identity. I tried to do it democratically, and it was not successful."[49]

Today the tensions are still evident in their recording; in the same way that the stylistic eclecticism of late Beatles recordings revealed a growing split between John Lennon and Paul McCartney, the United States of America's album is similarly diverse, often juxtaposing the highbrow and lowbrow within a single song. Were the United States of America a rock group with techniques appropriated from experimental art music (which would make them one of America's first progressive rock bands), or were they a new music ensemble from the cloisters of academia mounting a naive foray into the world of rock? Moskowitz asserts, "On this seemingly academic debate did the USA's fortunes hinge, even though no one ever articulated it as such. We were busy making the music and not analyzing it. Perhaps we should have been a bit more tidy in our thinking because confusion over first principles was truly at the root of the group's problem. Expectations on the part of the record company, agents and band members themselves that we be able to 'boogie' our way into the hearts of the mainstream public while remaining avant-garde were impossible to fulfill."[50] In retrospect, she adds, "I wanted us to do something new and unique while we had the chance. I sided with Byrd in his attempt to lead this effort, since my own background (or lack thereof) led me to be more comfortable with the simpler, more lyrical and melodic aspects of our work. Under my direction, the band would have had no edge, I'm afraid. Under Byrd's direction, it might not have had much heart. The strange thing is, we enjoyed and could live with this ambiguity rather easily. . . . The rest of the band may have needed more resolution."[51]

Unable to resolve such questions, the group splintered in the summer of 1968, within months of the album's release.[52] Caught in irreconcilable tensions between the idealism of theory and the pragmatism of practice, the breakup of the United States of America reflects similar tensions within the counterculture of 1968, as the slogans of the movement changed from "we can change the world" to "the whole world is watching" within the year.

"Stranded in Time": A Postscript

The band members followed different paths after the group's dissolution. Gordon Marron has continued an active career as a session violinist, performing on albums by Van Dyke Parks and jazz singer Diane Schuur. Craig Woodson has taken his experience playing experimental percussion to schools, where he conducts workshops on experimental musical instrument construction; in 1997 he participated in a residency program with the Kronos Quartet. Dorothy Moskowitz was a member of Country Joe McDonald's *All Star* Band from 1972 to 1973, which featured ex-members of Big Brother and the Holding Company and other players from the Bay Area. She now composes music for children's and adult theater in the San Francisco area.

Little has been heard from bassist Rand Forbes, although Joseph Byrd's career has been somewhat more visible, if erratic. After Byrd's post-USA solo album with the Field Hippies, he pursued his research interests in old-time musical Americana, culminating with the release of the six-album *Popular Music in Jacksonian America* (Musical Heritage Society, out of print). He was also active as an arranger for films (George Roy Hill's *The Long Riders* and Robert Altman's *Health*, among them), and as a composer of electronic/orchestral-style background music for television commercials, leading to eleven CLIO Awards. Byrd also made two albums for the Takoma label in the 1970s, consisting of synthesized renditions of marching tunes and Christmas carols. He also produced Ry Cooder's *Jazz* album in 1978, a collection of ragtime and vaudeville tunes. In 1986 Byrd moved to rural northern California and formed the Jewish Wedding Band, a Klezmer group later named Catskills Revival. This endeavor led Byrd to research the history of Jewish music in America; his research skills were now directed toward locating and learning forgotten pieces from the Yiddish stage and films. The group maintains an active touring schedule and recently released a CD, *Songs of Love and Chutzpah.* In 1998, the children's-music label Music For Little People approached Byrd to create a new Hanukkah album for children; the result, *A Child's Hanukkah with The Jewish Wedding Band,* was the year's top-selling album in its category.

Most recently, Byrd has launched LogoMusic, an Internet firm that develops musical "signatures" and other soundtrack material for corporate websites. The company is in the process of developing a clip music library, a collection of small pieces in virtually every conceivable style, for corporate clients and small website owners to nonexclusively license. According to Byrd, this endeavor finally brings together the longstanding interests of his life's work: [E]verything is coming together: eclecticism, once my Achilles' Heel, is a huge advantage; my scoring experience and knowledge of music styles and orchestration comes in very handy; and my old trick of using technology to my advantage is at the very center of the project."[53]

Today the United States of America is a nearly forgotten footnote in rock history, the victims of a historical oversight proportional to the innovation displayed on its single album. Had the group been on the scene longer, things might have been different. A song lyric Moskowitz wrote for one of her recent theater productions seems applicable for the renewed interest in the United States of America some thirty years after its brief flourish:

Great Unknowns of History

> We are the great unknowns of history
> We were heroes in our prime
> Our lives remain a mystery
> We didn't stand the test of time,
> All the deeds we did'll live on and on
> We were notable in our day,
> But if you don't remember us
> We'll become anonymous and be forever fading away.[54]

Notes

An earlier version of this chapter was presented at the (Sonneck) Society for American Music annual conference in Fort Worth, Texas, March 14, 1999.

1. Elliot Schwartz, *Electronic Music: A Listener's Guide* (New York: Praeger, 1973), 178.
2. See, for example, Barney Hoskyns, *Waiting for the Sun: Strange Days, Weird Scenes, and the Sound of Los Angeles* (New York: St. Martin's Press, 1996), 125, 126; and Jim DeRogatis, *Kaleidoscope Eyes: Psychedelic Rock from the '60s to the '90s* (Secaucus, NJ: Citadel Press, 1996), 110.
3. Joseph Byrd, personal communication with the author, June 24, 1999.
4. Edward Macan, *Rocking the Classics: English Progressive Rock and the Counterculture* (New York: Oxford University Press, 1997), 144.
5. Ibid., 147.
6. This detail was apparently fabricated by Columbia to enhance Byrd's hippie credentials. According to Dorothy Moskowitz, "There was a very modest seaside duplex apartment which we shared with singer Gayathri Rajapur. Students, obscure artists and occasionally famous people came to dinner, but there was never a commune" (Dorothy Moskowitz Falarski, personal communication with the author, July 22, 1998).
7. N.a., liner notes to Joe Byrd and the Field Hippies, *The American Metaphysical Circus* (Columbia Records, 1969).
8. Byrd, June 24, 1999.
9. Ibid.
10. Quoted in "The Invaders," *BMI: The Many Worlds of Music*, July 1968, 13.
11. Joseph Byrd, telephone interview with the author, June 30, 1999.
12. Joseph Byrd, personal communication with the author, June 23, 1999.
13. Dorothy Moskowitz Falarski, personal communication with the author, June 22, 1998.
14. Ibid.
15. Dorothy Moskowitz Falarski, personal communication with the author, June 24, 1998.
16. Falarski, June 22, 1998.
17. Richie Unterberger, *Unknown Legends of Rock 'n' Roll* (San Francisco: Miller Freeman Books, 1998), 367.
18. Falarski, July 22, 1998.
19. Ibid.
20. Unterberger, *Unknown Legends*, 365.
21. Byrd, June 30, 1999.
22. Ibid.
23. Byrd, personal communication with the author, August 6, 1999.

24. Ibid.

25. Byrd, June 23, 1999.

26. Byrd, June 30, 1999.

27. Richard Kostelanetz, "The United States of America." *The Fillmore East: Recollections of Rock Theater* (New York: Schirmer, Books, 1995), n. p.

28. Byrd, June 23, 1999.

29. N.a., liner notes to *The United States of America* (Edsel EDCD 541, 1997).

30. Kostelanetz, "United States," n. p.

31. Lilian Roxon, *Lilian Roxon's Rock Encyclopedia* (New York: Grosset and Dunlap, 1971), 502.

32. Unterberger, *Unknown Legends*, 368.

33. Although the Beatles made use of backward tape effects in songs such as "I'm Only Sleeping" and "Tomorrow Never Knows" (both 1966) and used electronic keyboards such as the Mellotron on earlier songs such as "Strawberry Fields Forever" (1967), the United States of America used electronic sound for purely textural purposes, in a manner that is far less referential of conventional instruments. Compare, for example, the backward guitar sounds in "I'm Only Sleeping"—still melodic in character and recognizable as an electric guitar—and the "faux flute" Mellotron sounds in "Strawberry Fields Forever" with the aggressive shrieks and swooshes in the USA's "Garden of Earthly Delights." On the other hand, it is interesting to compare the USA's tape-loop collage that concludes their album with the Beatles' "Revolution 9" from the "White Album" (released after the USA album).

34. A ring modulator is an electronic processing device that takes inputs from two signal sources and sends out only the sum and difference tones resulting from the two inputs. If the two input signals are a consonant interval, the result is a bell-like metallic tone; this can quickly turn to a harsh growl if the two inputs are in a dissonant relationship to one another. If one of the signal sources is a variable oscillator (the other being the vocal), a sweep of sounds is possible.

35. Roxon, *Encyclopedia*, 502.

36. Kostelantez, "United States," n. p.

37. Byrd, June 23, 1999.

38. Ibid.

39. "The American Metaphysical Circus," Words and Music by Joseph Byrd.© 1968 (Renewed 1996) EMI Blackwood Music Inc. All Rights Reserved. International Copyright Secured. Used by Permission.

40. Joseph Byrd, personal communication with the author, June 24, 1999.

41. A chromatic mediant progression involves two chords that are both major or both minor, the roots of which are a major third or minor third apart

(for example, C major to A-flat major). Examples of such a progression can be heard in the conclusion of the "Gretchen" movement of Franz Liszt's *Faust Symphony*, as well as "Neptune: The Mystic" from Gustav Holst's orchestral suite *The Planets.*

42. Stockhausen used ring modulators in some of his compositions during this period, most notably *Mikrophonie II* (1965) and *Mixtur* (1964, rev. 1967).

43. Byrd distances his work with the USA from Zappa's with the Mothers. In an e-mail from August 4, 1999, he wrote,

> The thing that really set me apart from Frank Zappa was that he was like [L.] Ron Hubbard, another cynical genius who set up a way to milk the system, while seeming to be apart from it. Frank was until 1966 a highly-paid studio musician, the top gun (double scale) lead guitarist in LA, and he realized that he was going nowhere in terms of his own talent and his future. He chose a niche.... The niche was: Offend The Parents. If it was cynical, he certainly was never hypocritical about it, he looked around, he saw the availability of the Anti-Parent, and he grabbed it and never looked back....
>
> Now, none of this is criticism of Zappa's work, which outgrew the planned outrageousness as he evolved, and I have only admiration for the musicianship that led him to seek out Varese's music and try to integrate it with his own.... I am less at one with general opinion about the later stages of Zappa's work; yes, he did become the legend he wanted to be, but his brilliance became subsumed in what I think was a self-referential loop of schizophrenic rebellion and seeking acceptance. Interesting man.

44. Falarski, June 24, 1998.

45. Byrd, June 23, 1999. The tune is, in fact, "Sunshine in my Soul," music composed in 1887 by John Robson Sweney (1837–1899).

46. Falarski, June 22, 1998.

47. Kostelanetz, "United States," n.p.

48. Unterberger, *Unkown Legends*, 368.

49. Kostelanetz, United States," n.p.

50. Falarski, June 24, 1998.

51. Dorothy Moskowitz Falarski, personal communication with the author, June 29, 1998.

52. According to Byrd, there were also more mundane factors involved in the group's breakup. Their manager, Malcolm Terrence, encouraged by Janis Joplin's solo success after leaving Big Brother and the Holding Company, apparently formed an alliance with David Rubinson to nurture a solo career for Moskowitz, whose material had begun to take on a "softer, smoother, less edgy sound" (Byrd, June 24, 1999). Hopes for Moskowitz's solo career, plus the general lack of commercial success accorded the USA album, led to Byrd's ouster from Columbia. Columbia retained the rights to the group's name, but nothing further came from the USA.

53. Joseph Byrd, personal communication with the author, August 6, 1999.
54. Dorothy Moskowitz Falarski, "Great Unknowns of History." Copyright 1998, Jessimel Music, BMI. Used by permission.

References

Byrd, Joseph. Personal communication with the author, June 23, 1999.
————. Personal communication with the author, June 24, 1999.
————. Telephone interview with the author, June 30, 1999.
————. Personal communication with the author, August 4, 1999.
————. Personal communication with the author, August 6, 1999.
Byrd, Joe, and the Field Hippies. *The American Metaphysical Circus*. Columbia Records, 1969. Liner notes.
DeRogatis, Jim. *Kaleidoscope Eyes: Psychedelic Rock from the '60s to the '90s*. Secaucus, NJ: Citadel Press, 1996.
Falarski, Dorothy Moskowitz. Personal communication with the author, June 22, 1998.
————. Personal communication with the author, June 24, 1998.
————. Personal communication with the author, June 29, 1998.
————. Personal communication with the author, July 22, 1998.
Hoskyns, Barney. *Waiting for the Sun: Strange Days, Weird Scenes, and the Sound of Los Angeles*. New York: St. Martin's Press, 1996.
"The Invaders." *BMI: The Many Worlds of Music*, July 1968, 13.
Kostelanetz, Richard. *The Fillmore East: Recollections of Rock Theater*. New York: Schirmer Books, 1995.
Macan, Edward. *Rocking the Classics: English Progressive Rock and the Counterculture*. New York: Oxford University Press, 1997.
Roxon, Lilian. *Lilian Roxon's Rock Encyclopedia*. New York: Grosset and Dunlap, 1971.
Schwartz, Elliot. *Electronic Music: A Listener's Guide*. New York: Praeger Publishers, 1973.
The United States of America. Edsel EDCD 541, 1997. Liner notes.
Unterberger, Richie. *Unknown Legends of Rock 'n' Roll*. San Francisco: Miller Freeman Books, 1998.

Discography

The Beatles, *Sgt. Pepper's Lonely Hearts Club Band*. Capitol CDP 7 46442 2, 1967.
Joe Byrd and the Field Hippies, *The American Metaphysical Circus*. One Way CD 26792, 1969.

The Byrds, *The Notorious Byrd Brothers*. Columbia/Legacy CK 65151, 1968.
Emerson Lake and Palmer, *Brain Salad Surgery*. Rhino CD R272459, 1973.
King Crimson, *Lizard*. Atlantic SD-8278, 1970.
Pink Floyd, *Atom Heart Mother*. Capitol CDP 7 46381-2, 1970.
———. *Dark Side of the Moon*. Capitol CDP 7 46001-2, 1973.
Renaissance, *Scheherazade and Other Stories*. Repertoire REP 4490-WY, 1975.
The United States of America, *The United States of America*. Edsel EDCD 541, 1968.
Rick Wakeman, *No Earthly Connection*. A&M SP 4583, 1976.

part 2

Analytical
Perspectives

Pink Floyd's "Careful with That Axe, Eugene"

Toward a Theory of Textural Rhythm in Early Progressive Rock

John S. Cotner

In this study, I analyze one of Pink Floyd's most popular recordings, the 1968 studio track "Careful with that Axe, Eugene."[1] First, I give the work's historical background. Second, I analyze structural and nonstructural features, drawing on Wallace Berry's (1976) methods for evaluating musical texture, and Eytan Agmon's (1997) procedures for analyzing rhythmic durations. Third, I propose a theory of textural rhythm specific to the studio track. I argue that "Careful with that Axe, Eugene" (hereafter, CAE) represents the successful convergence of particular improvisational idioms and conceptual strategies that the group had begun to develop in their first two albums. The studio recording reveals a dynamic textural rhythm of affective depth: on one plane, a kind of heterophonic "infrastructure"; on another, an expansive stereophonic "soundscape." Aspects of the amplified rock medium, musical language, and recording treatment continually transform the sonic environment and engage the listener experientially in the unfolding structure of the recorded musical work.

Historical Context

In 1968 Pink Floyd released a single with two rather unusual recordings. Nicholas Schaffner tells us that "Point Me at the Sky" (the A-side) was relegated to obscurity soon after its release, whereas "the B-side's throwaway jam [CAE] ... survived as a minor Floyd classic—and yet another milestone in the development of the band's distinctive sound."[2] This same B-side track later appeared on *Relics* (1971), an album of early studio gems spanning the years 1967 to 1971. Even though CAE was not released on any of the studio albums preceding *Relics*, an elaborate live version, performed at Manchester College, appears on the double LP *Ummagumma* (1969). The band also recorded another studio version, similar in form and content to the Manchester performance yet retaining the basic musical and aesthetic markers of the original studio single. Retitled "Come in Number 51, Your Time's Up," this rendition was originally included on the soundtrack to Michaelangelo Antonioni's film *Zabriskie Point* (1970). Shortly thereafter, the film *Pink Floyd at Pompeii* (1972) was released, capturing parts of a live performance from October 1971 that featured a rendition of CAE among other earlier pieces, along with footage of the *Dark Side of the Moon* recording sessions.[3]

As with a good portion of Pink Floyd's musical projects during the late 1960s, the history of CAE suggests its origin in live performance, as a vehicle for theatrical, musical, and psychedelic exploration. In fact, Pink Floyd's live shows were evolving programmatic structures of greater aesthetic sophistication and continuity, as the music became part of a larger, more profound multimedia experience. Nicholas Schaffner tells us that these live performances were "augmented not only by films but also by a plethora of inventive visual effects" and that "[d]uring the group's July 1969 return to the Royal Albert Hall—dubbed 'More Furious Madness from the Massed Gadgets of Auximenes'—someone materialized in a gorilla outfit; a cannon was fired; and the program climaxed with the explosion of a pink smoke bomb. In concerts such as this, the Floyd were already structuring their performances in the guise of two album-length song cycles, called *The Man* and *The Journey*."[4]

It is in the context of *The Journey* suite that "Careful with that Axe, Eugene" was transformed into "Beset by Creatures of the Deep," indicating that the band and listening audiences viewed the extramusical connotations of the piece as changeable. That is, the studio track, like many of their longer works at the time, could potentially signify a range of implicit programs due to its open-ended design, improvisational aesthetic, and ambiguous linguistic markers. Still, I assert that when CAE was designed in the recording studio, its programmatic and affective content was, to a certain extent, idealized; even though subsequent live versions dramatically vary aspects of the original studio track, these renditions are successful only insofar as they elaborate rather than nullify the principal musical and extramusical markers of the original recording.

Schaffner also relates a revealing interview between the band's guitarist David Gilmour and David Fricke regarding the 1968 studio single "Like other such Floyd efforts, 'Careful with that Axe, Eugene' consisted of, in Gilmour's words, 'basically one chord. We were just creating textures and moods over the top of it, taking it up and down . . . it was largely about dynamics.' This time the predominant mood was that of menace and fear—which became increasingly pronounced and effective as 'Eugene' developed into another long-term concert staple. . . . In comparison with the Floyd's subsequent eerie live renditions, the original track was, as Mason put it, 'extremely mild, jig-along stuff.'"[5]

Schaffner's notion that "other such Floyd efforts" exist, such as "Set the Controls for the Heart of the Sun" (1968), suggests that it would be worthwhile to compare similar works among their recordings. Additionally, his point that the band more fully explores connotations of "fear" and "menace" in concert performances infers that those states of mind were originally brought to consciousness in the 1968 studio recording. Yet Gilmour's uncomplicated analysis ("basically one chord"), along with Mason's disinterested characterization ("extremely mild, jig-along stuff"), seems to oversimplify, perhaps undercut, and hardly clarify the encompassing aesthetic effectiveness of the track; and illustrates most explicitly the expressive ambiguity of the musical work for performer and listener alike.

Medium

Pink Floyd's sound in CAE builds from the conventional rock ("power") trio of drum kit, electric guitar, and bass, with Hammond organ completing the core instrumental lineup.[6] To this ensemble vibraphone is added; more than a novelty, it is integral to the spatial, timbral, and textural unfolding of the work. Along with the instrumental source sounds are three discrete vocal characterizations: voice 1 sings open vowel sounds in a melismatic style; voice 2 whispers the phrase, "Careful with that axe, Eugene" (the dominant linguistic moment of the track); and voice 3 takes the shape and tone color of anguished shrieks, repressed screams. A fourth kind of dramatic vocal feature juxtaposes nondescript human sighs with indeterminate high-pitched, nonhuman sounds.

From the first several beats onward, the treatment of source sounds in the recording mix creates a sonic structure that parallels the musical infrastructure. This multitrack orchestration is achieved by means of recording treatments such as:

1. echo (delay) in combination with reverberation, giving the illusion of multiple, juxtaposed ambient spaces;
2. wide panning across right and left stereo channels;
3. source sound locality within the stereo spectrum;
4. timbral modifications including distortion, compression, and phase shifting;
5. exaggerated dynamic contrasts among source sounds.

This "rhetoric of the mix," a contrapuntal treatment of the stereo image, creates the illusion of spatial depth, width, and distance.

Figure 3.1 illustrates the entry of primary source sounds across the stereo image of CAE (5:41 in total length). It provides an allegory for what William Moylan calls the "perceived performance environment" characterized by "a two-dimensional area (horizon plane and distance), where the performance is occurring: the sound stage."[7] The passage of time is measured in seconds along the top of the diagram, and a description of symbols is given in the key. Source sound entries are designated with Arabic numerals in square brackets.

Cross-referencing figure 3.1 with figure 3.2a, below, the bass guitar enters first, *pianissimo*, occupying a position at the center of the stereo spectrum. Alternating octaves D^2–D^3, the bass sets in motion the underpinning ostinato (or drone) that solidifies D as pitch center. It establishes the tempo (approximately ninety-two beats per minute),

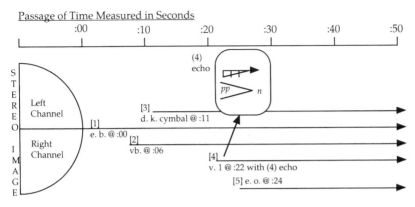

Passage of Time Measured in Seconds

Key

1. *Source Sounds:* electric bass = e. b.; vibraphone = vb.; drum kit cymbal = d. k. cymbal; voice 1 = v. 1; electric organ = e. o.

2. *Order of Source Sound Entries:* Arabic numbers in square brackets denote entries (i.e., [1], [2]).

3. *Echo Effect (Delay):* the shadow component of v.1. is denoted with parenthesis (4) as opposed to square brackets.

4. *The Rate and Direction of Echo:* qualified with the symbol ⊏⊤⊤⊤→ ; here, a sequence of approximately three discreet echoes is demonstrated. The rate of decay and corresponding dynamic diminuendo of the voice 1 echo (4) to silence is indicated *ppp* ⟩ *n* .

Fig. 3.1. Initial sequence of source sound entries (labeled numerically), and abstract representation of voice 1 echo effect within the stereo image.

fixing the quarter note as the unit of metric continuity, and projecting the prevailing two-bar phrase pattern. As shown in figure 3.2b, the vibraphone enters at 0:06 (m. 3),[8] with its motor on a medium setting, and introduces a melodic-harmonic "motto" comprised of six pitches D^4–A^4–C^5–D^5–D^4–E^4. The motto outlines the dorian/aeolian modality of the recording, and gradually sustains a wash of color that prolongs a D minor seventh sonority. This vibraphone motto foretells the long-range harmonic dimension of the musical texture.

Bass drum and ride cymbal join the vibraphone and bass guitar at about 0:11 (m. 5). The crisp rhythmic pattern (0:11) at the bell of the ride cymbal complements the bell-like timbre of the vibraphone. By contrast the bass drum enters hesitantly, holding back, a muffled rhythmic sensation. The drum kit is comprised of multiple percussive accessories (snare, bass, floor tom[s], cymbals and high-hat, etc.), each adjunct element functioning within a composite timbral-rhythmic textural layer (what I refer to as a textural *strand*). The drum set works in

Fig. 3.2. (a) electric bass octave ostinato (drone) as the prevailing 2-bar hyper-metric unit; (b) vibraphone motto; (c) excerpt from opening electric organ theme.

tandem with bass guitar to create a metric substructure of considerable forward momentum; dotted rhythms are handled somewhat freely, giving the impression of triplet subdivisions that "jig" and "swing." As the work proceeds, percussive embellishments become more elaborate, and syncopation is emphasized. Still, the repetitive R and B, off-beat accents endure throughout most of the recording.

It is possible to hear this opening eight-bar series of source sound entries (roughly 0:00–0:22) as a single upbeat, or anacrusis to the voice 1 and electric organ entrance at 0:23 (m. 9). Voice 1 enters, barely audible, on the downbeat of measure 9, enhanced with reverb and echo in combination with subtle wide panning. Immediately, the listener perceives that voice 1 moves across the stereo horizon from right to left, then casually drifts into the depths of psychic space. The direction of echo decay is symbolized in figure 3.1, with an arrow extending through time, from stereo right to stereo left, toward an abstract spatial field within the larger stereo image. Further, the sequential entry of sound sources and their adjacency in the stereo image reinforces the illusion of spatial depth within the ever-shifting soundscape of the recording.

Figure 3.2c provides an excerpt of the electric organ's opening theme as it appears from 0:23–0:49 (mm. 9–18). In measure 9 it breaks from a sustained D^4, elaborating a dorian/aeolian melodic gesture with phrygian coloring, and gradually increasing in loudness. Like the other source sounds, the organ functions in a semi-improvisational capacity: now developing a modal theme, later providing an arpeggiated accompanimental layer; and, during the latter half of the track, loosening exuberant flourishes and dissonant pitch clusters in the lower registers.

The organ line reveals something of the formulaic treatment of scale and rhythm evident between lead guitar, vibraphone, electric organ, and voice 1:

1. inflection of the dorian/aeolian scale content; a kind of modal mixture exploiting F-sharp, C-sharp, and E-flat;
2. recurring pentatonic patterns emphasizing the ascending series A–C–D or descending series F–D–C;
3. mostly symmetrical, even subdivisions of the quarter note into eighth-note and sixteenth-note patterns;
4. sequential patterns building from the quarter note into two- and three-bar melodic gestures;
5. emphasis on the sonorous tenor register, particularly the series of diatonic pitches spanning the A^3–F^4;
6. phrase groupings that begin and end on the modal center D or fifth degree A;
7. minimal ornamentation, usually in the form of grace notes, trills, and mordent-like figures.

The experienced listener might potentially hear these formulas as indirect references to medieval modal practices, and, at a residual symbolic level of meaning, suggestive of something ancient, sacred, or mystical. These associations, along with the hypnotic drone (a remnant of both East Indian and blues practice) easily play into the psychological drama of CAE precisely because such stylistic traces are precariously encoded within the recording.

Texture

Albin Zak defines *texture* as "the quality of sound that resides in the relationships created by the interaction of a track's constituent elements. . . . This 'overall quality' is the general character of the musical gestures; it encompasses among other things timbre, dynamics, rhythm, ambience, pitch range, harmonic spacing, and spatial placement of constituent sounds. Creating and molding textures entails bringing all these elements into a desired balance that involves a complex set of proportions and angles of intersection."[9]

Zak's concept of musical texture is multifaceted, and well-suited to the analysis of rock recordings, especially works such as CAE, which explore unusual ways of elaborating a musical texture within the stereophonic soundscape.

In figure 3.3a, the initial entry of voice 1 at 0:23 (m. 9), full of affective premonitions, subtly foreshadows changes in the textural rhythm of CAE as the source sound configuration increases in diversity from one to five elements: electric bass, vibraphone, electric organ, drum kit, and voice 1. According to Wallace Berry, *textural diversity* is "that textural parameter, quantitative and measurable, conditioned by the number of simultaneous or concurrent components and by the extent of vertical 'space' encompassing them. . . ."[10] Thus, at measure 9, a faint, though stirring, textural change occurs; that is, the textural diversity now consists of six components: four pitched source sounds enhanced by two parallel sonic-timbral modifications, or what I call "shadow" images. Additionally, this event presents a subtle indication of the heterophonic interaction between source sounds so prevalent across the musical infrastructure. By *heterophony* I mean a musical texture in which the individual lines differ in one or more elements (say,

Fig. 3.3. Transcription of voice 1 (v.1.), vibraphone (vb.), electric organ (e.o.), and electric bass (e.b.), 0:20–0:28 (mm. 8–10): (a) reduced score; (b) corresponding textural diversity/density values for definite-pitched source sounds and shadow components. Note: with respect to shadow components, (1e) signifies voice 1 echo effect, and (1s) signifies vibraphone sustain (motor on medium); and concerning stereo panning, R refers to right channel, L to left channel.

rhythm, timbre, and pitch), but retain their resemblance in others (say, intervallic content and motion). Unlike polyphony, lines in a heterophonic texture never assert total independence from one another; and unlike homophony, lines maintain a degree of linear integrity that negates total vertical conformity.

Synchronous with our awareness of textural diversity is an awareness of *textural density*, illustrated in figure 3.3b. Berry explains, "Density as the number of sounding components is the *density-number*; density as the ratio of the number of sounding components to a given total space is the *density-compression*."[11] On the downbeat of m.9, vibraphone and organ collide on the major second interval E^4–D^4. Voice 1, oscillating about the minor second E^4 and F^4, seems to originate from within the tail of the vibraphone's sustained E^4, disturbing the meter but maintaining continuity by doubling the vibraphone at the unison.

Figure 3.3b shows that the incidence of echo on voice 1—what Zak might call a "ghost image"[12]—pulls away from its sustained source at a pulse narrowly ahead of the eighth note (a delay time of about 250–300 milliseconds), transforming the E^4–F^4 melodic dissonance into a new layer of harmonic dissonance. The *echo* treatment of voice 1 is symbolized with the letter *e* attached to the diversity value *1*, suggesting a timbral trace of the melismatic vocal signal. Likewise, the residual E^4 of the vibraphone is represented as a shadow component with the letter *s*, symbolizing *sustain*. These two shadow images are denoted below the score with parentheses to indicate their function as textural thickeners having an illusory extramusical capacity. Together, they connote a divergent reality: perhaps madness, or the mystical potential of LSD-induced aural/visual hallucinations, or an even more abstract metaphysical state of consciousness. As a point of clarification, then, a textural *strand* is the combined effect of a source sound signal and its complex shadow image (its sonic-timbral modifications and treatment in the stereo image, such as panning, phase, echo, and distortion).[13]

Moreover, between organ, vibraphone, and voice 1, the density-compression is that of a minor third, while the range between bass guitar D^2 and voice 1 F^4 (lowest and highest sounding pitches) is over three octaves: a fairly wide and sonorous harmonic field. These relations are quantified below the grand staff with diversity values for the distinct textural strands in figure 3.3b. Textural diversity among the definite pitched instruments decreases in measure 10, as the residual echo from voice 1 leaks across the metric seam between measure 9 and measure 10. Voice 1 descends from F^4 to D^4, diminishing to silence before measure 11; hence, the density-compression between organ and voice contracts to a unison D^4 on the downbeat of measure 10, immediately before the organ begins its long-range melodic idea with phrygian inflection.

Figure 3.4 sketches the outer voice contrapuntal profiles of voice 1 and organ at 0:50–0:58 (mm. 19–22). These parts follow a downward contour, against the octave drone of the bass guitar, to beat four of measure 21: a moment of harmonic convergence and rhythmic accentuation on octave Ds. The two lines descend across a two-octave range from D^5 to D^3, prolonging an embellished D minor seventh sonority. Arabic numerals between the staves in figure 3.4 measure the series of vertical intervals between voice 1 and organ, suggesting a degree of bilinear coherence through the proliferation of sixths, fifths, and octaves. This type of heterophonic continuity proves to be one of the features that gives CAE its rhetorical persuasiveness, an expressive mannerism that depends as much on the musicians' agreed-upon constraints to the improvisational process as their sense of long-range purpose.

The improvisational and formulaic interaction between source sounds in CAE projects a textural rhythm of affective depth. This sort of textural rhythm involves an obligatory tension between meter and phrase grouping among definite-pitched source sounds. Eytan Agmon has developed a method for plotting musical durations that is useful in evaluating the textural rhythm in experimental ambient rock recordings such as CAE.[14] First, I introduce aspects of Agmon's method, then adapt the procedure to specific passages in the studio recording of CAE. Figure 3.5 provides a notational key to the durational analyses in figures 3.6 through 3.8.

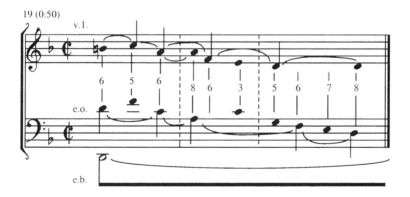

Fig. 3.4. Reduction of voice 1 (v.1.) and electric organ (e.o.) outer voice contour with harmonic intervallic content.

a. closed duration:

b. pseudo-duration:

c. metrical duration

d. antimetrical duration:

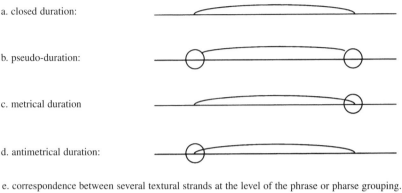

e. correspondence between several textural strands at the level of the phrase or pharse grouping.

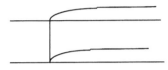

f. correspondence between several textural strands; articulate long-range metric and/or textural goals.

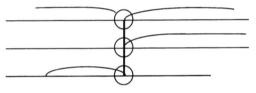

g. implicit conflict between metrical and antimetrical durations:

meter

antimeter

Fig. 3.5. Notational key to the durational analyses in figures 3.6–3.8. Nomenclature adapted from Agmon (1997).

Agmon defines four kinds of musical durations: (1) closed; (2) open; (3) metrical; and (4) antimetrical. Referring to figure 3.5a, a *closed* duration contains both attack and release points; such durations are rare in CAE. Perhaps most problematic is the notion of the *pseudo-* or *open duration*, as illustrated in figure 3.5b. Agmon argues that *pseudo-durations* "are seen, passively, as the time span that separates the release of one note from the attack of the following note; this time span, however, is not defined as a duration in its own right."[15] He further explains that the pseudo-duration is typically perceived in the mind of the listener as a "mental beat" symbolized by means of a rest in the written score, and often corresponds with an anacrusis.[16] Yet with regard to a musical work such as CAE whereby the recording is the "primary text," Agmon's observation that "rests may be often seen in terms of texture, articulation, and even timbre," takes on new significance. "Shadow" effects (such as echo, reverb, distortion, and phase) and recording treatments such as panning and source sound position in the stereo image can significantly alter one's perception of phrase grouping in relation to meter. Some melodic lines, for example, lack both a definitive attack and release point due to the use of echo in combination with panning and dynamic contrasts. Thus, the pseudo-duration seems to be an essential property of the textural rhythm in CAE.

However, the relation of phrase grouping to meter is such that the majority of durations are *metrical* in CAE as shown in figure 3.5c. This type of duration contains an attack point, but lacks a release. For instance, echo enhances the unison doubling of the voice 1/lead guitar melodic trajectory, consistently obscuring the ends of phrases. By comparison, the *antimetrical* duration, seen in figure 3.5d, is a "mirror-image" of the metrical duration since it lacks an attack but contains a point of release. Therefore, the listener must mentally fill in the implied point of attack; Agmon notes that "usually, however, the attack of an anti-metrical duration exists physically, perhaps as a sort of 'rhythmic complementation', in another part."[17] Indeed, "rhythmic complementation" is a pertinent feature of the textural rhythm in CAE and could be expanded to include parallel timbres and recording treatments, and shared melodic formulas among the linear-oriented source sounds, particularly electric organ, lead guitar, and voice 1.

Figure 3.5e–3.5g depict some of the modifications I have made in order to account for unique aspects of the composite textural rhythm of CAE. Correspondence between several textural strands at the level of the phrase and phrase grouping is denoted with a thin vertical connecting line, as illustrated in figure 3.5e. These events commonly involve a rhythmic or metric accent made emphatic through harmonic, melodic, registral, timbral, and/or dynamic means. In figure 3.5f, correspondence between multiple textural strands at the level of the phrase grouping is illustrated with a thick vertical connecting line; these events mark long-range structural-textural coordinates, and usually involve some kind of metric accent, rhythmic complementation, melodic goal, timbral transformation, or combinations of these factors.

One of Agmon's most appealing contributions to the study of rhythm concerns the conflict between meter and grouping that results when the two elements are "out of phase" with one another. He writes, "I believe that the typical metre/grouping conflict is better described as a metre/*shadow-metre* conflict, that is, a conflict between two metrical divisions of the same musical duration, a primary division (metre) and a subsidiary one (shadow metre). . . ." Conversely, metrical and anti-metrical duration are "*qualitatively different* types of durations;" hence, "it seems theoretically possible to have a conflict between metrical and antimetrical durations even when their attacks and releases happen to coincide."[18] This scenario is illustrated in figure 3.5g: the two types of durations on the musical surface suggest an antimetrical duration at the level of the phrase grouping. The conflict between meter and antimeter is a critical aspect of the textural rhythm, and takes on significance as a rhetorical code that lends affective immediacy to the psychological drama of the recording.

Voice 3 begins a series of drawn out, horrific shrieks just prior to David Gilmour's extended vocal/guitar solo. An extra- (or "para"-) linguistic layer of dark and disturbing affect, suggestive of something pathological and violent, voice 3 immediately intensifies the ambiguous meaning of voice 2's preceding whispered phrase ("Careful with that axe, Eugene") at 1:35 (m. 35), and signals the beginning of Gilmour's solo at 1:50 (m. 41). I am calling this solo passage a *textural strand* due to the combined effect of unison doubling and timbral-sonic treatment ("shadow components") of the distinct vocal and guitar source sounds in the stereo image. Further, the vocal/guitar strand originates from stereo right, while residual echo and feedback loops perpetually bleed into stereo left. The effect is at once eerie and engaging, encoding the textural rhythm of the track with a new layer of psychological discord.

Figure 3.6 sketches the durational profile of the voice 1/lead guitar textural strand, at roughly 1:50–3:26 (mm. 41–79). Pitches are represented by notes half their actual durations (that is, a sounding half note

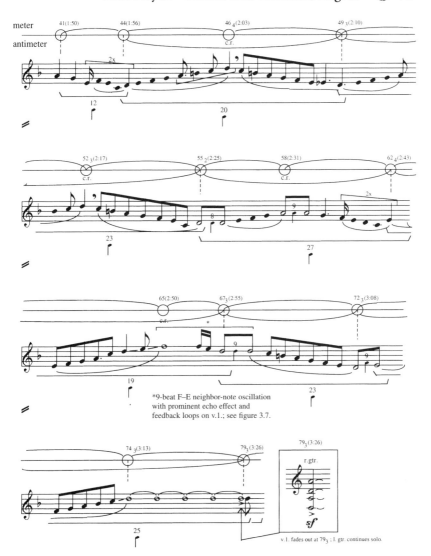

Fig. 3.6. Melodic and durational profiles of the voice 1/lead guitar (v.1./l.gtr.) textural strand spanning 1:50–3:26 (mm. 41–79). Note: c.r. = contour reversal; 2x = recurring pattern repeated twice; ' = breath in vocal line; subscripts attached to measure numbers denote beat within the designated bar (other than downbeat).

has a quarter note written value, and so on; actual rhythmic values smaller than an eighth note are indicated with stemless noteheads). Periods of rhythmic "ebb" in the melodic "flow" of the voice 1/lead guitar trajectory are accounted for by a symbol giving the approximate number of quarter-note beats bridging beamed half notes on the staff. These events correspond with ambiguous boundaries between musical durations within phrase groupings.

Out of Gilmour's vocal/guitar doubling emerges a melodic trajectory that cuts across the structural midframe of the track. Voice 1 and lead guitar signals, especially in terms of rhythmic inflection and gestural nuance, coordinate to such a degree that the listener may reasonably conclude that Gilmour performed both lines at the same time; the technique is idiomatic to the blues and some jazz, and the guitarist incorporated both styles in his improvisations.

At 1:50 (m. 41), a recurring pattern is stated twice (bracketed and marked "2x") which constitutes a twelve-beat phrase having the conduct of a metrical duration. Syncopation across the barline at 1:56 (m. 44) eliminates a clear release, and propels the melodic line forward, as Gilmour's improvised solo unfolds in balanced, wave-like phrase groupings ranging from roughly twenty to twenty-seven beats. The first twenty-beat phrase grouping, at 1:56–2:10 (mm. 44–49$_3$), lacks an equivocal attack but contains its release (an example of an antimetrical duration). The melodic trajectory ascends an octave through a pure dorian scale to the crest of its first wave, momentarily stressing D^5 at 2:03 (m. 46$_4$); this pitch articulates a contour reversal (marked "c.r."), whereby the melodic trajectory changes direction downward to D^4 at 2:10 (m. 49). This change in melodic direction transforms the twenty-beat antimetrical duration into two shorter ones. Yet the fact that the contour reversal at measure 46$_4$ occurs on a weak beat, and is followed by a rest on the downbeat of measure 47, suggests that the ascending gesture of the first wave spanning 1:56–2:03 (mm. 44–46$_4$) is a pseudo-duration, lacking both attack or release points. The crests of the two succeeding melodic waves, at 2:17 (m. 52$_3$) and 2:31 (m. 64$_4$), are also articulated by contour reversals, and have the conduct of pseudo-durations. In each of these instances, both voice 1 and lead guitar fail to stress the beat with a degree of clarity that affirms the coordination of attack and release points at the moment of contour reversal. The manner of surface conflict between meter and grouping at the boundaries of phrases in the voice 1/lead guitar textural strand complements similar idiomatic treatment by the vibraphone, electric organ, and rhythm guitar.

The recurring pattern heard earlier at 1:50 (m. 41) is repeated toward the end of the antimetrical duration spanning 2:25–2:43 (mm. 55_2–62_4), and initiates a series of connected nineteen-, twenty-three-, and twenty-five-beat phrase groupings that encompass the highpoint of the track. Focusing on the circled region in figure 3.6, the vocal/guitar melodic trajectory reaches upward to its apex, the sustained seven-beat neighbor oscillation between F^5 and E^5 spanning 2:50–2:55 (mm. 65–67_3); figure 3.7 magnifies this climactic moment. While the pitch content of the neighbor-note oscillation is identical for voice 1 and

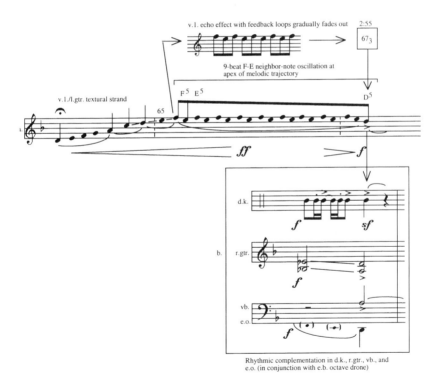

Fig. 3.7. Voice 1/lead guitar textural strand at apex of melodic trajectory, 2:50–2:55 (mm. 65–67); (a) sketch of v.1./l.gtr. textural strand; (b) rhythmic-metric complementation in d.k., r.gtr., vb., and e.o.

lead guitar, volume, echo, and residual feedback loops saturate the sonic environment. Consequently, the extreme amount of sonic-timbral saturation overcomes a potential attack on F^5 at 2:50 (m. 65); for the same reasons a clear release on D^5 at 2:55 (m. 67_3) is also ambiguous. Thus, the climactic neighbor-note oscillation resembles a pseudo-duration, and delays the change in melodic direction. Nonetheless, rhythmic complementation in the other source sounds at m. 67_3 provides a metric accent that alters the textural rhythm: the vocal/guitar strand gradually descends to D^4, then rises stepwise again to D^5, gliding there as voice 1 echo feedback loops cascade across the stereo image from right to left channels, fading out at 3:26 (m. 79_3). In figure 3.6, the rhythm guitar articulates this moment, as voice 1 drops out of the texture, and lead guitar continues its solo.

The graph shown in figure 3.8 portrays the period of textural saturation and structural emphasis coinciding with the apex of the vocal/guitar trajectory at roughly 2:25–3:26 (mm. 55–79_3). As illustrated, this event also marks the end of textural "progression" and the beginning of textural "recession" to the end of the track. Indeed, the gradual rise and fall of textural intensity across the formal breadth of CAE recalls Berry's concepts of *progression* and *recession*: an extended duration of textural growth (progression) toward maximal density and diversity, followed by a comparable duration of textural simplification (recession) to minimal diversity and density.[19]

Further, the encompassing textural rhythm of the track effects one's perception of structure in a number of ways. I tend to interpret the overall design of CAE along the following lines. First, the period of textural progression from roughly 0:00 to 1:34 implies a broad structural downbeat or thesis—what Berry would term an *initiative impulse*. Second, the period of textural saturation and structural emphasis connected with the apex of Gilmour's vocal/guitar solo from about 1:34 to 3:26 connotes "accent-delineated thrust (motion, energy), in a sense absorbing the force of the initiative impulse, reacting to its accentual 'energy' and predominance"[20]—a *reactive impulse*. Finally, the period of textural recession from roughly 3:26 to the end of the track suggests an upbeat or anacrusis, an *anticipative impulse*.[21] What is more, the dynamic shape of the track outlines a long-range crescendo, increasing in loudness toward the vocal/guitar apex and textural saturation, fol-

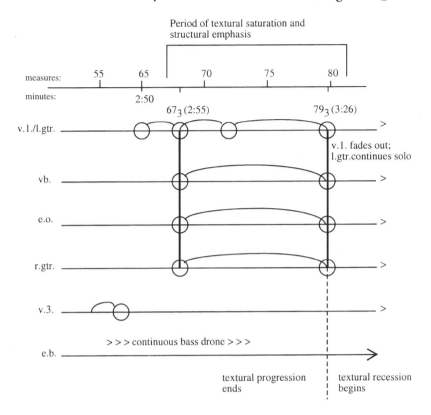

Fig. 3.8. Composite textural rhythm of definite-pitched source sounds from 2:25–3:26 (mm. 55–80). The period of textural saturation and structural emphasis is bracketed; end of textural progression ends, recession begins. (See keys to figures 3.1 and 3.5 for nomenclature.)

lowed by a gradual diminuendo to silence across a duration of almost two and a half minutes.

The unmeasured aleatoric final seconds of the track are open ended, leaving the listener without a clear sense of metric closure and anticipating a definitive resolution that never occurs. Indeed, the sigh at the end of the track suggests a release point for everything that came before; however, its almost inaudible conduct, though a subtle release, fails to adequately substitute for a point of release that never comes. The question, then, is, "If the conclusion of the piece suggests an antic-ipative impulse, what is it anticipating?" It anticipates the unknown, a vast, empty spatial presence—perhaps symbolic of a psychological void, a crisis of personality or ego. These connotations would align with the general psychedelic quality of the recording.

On the other hand, the beauty of the piece is that it allows for multiple readings. For example, the first half of the track could also imply a large-scale anacrusis to the climactic event, which could articulate an initiative impulse. This interpretation raises different questions: Do we discard the "motion/energy," the "absorption of the force" of the initiative impulse, or the void of the unmeasured ending? Does it function as a reactive impulse, absorbing the initiative impulse? These questions about the flow of textural rhythm in relation to large-scale impulses play effectively into the psychological openness and unresolved psychic tension of the track.

Conclusion

In *Rocking the Classics: English Progressive Rock and the Counterculture* (1997) Edward Macan provides an overview of the stylistic parameters of progressive rock, distinguishing between two "waves" of English progressive rock. The first wave, 1967–71, included psychedelic bands such as the Nice, the Moody Blues, and Pink Floyd and "actually represent a proto-progressive style. . . ."[22] The second wave, 1971–76, included King Crimson, Jethro Tull, and Van der Graaf Generator and according to Macan constitutes the "golden age" of English progressive rock. The first wave is a direct outgrowth of psychedelic rock, the Beatles' album *Sgt. Pepper's Lonely Hearts Club Band* (1967) being the principal catalyst of change, in which "many of the elements that later characterized English progressive rock first appear."[23] With this chronology in mind, I would like to revisit Macan's concept of psychedelic ("proto-progressive") rock, and reconsider its impact on current notions about "progressiveness in rock."

According to Macan's interpretation, psychedelic rock can be organized into three branches ("wings") of style growth. The third wing is characterized by a group of subgenres: (1) a symphonic extension of classical influences; (2) the concept album as a kind of "programmatic song cycle"; and (3) the instrumental multimovement suite, a "large-scale programmatic form drawn from classical music." He further distinguishes The Nice and Pink Floyd as two English bands who experimented extensively within these subgenres, particularly the multimovement suite, noting, "Indeed, it was an interest in creating lengthy instrumental soundscapes that led these two groups to bring yet another large-scale programmatic form drawn from classical music. The multimovement suite, as employed by late-nineteenth-century and early-twentieth-century composers, is (usually) an instrumental piece in several distinct movements that attempt to convey an extramusical source of inspiration (the 'program') by using music to 'paint' a picture, 'narrate' a story, or 'describe' a philosophical concept."[24]

While one might question Macan's assertion that these two bands annexed the multimovement suite from its historical and cultural context, we can safely conclude that Pink Floyd and the Nice (like their contemporaries such as the Beatles, the Moody Blues, and Procol Harum) were at once inspired and challenged by the weight of the European art music tradition—though these two groups took rather divergent experimental courses.

Generally, the descriptor *progressive* is based on the root concept *progress,* which, as David Brackett, Bill Martin, and others explain, refers to *development* and *growth* by accumulation.[25] Rock music of the 1960s and 1970s that appropriates a compositional mentality and alludes to older styles of art music is typically lumped into this category, for "cultivated" music is associated with notions of large-scale structural coherence, thematic and harmonic growth. The rational musical systems associated with Classical and Baroque genres—such as sonata principle, theme and variation, song cycle, and multimovement suite—are realized in one form or another in the music of bands such as Pink Floyd, Genesis, and King Crimson. *Progressive,* then, seems to be equated with explicit references to aspects of art music.

In response, I argue that by 1966 the degree of social and artistic dialogue among rock musicians in the United Kingdom and United States had dramatically accelerated. For bands such as the Beatles, the Byrds, and the Beach Boys, the idea of fusing elements of cultivated (composed) music with rock, a vernacular (oral) musical tradition, was already seen as a convention within the emerging rock aesthetic. That late 1960s and 1970s progressive rock evolved out of psychedelic (or "acid") rock is indisputable; however, I question the notion that either psychedelia or progressive rock are well-formed genres to begin with. The dominant view among scholars and journalists is that the experimental projects of bands such as the Nice, Pink Floyd, and the Jimi Hendrix Experience in the mid to late 1960s are quite removed, aesthetically and ideologically, from archetypal English progressive rock. Psychedelic rock is usually distinguished from progressive rock in that the former style was directly mediated by the counterculture, whereas the latter formation drew only indirectly from that earlier source. While it is a fact that some early 1970s English bands, some of the time, took a unidirectional course into the harmonic and structural domains of European art music, I question the long-standing tradition that one can identify a site of "authenticity" for progressive rock.

Indeed, Richard Middleton and Allan Moore make clear the fact that progressive rock is "heterogeneous by design," and "contradictory." Middleton goes so far as to question the notion that it is a "phenomenon" at all.[26] A number of factors underline the inherently contradictory quality of so-called 1960s and 1970s progressive rock. Part of the problem lies in the fact that many of the albums by English progressive bands include simple, blues-influenced rock songs and ballads intermingled among longer suites, forming song cycles that increase rather than resolve the tension at the aesthetic boundaries of "art" and "rock." Yet a more provocative problem is the widespread implication that in order for a rock musical work to be "progressive," it must refer explicitly to classical sources be they formal, instrumental, conceptual, or technical. Sometimes this results in the reification of rock as art music, neutralizing, through analysis, the intrinsic impurities and discrepancies, subject matter, and residual social effects that make this music rock in the first place. Bruce Baugh presents a strong argument that most attempts to combine rock with "classical" music result in a kind of misguided formalism on the part of performer and receiver alike: "To the extent art rock succeeded, it did so because it was rock, not because it was art."[27] Even though I disagree with some of his points, Baugh's distinction between the *form* and *matter* of music is pertinent to any study of experimental trends in popular and rock music. Indeed, his views support my claim that "progressiveness in rock" moves continuously between explicit and implicit references to genres and strategies derived not only from European art music, but other cultural domains (such as East Indian, Celtic folk, and African) and hence involves a continuous aesthetic movement between formalism and eclecticism.

Successful progressive rock, then, does not seek so much to neutralize the aesthetic contradictions arising from the fusion of cultivated and vernacular sources. To the contrary, progressiveness should be viewed more broadly, not as a genre or style per se, but as a "frame of mind"—a mannerism whereby the artist elaborates a concept, to varying degrees, through both magnification and accumulation, variation and development.

This allows us to acknowledge the fact that sometimes progressive rock fails to integrate classical sources; and sometimes, as in the Beatles' "A Day in the Life," the fusion seems to create a new aesthetic standard; one emerging at the level of the opus, but dissolving at the level of the genre. Viewed this way, the kinds of formal and thematic complexity and growth associated with art music comes into conflict with the improvisational, profane, and confrontational ideology of rock. Progressiveness, then, cannot exist without a comparable transgressive tendency, an attention to the mind/body conflict that allows rock to thrive as music for both dancing and listening, individual and collective expression, antiestablishment sentiment within the dominant cultural environment.

Into this reinterpretation of progressiveness in rock, I return to Pink Floyd's "Careful with that Axe, Eugene." In most outward appearances, the studio recording can easily be categorized as psychedelic rock: it suggests a countercultural tendency, exploiting formal open-endedness, and a kind of expanding-present consciousness associated with LSD experimentation; it makes use of a steady drone around which instruments improvise extended passages, also alluding to alternative "non-Western" sources. But, on a more covert level, the track manifests subtle means of variation and development, a *progressive* tendency that is more than merely "experimental."

The implicit manner of progressiveness in "Careful with that Axe, Eugene" is actualized most cogently in the area of musical texture. Source sounds extemporize within a prescribed modality, building-up a largely heterophonic infrastructure; musical lines indirectly infer simple motor rhythms and melodic sequences associated with baroque symmetry, and the stereo image forms a multidimensional conceptual space within which musical ideas enlarge and diminish. Additionally, the conflict between phrase grouping and meter that results from timbral-electronic and textural considerations combines with unusual extralinguistic vocal elements to create a strange and elusive psychological drama. It is music for listening and contemplation, deeply preoccupied with the formal and material aspects of sound, and as covert in its progressive signs as its transgressive subject matter. I suggest that "Careful with that Axe, Eugene" gains aesthetic persuasiveness precisely because it understates its progressiveness; the exploration of textural rhythm within a complex sonic soundscape brings musical and extramusical images to fruition in a way that is not matched by its successors.

Notes

1. This article is based on the paper entitled "Pink Floyd's 'Careful with that Axe, Eugene' (ca. 1968): A Study in Genre, Medium, Texture, and Structure," which was presented November 11, 1999, at the Twenty-Second Annual Meeting of the Society for Music Theory in Atlanta, Georgia.

2. Nicholas Schaffner, *Saucerful of Secrets: The Pink Floyd Odyssey* (New York: Delta Books, 1992), 139.

3. A detailed comparative analysis of studio and live versions of CAE would be a logical extension of this study. I begin such a comparative analysis of the studio track with both Pompeii and Manchester performances in my dissertation, provisionally titled "Archetypes of Progressive Rock, ca. 1966–1973."

4. Schaffner, *Saucerful of Secrets*, 139.

5. Ibid., 139.

6. Two psychedelic bands of the mid-1960s, Cream and the Jimi Hendrix Experience, are representative "power" trios who undoubtedly had an impact on Pink Floyd and other groups, such as Led Zeppelin, ZZ Top, and Rush, among others.

7. William Moylan, *The Art of Recording: Creative Resources of Music Production and Audio* (New York: Van Nostrand Reinhold, 1992), 207–8.

8. Since the recorded musical work is the "primary text" rather than a score of arrangement, I will usually refer to musical events by their clock-time designations, providing measure numbers (hence "m.3" here) in order to clarify the location of events within the metric substructure. At times I

refer only to measure numbers or minutes depending on the context of the discussion.

9. Albin Zak, "The Poetics of Rock Composition: Multitrack Recording as Compositional Practice" (Ph.D. dissertation, City University of New York, 1997), 90.

10. Wallace Berry, *Structural Functions in Music* (Englewood Cliffs, N.J.: Prentice-Hall, 1976), 191.

11. Ibid., 209; emphasis added.

12. Zak, "Poetics of Rock Composition," 108–9. Zak's notion of a "ghost" image is connected to the effect of echo on a given source sound, whereas my idea of a "shadow" image merely stresses the combined effect, the *complex* of multiple timbral-sonic modifications to a source signal; thus, a "ghost" image is a component of the "shadow" image.

13. This is a modification of Wallace Berry's method for representing textural diversity values. He writes in chapter 2, "Texture," note 3, "In this symbolization, the actual vertical alignment of voices is not necessarily represented. Parentheses may denote a component having independence or substance in some way restricted" (Berry, *Structural Functions,* 188). In CAE shadow components give spatial and directional depth to the textural rhythm; they also provide semantic depth by enhancing the listener's illusion of increased psychological engagement.

14. See Eytan Agmon, "Musical Durations as Mathematical Intervals," *Music Analysis* 16 (1997): 45–75; see also Wallace Berry's *Structural Functions.*

15. Agmon, "Musical Durations," 55.

16. Though the terms seem similar, an *anacrusis* is different from an *upbeat,* as Fred Lerdahl and Ray Jackendoff assert: "Grouping and meter can be in or out of phase in varying degrees. To clarify this point, we define *anacrusis* as the span from the beginning of a group to the strongest beat in the group. (The term *upbeat* will not do here, since beats do not have duration; an anacrusis can include many upbeats at various levels.)" (30); see Lerdahl and Jackendoff *A Generative Theory of Tonal Music* (Cambridge: MIT Press, 1983).

17. Agmon, "Musical Durations," 63.

18. Ibid., 64; emphasis in the original.

19. Berry, *Structural Functions,* 184–90.

20. Ibid., 327.

21. Ibid. Berry describes (in chapter three, "Rhythm and Meter," note 24) the reactive impulse as follows: "The physical analogy of an object set in motion, impelling another object, which sets in motion another, etc., is tempting; the diminishing force in such a series seems distinctly parallel to that perceived in the relations of impulses within the metric unit."

22. Edward Macan, *Rocking the Classics: English Progressive Rock and the Counterculture* (New York: Oxford University Press, 1997), 23.

23. Ibid., 20.

24. Ibid., 21.

25. See David Brackett, *Interpreting Popular Music* (Cambridge: Cambridge University Press, 1995); see also Bill Martin, *Listening to the Future: The Time of Progressive Rock, 1968–1978* (Chicago: Open Court Press, 1998).

26. Richard Middleton, *Studying Popular Music* (Buckingham: Open University Press, 1990), 28; see also Allan Moore, *Rock: The Primary Text; Developing a Musicology of Rock* (Buckingham and Philadelphia: Open University Press, 1993).

27. Bruce Baugh, "Prolegomena to Any Aesthetics of Rock Music," *Journal of Aesthetics and Art Criticism*, 51, no. 1 (1993): 25.

Progressive Rock As Text

The Lyrics of Roger Waters

4

Deena Weinstein

Progressive rock is rather less than a genre and a lot more than one, too.

It is less than most popular music genres because its defining feature is not a set of concrete sonic elements, such as particular rhythms or instrumentation. Instead, progressive rock is distinguished by a conceptual trope: the appropriation of nonpopular musical forms. Typically, the sources are European "classical" music, jazz, and avant-garde music. What these three types have in common is not their sonic qualities. They are tightly linked, at least at the time of progressive rock's origins in the late-1960s, on an abstract level: they are the major extant representations of "high art" musical forms, associated socially with the upper middle class. (Jazz, of course, originated as anything but "high art," but in the post–World War II years its Beat champions and the loss of its original audience altered its class associations.)

Progressive rock's conceptual unity gives a strong clue about its extramusical import. So does the fact that the early progressive rock bands were supported by their tours of the college circuit (at that time defiantly non-working class) in England. Paul Stump states that the "redbrick colleges practically kept Progressive alive, and helped create an audience for Progressive as a lifestyle, as a separate culture, a signifier for a newly-defined 'other.'"[1]

Progressive rock is also more than a genre; rooted in the upper-class and white-collar regions of Britain,[2] it was, at least in the era of its formation and initial crystallization, an expression of a sociocultural movement, specifically an attempt to put forth claims of value for the upper middle class.[3] Edward Macan writes, "Obviously, a style like progressive rock, with its references not only to classical music but also to the art and literature of high culture, was not going to spring from a working-class environ. Its emergence depended on a subculture of highly educated young people."[4]

This class-oriented movement was centered in British society, where class was (and perhaps still is) a central issue. It did not find resonance in the United States, attracting far fewer fans and fewer musicians. Yet it was part of the wider particularist validation movements that had parallels in the United States. These replaced the failed universalist movements that characterized the 1960s, namely the civil rights movement and the counterculture/youth/free speech/antiwar movement. The turning point came in 1967–68, when a series of events made universalist hopes turn sour, including the murder of Martin Luther King Jr., the drug casualties overrunning San Francisco's Haight-Ashbury, and the state repression of youth in Chicago, Mexico City, Paris, and Prague.

The reaction to these failures were movements validating particular groupings: women (women's liberation); blacks (black power); gays; and, by the mid-1970s in the United States, various ethnic groups ("roots"). Progressive rock can be seen as a cultural variant of these contemporaneous movements.[5]

That progressive rock was a class-based social movement is underscored by the scorn and vitriol heaped upon it by the British-based punk rockers of the latter half of the 1970s. They were also a class-based movement, championing the working class. (Take, for example punk's code: its non-upper-class speech and ragged clothing are but two symbolic expressions of its class affiliation.)

Rock music, of which progressive rock is a form, distinguishes itself from "pop" by its claim to authenticity. Initially, for "British Invasion" bands such as the Rolling Stones and the Beatles, or for Bob Dylan, that authenticity came from incorporating the otherness of "authentic" groups, particularly blacks and rural whites. Those groups were seen to be "real" because they and their music were thought to be outside commercial fabrication. Progressive rockers also needed authenticity; after all, they shared in the prevailing "rock" ethos. But instead of taking their predecessors' route of "prestige from below," they went the way that the upper-middle class, or the nouveau riche, always do—emulating the upper classes, especially in their artistic tastes; for example, late-nineteenth-century "robber-barons" decorated their homes with "classic" art. Discussions of progressive rock always indicate how its practitioners overtly announced their upper-middle-class backgrounds and made frequent references to the music, art, and literature of high culture.[6]

Progressive rock's fusion of "high" and "low" art forms was not a unique move. The pop art style, working in the opposite direction, imported pop culture iconography into "serious" art. Think here, for example, of Andy Warhol's Marilyn Monroe and Campbell's Soup paintings. Within rock itself, the binary of high and low art had already begun to be dissolved in the 1960s by Bob Dylan and those who followed in Dylan's wake, such as Simon and Garfunkel and John Lennon. Progressive rock can be understood as belonging to the postmodernist movement, which came into being at the same time and championed transgressing the boundaries of high and low culture.

Progressive rock is often called "art rock," particularly in the United States, where critics and musicians have not gone to art school and learned the romantic ideology that privileges innovation (progressivity) over stagnation/imitation. As Stump argues, progressive rock is more than a sonically defined genre: "The music is NOT all that matters. The ideology—the Progressive ideology—or artistic idealism in British pop music trails a continuous *cultural* thread back to the 1940s."[7]

Progressive rockers borrowed high art to decorate their own endeavors. Because "classical," jazz, and experimental musics only share an abstract unity under the category of "high art," the genre that appropriated them allows for some play by noncreators: that is, writers can play with the genre, which is what I propose to do here. Specifically, I want to address "high art" elements that go beyond strictly musical forms, in particular, lyrics. Progressive rock, after all, is a rock genre, and rock is a song-based formation in which lyrics play an integral part.

The Case of Pink Floyd

I believe that Pink Floyd, which is already designated as a progressive rock group by many commentators on the basis of its music, should also be considered as one on the basis of its lyrics. In order to do so, I need first to distinguish among the bands that are designated as "Pink Floyd." There are at least four groups going by that name; the first and the last will not be included here for lyrical analysis.

The earliest version of Pink Floyd was a mid-1960s experimental psychedelic band centering on the writing and performing of guitarist/singer Roger "Syd" Barrett, a charismatic front man as well as a creative composer. The three other members of that original line-up were bassist Roger Waters, drummer Nick Mason, and keyboardist Richard Wright. All four young men lived in the London area and attended British art schools.

Attendance at art schools, which some writers have called colleges for middle-class misfits, is something that many progressive rockers and, indeed, British band members in general—such as John Lennon, Keith Richards, and Eric Clapton—had in common. Simon Frith and Howard Horne indicate the art school impact on music, noting that "in the 1960s art school students became rock and roll musicians and in doing so inflected pop music with bohemian dreams and Romantic fancies and laid out the ideology of 'rock'—on the one hand a new art form, on the other a new community."[8] Stump, writing specifically about progressive rock, agrees: "The art-school tradition with its championing of individual creativity, genius and Romantic personal adventurism in the arts, informed many strands of British popular music, but a specific coincidence of cultural, social and economic conditions in the mid- and late 1960s facilitated the making of music for music's sake."[9]

When Barrett withdrew from the band (and from the world, due to schizophrenia) ending Pink Floyd's first incarnation, he was replaced by his friend and sometime guitar instructor, David Gilmour. Gilmour had not gone to art school, but had worked as a male model and had played with other rock bands.

The post-Barrett band, the second Pink Floyd, was a mixed bag, encompassing both experimental/psychedelic and progressive rock, and within this bag are the works that generally classify the band soni-cally as progressive rock (mainly through its appropriation of avant-garde experimental music, particularly musique concrète).

The fourth and latest version of Pink Floyd (what some fans call Pink Fraud and Pink Void because they have a specific response to the query "Which one is Pink?": Roger Waters) consists of Wright, Mason, and Gilmour. Guitarist Gilmour is the Waterless Floyd's main man, as singer and composer (although he gets help from others outside the band in both areas). No one, especially Gilmour, would argue that the lyrics of this version of Pink Floyd are anything resembling high art, or are even good lyrics.

My focus will be on what I classify as the third Pink Floyd, which created a set of albums beginning with *Dark Side of the Moon* in 1973 and ending with *The Final Cut* in 1983. This Pink Floyd has all of the same personnel as the post-Barrett band,[10] but, after Barrett's departure, the band's second incarnation made albums in a variety of styles based on music and lyrics written by different members. In contrast, the albums of the third incarnation were all based on lyrics (and much of the music, but that is not of interest here) written by Roger Waters. Indeed, Waters has recognized that lyrics are central to his works: "What was important about that record [*Dark Side of the Moon*] is what it was *about,* in my view. The recording was very ordinary, *really.*"[11] So, it is Waters's lyrics that are, I will argue, deserving of the designation of high art, for the following four reasons:

1. They encompass a well-developed artistic vision that tran-scends specific songs or even albums.
2. There is a consistent set of images and metaphors that are found in this body of work, as well as specific high-art influ-ences and appropriations.
3. Each album constitutes a thematic whole—a "concept album" rather than a collection of songs—and each album takes a dif-ferent form.
4. In addition to these formal characteristics, Waters's lyrics are appropriations of themes that are staples of the high modernist art associated with cultural pessimism, turn-of-the-twentieth-century British romanticism, and existentialism.

This is not to say that Waters's words were particularly *appreciated* as high art, or appreciated on any level by most listeners. Nor were they understood well. The rock critic establishment, for the most part, hated them. Its damnation of Waters's work centered on the fact that his lyrics did not provide the listener with any hope or optimism, and that they only projected a "grim misanthropy."[12] The *Rolling Stone* reviewer of *Wish You Were Here* is typical, summing up Waters's view as "defeated cynicism" and complaining that he offers "not so much as a hint of liberation...."[13] In the next decade, in the same magazine, another critic, Kurt Loder, lamented that "Waters is just constitutionally incapable of relating a happy state."[14] A *Chicago Tribune* critic summarized and damned his lyrics as providing "darkly cynical views of life and the human condition...."[15] And another from a 1992 interview in *Q* magazine: "Waters, the Mister Glum who refuses even to sniff at his brimming beaker of beer, is the gloomiest man in rock. He's enough to depress a gadfly."[16]

Waters's lyrics for the third Pink Floyd were written after the youth movement—the counterculture, with its universalist utopian dreams—was soundly defeated. Similar "downer" vibes were alive in other post-'60s music, especially in what became known as heavy metal (a replacement for an earlier term, "downer rock," that was tossed at groups like Black Sabbath), which the critics detested as well.[17]

While the rock critics demand truths—authenticity—from musicians, their criticisms of Waters indicate that they only want to hear *some* truths—the happy, redeeming, or uplifting ones. When there is no optimism to be gained from artists' authentic expressions, they are dismissed as egotistic or neurotic, the outpourings of sick minds. For example, Loder advised that Waters "should have a long session with his therapist before making any future public utterances about the human condition."[18] A 1983 review referred to Waters as writing "rock's most neurotic lyrics...."[19] David Fricke, writing in *Rolling Stone* in 1984, slighted Waters's work as "confessional."[20] A Chicago critic dismissively contended that *Wish You Were Here* is "about how awful life became for Waters after *Dark Side of the Moon*'s success; and *The Wall*, of course, was a two-record set on just that same subject." In sum, Waters "confused his terrors, his problems, with those of the world generally...."[21]

That critics disliked Waters's lyrics because they lacked any hope that human beings could be redeemed is demonstrated by the reversal that they almost universally made when they evaluated *The Final Cut.* Typical was Loder, who in a review entitled "Floyd's Artistic Epiphany" wrote, "Dismissed in the past as a mere misogynist, a ranting crank, Waters here finds his focus at last, and with it a new humanity."[22]

Beyond their lyrical content, there were other reasons for the critical dismissal of Waters's work. One was the punks' selection of Pink Floyd as the enemy, the premier exemplar of the culture against which they were revolting. Given the antibourgeois ideology of the punks, their choice of a progressive rock group was right on. Choosing a band that was massively popular was a fine bit of rhetoric, too. Nicholas Schaffner notes that by the end of 1976, "critics [had] made common cause with the punk revolution."[23]

Then, too, the seriousness with which the progressive rock groups took themselves did not win them friends; *pretentiousness* was punk's invidious term. That Waters, or any other member of Pink Floyd in the 1970s, was standoffish toward the press and refused to sit for pictures and interviews cheerfully also did not endear them to the rock magazine crowd. Waters, especially, did not suffer fools gladly, and the rock press demands pandering.

Another reason for the negative reaction to Waters was the contrast between him and his predecessor, Syd Barrett, who came straight out of rock's central casting department. Barrett was handsome, charismatic, and charming; Waters was none of these. Barrett's lyrics were hardly pessimistic. (Of course they were hardly optimistic either; they are best described as whimsical, childlike, or "out there.") And Barrett won the hearts of all rock appreciators because he performed that great charismatic career move (perhaps even better than death at an early age from excess): he went mad. Barrett was seen as an "acid casualty" and certainly he did ingest more than his fair share of LSD—more than a small city's fair share. But whether the LSD was the cause, or merely hastened the onset, of his schizophrenia (or indeed, had anything to do with it) is not known. The myth remains, and that myth is more than enough. Waters, in stark contrast, took a few hits of LSD at best, and was maddeningly rational.

Fans may have loved Waters's songs, but not because they (or the critics for that matter) understood their lyrics. Cliff Jones, for example, reports that the song "Money," which bemoans the way that lucre corrupts us, was misunderstood. On tour in the United States, Waters realized that his fans "believed that he'd been celebrating the fact that money allows you to buy professional sport teams, stay at luxurious hotels and eat expensive foods."[24] The hit single from *The Wall*, "Another Brick in the Wall, part 2," was misinterpreted as a slam against education, "much to Waters's chagrin."[25]

Lyrics have never been much of a selling point for rock anyway. They're ignored, misinterpreted, or misheard. When words are grasped, it is fragmentarily through phrases or a chorus rather than as the full lyrical text. Fans and fan-pandering critics attempt interpretations, but they tend to be superficial and naive. They hear the singer's "I" as a literal reflection of the author, indicating a failure to see that art may be something beyond giving vent to one's personal feelings and experiences. Were these critics and fans to read *Moby Dick* they would think that Herman Melville *was* Ishmael ("Call me Ishmael"). They mainly interpret lyrics psychologically, not artistically. Such romantic readings, catering to celebrity, have fueled the popularity of the innumerable interviews in rock magazines and their ubiquitous video counterparts such as VH1's *Behind the Music* program, as if learning about the musician's favorite drugs or his high school pranks provide insightful clues to his art. Sometimes, of course, they do.

Waters's lyrics were read as if they were about, and *only* about, his personal life and feelings. The tendency has been to conflate Waters's (supposed) psychological motivation with his creative work, as if dyspepsia and depression *are* works of art. Rock fans and critics have not heeded Foucault's argument that an author is not a human being, but a subject position. For Foucault, the author is "created by the text," which is the opposite of the VH1-profile romantic fantasy of a text created by a "life."

My argument that Waters's lyrics for Pink Floyd's albums, beginning with *Dark Side of the Moon,* are examples of high art does not address the issue of whether or not they are *great* examples of high art. The case made here opens up possible exploration of other examples of high art lyrics in rock. The presence of high art lyrics in progressive rock has been acknowledged, but few of the writers who have detailed the genre's code have claimed that they were a defining feature.[26] Stump cites King Crimson's *In the Court of the Crimson King*, released in 1969, as the first fully progressive rock work. After defining its sonic features at length, he adds: "Rococo, Romantic imagery saturates [Pete] Sinfield's lyrical input."[27] Sinfield himself says, "'As for lyrical influences, they went perhaps, beyond Dylan and went back to Rimbaud and Verlaine and people like that. . . . I was more interested in Kerouac, I suppose, but who wasn't?'"[28]

One might argue that Waters's artistic vision went beyond words or music. He was greatly interested in the concert, beginning with the innovative light shows and proceeding through the massive undertaking of the concert for *The Wall*. Stump notes, "Clearly what was at stake here was no longer simply music, but the entire artistic realm, a striving towards *Gesamtkunstwerk* that the modernist pioneer and archangel of Romanticism, Richard Wagner, would have recognized; music, once again, sat at the centre of a multi-artistic endeavour."[29] It should be noted that currently Waters is working on an opera.)

High Cultural Form

In its formal dimension, modernist art strives to encompass diversity in unity. Modernism is aware that the world is multidimensional, containing loose ends, contradictions, and irreducible variety, especially in the sphere of human relations. Yet modernism does not surrender to diversity; rather, it strives for generous unities that do not oversimplify, but still evince coherence. Examples of this tendency abound, such as the romantic symphonic works of Pyotr Ilich Tchaikovsky and Gustav Mahler, and Richard Strauss's tone poems; the cubist experiments of Pablo Picasso; Fyodor Dostoevsky's novels; Friedrich Nietzsche's aphoristic philosophy; and Georg Simmel's formal sociology, which partakes as much of art as of science. Moreover, in the modernist paradigm, the single work is continuous with the creator's entire oeuvre, at least during the same creative period. That is, there is a systematicity to the artist's creations.

In pop music, any systematicness is found in the sonic elements, the so-called signature sound of, for example, Chuck Berry's guitar riffs, the distinctive vocal timbres of Bob Dylan or King Diamond, and so on. In these cases, the systematicness is simple and does not come close to the standards set by high modernist art. In the case of even the most interesting rock lyricists, such as John Lennon, the themes across the writer's canon do not display coherent meaning; but Roger Waters's lyrics do.

Concept Albums

All of the albums of Pink Floyd's third incarnation contain sets of songs with diverse lyrics that are unified around a specific theme. These so-called concept albums, which Stump asserts are the "key to the founding of Progressive aesthetics,"[30] are given various shapes by Waters. The first of them, *Dark Side of the Moon,* is rather nakedly philosophical, speaking in abstractions: "Time," "Money," "Us and Them." In contrast, *Wish You Were Here* focuses on a specific institution, the rock business, addressing the dichotomy that is central to rock's ideology: art and commerce.[31] The songs on the next album, *Animals,* discuss the human condition in the form of an allegory, similar to George Orwell's *Animal Farm,* but instead of deflating the socialist ideal, as Orwell did, Waters aims his arrow at the heart of modern capitalist society. Each of the songs describes the plights of various types of people from the cunning, self-serving "Dogs" and the moralist oppressor "Pigs," to the ever and always easily fooled masses, the "Sheep."

The almost two dozen songs on Waters's most ambitious project, *The Wall,* are united in still another way—as a narrative. The lyrics tell the story of Pink, a boy whose father dies in World War II, and who becomes, in spite of and perhaps because of his psychiatric problem, a rock star. The last album that Waters did with Pink Floyd, *The Final Cut,* focuses on the absurdity of war in general, and in particular on the Falkland Islands War that Britain fought with Argentina.

Waters's solo albums are also conceptual. *The Pros and Cons of Hitchhiking,* written at the same time as *The Wall,* is about relationships between men and women, and especially the problem of fidelity; the songs are linked to one another as a dream sequence. *Radio Kaos* and *Amused to Death,* which were conceived in Waters's post-Floyd period, fall into the movement of postmodern cultural criticism, detailing the ways in which mass media help and hinder genuine communication.

Recurrent Imagery

The systematicness of Waters's lyrics extends far beyond each and all of the concept albums. Running through them is a set of images, metaphors, allusions, and metonyms that extend from his earliest lyrical forays through his later solo work. The recurrence of these elements, such as images of the sun and moon and allusions to madness, war, and the music business, function like a composer's signature sound in classical or popular music. Waters's lyrics have formal features, such as his use of lists, that also provide unity to his distinctive songs.[32]

Waters's allusions to war pervade all periods of his work. For Waters, war is both a concrete reference and a metonym for human relations in a more general sense. His innumerable references to war begin with "Corporal Clegg," from *A Saucerful of Secrets* (1968), the album on which Waters began to slowly assert his leadership role in the band. It is about a soldier who returns from the war bedecked with medals and a wooden leg. He is missing more than his limb, however: the shell-shocked veteran has also lost his mind. In "Us and Them" (*Dark Side of the Moon*), Waters describes the front-line soldiers who were sent to their deaths by safe-in-the-rear generals. *The Final Cut* and *Amused to Death* both focus on the idiocy of war. Those in command deserve commitment into a mental hospital for the criminally insane, the Fletcher Memorial Home (named for Waters's father Eric Fletcher Waters, who was killed in World War II when his son was an infant). Another basis for Waters's use of war referents is the influence of Rupert Brooke, whose poetry Waters read while at school.[33] He incorporates the line, "in the corner of some foreign field," from Brooke's most famous poem, "The Soldier," in the lyrics for "The Gunner's Dream" on *The Final Cut*. Waters was also part of the youth culture that opposed the Vietnam War.

Another signifier that spans many of Waters's songs is the music business. Like war, it refers to its primary meaning but also serves as a methaphor for human relations. "Cymbaline," from the 1969 soundtrack *More*, foreshadows Waters's more extensive attacks on the rock business, describing managers and agents on the phone selling pictures of the band to magazines. "Have a Cigar" (which critic Jim DeRogatis calls "a sarcastic comment on greedy music moguls"[34]), and the whole album on which that song appears, *Wish You Were Here,* is a vicious diatribe against the business, showing how it damages the artist. One of the pigs in "Pigs (Three Different Ones)" (from *Animals*), the "cheating" and "lying" one, stands for music executives. The theme is explored at greater length in *The Wall* and in the full-length movie based on the album.

Waters is often seen by critics as a hypocrite who disingenuously decries the rock business while avidly pursuing and succeeding in capturing its rich rewards. Waters has attempted to demolish this misreading, but he seems to have had little success. Schaffner is one exception, recognizing that Waters harbors these opposing elements within himself. "Have a Cigar," he explains, is about "the battling elements within [Waters's] own contradictory character" including an "avaricious" side. "The song slips in and out of both personae."[35] Schaffner goes on to state that "Waters allows that he, too, is something of a 'dog.'"[36]

Metaphors of the sun and the moon also thoroughly pervade Waters's lyrics. A few of the songs with the sun in the title include "Set the Controls for the Heart of the Sun," written in 1967, and "Two Suns in the Sunset" from *The Final Cut.* The moon also figures prominently as an image, with a starring role in *Dark Side of the Moon.* These astral orbs are not derived from the "space rock" designation of the Barrett-era Floyd, but from another world altogether, the British poetic tradition. In this imagery Waters was again influenced by the celebrated nature-lover and paganist Rupert Brooke,[37] whose early pastoral poems are replete with allusions to the sun and the moon. Brooke's references follow from the wider romantic tradition as well as from his interest in ancient Egyptian religion. In both practices, the sun is seen as the giver of, or represents, life; the moon stands for a variety of "otherness," including the antithesis to life, death. "Eclipse" (from *Dark Side of the Moon*) features one of Waters's lists as lyrics; it is a list of everything "under the sun." But everything—that is, life—is "eclipsed by the moon."

The moon is *not-life,* as in another song on *Dark Side of the Moon,* "Brain Damage," where the living dead meet "on the dark side of the moon." The brain-damaged man in "Shine On You Crazy Diamond" (from *Wish You Were Here*) had "cried for the moon." The working title for *Dark Side of the Moon* had been *Eclipse (A Piece for Assorted*

Lunatics) [38]; the lunar imagery is directly related, in Waters's work as well as etymologically, to lunacy.

Lunacy, or any of Waters's other terms for dementia, is for him a human, albeit inhumane, social phenomenon that results from being isolated, unable to be with others. When we are denied a genuine emotional presence, we withdraw into ourselves and become unable to be there—a *there-being* (*Dasein*)—for anyone else, including ourselves.

Madness crops up in numerous places throughout Waters's oeuvre. It is found early on in the shell-shocked "Corporal Clegg" and in lines like "If I go insane" in "If" (from *Atom Heart Mother*). It plays a starring role in some albums, such as *Dark Side of the Moon, Wish You Were Here,* and *The Wall,* and a walk-on role in others.

Waters's lyrical recurrences to madness have been misread by fans and critics, who have given them a roman-à-clef reading; they take them as references to Syd Barrett, the charismatic "acid casualty" who was so crucial to Pink Floyd's early years. "Syd and I went through our *most* formative years together, riding on my motorbike, getting drunk, doing a little dope, flirting with girls, all that basic stuff,"[39] Waters recalled in a *Penthouse* interview two decades after Barrett was ousted from the band. However, in numerous conversations, Waters denied that his songs about madness are specifically about Syd. For example, "*Dark Side of the Moon* was an album about the universal condition of insanity," Waters stated.[40] In "A Rambling Conversation with Roger Waters Concerning All This and That" from the *Wish You Were Here Song Book,* Waters said, "'Shine On' [is] not really about Syd—he's just a symbol for all the extremes of absence some people have to indulge in because it's the only way they can cope with how fucking sad it is—modern life, to withdraw completely."[41] Storm Thorgerson, head of the design group Hipgnosis, who provided both the album art and the title to *Wish You Were Here* after long conversations with Waters, described its lyrics: "They seemed to be about unfulfilled presence in general rather than about Syd's particular version of it—and he certainly had his own unique brand. The idea of presence withheld, of the ways that people pretend to be present whilst their minds are really elsewhere, and the devices and motivations employed psychologically by people to suppress the full force of their presence, eventually boiled down to a single theme—absence: the absence of a person, the absence of a feeling."[42]

Artistic Vision

Beyond this set of metaphors, allusions, and metonyms, the major connection between the form and the content of Waters's lyrics is the vision of the human condition that informs his work. All of Waters's lyrics are of a piece, intellectually—developed by recurrence and intensification. They are expressions of a singular artistic vision, just as Fyodor Dostoevsky's fiction and Edgar Allan Poe's poems and stories are both diverse articulations of the same singular view.

Waters's lyrics have been seen mainly as a neurotic's plaint, best suited for a psychiatrist's couch. However, as I have hinted above, Waters's vision is not the emanation of some neurasthenic, but is fully within the parameters of modernist discourse that informed much of the 1960s zeitgeist.[43]

Waters's position is existentialist; it is embedded in a discourse whose roots are easily traced back to the work of Jean-Jacques Rousseau. They share the frustrated wish to unite fully with someone else. Rousseau explored this theme, especially in his *Emile* and *Reveries of a Solitary Walker*. For Rousseau, the tragedy, the pathos, is that ontologically each human being is separated from all others because each one of us is a separate center of consciousness—what he calls "amour de soi." Yet although our very being is constructed in ways that prohibit this desire, we want to unite with others. Even worse, the inequalities of civil society serve to separate us further, not only ontologically but socially. Civil society is represented in Waters's lyrics by references to money and business. It brings in the "amour propre," the love of self by invidious comparisons (the "house-proud town mouse" from *Animals*).

Rousseau's contrast between the noble savage—isolated and detached from others—and the civic being plays out for Waters as the conflict between the artist and business. As he once said in an interview, "I can't make a connection between what I do . . . writing songs and recording them, making films, putting on rock 'n' roll shows . . . I think that's intrinsically different than making automobiles. I don't see Dylan Thomas and Henry Ford as being in the same business."[44]

Rousseau felt that education should follow the impulses and desires of the child, standing in sharp opposition to the educational system damned in *The Wall,* where the young Pink's poetry, his display of emotions, is brutally repressed.

Waters was not directly influenced by Rousseau as much as by those high modernists working in the late romantic tradition, such as Thomas Hardy and Rupert Brooke, who have often been termed "cultural pessimists" and are contributors to "high culture." Parts of Brooke's and his contemporaries' (such as British novelist E. M. Forster's) works hark back to John Donne, the seventeenth-century poet whose "no man is an island" focuses on the crucial necessity for connection with others. But these high modernists see that connection is difficult, if not impossible.

The essence of Waters's artistic vision centers in the fundamental human necessity for authentic communication. The specifics of so many of his lyrics refer to how communication is blocked or shammed. It is a theme that resonated with his times, as characterized by John Lennon's "Isolation."[45] That song shares Waters's key metaphors of the sun and insanity, and addresses Waters's key conundrum: the connection with others, the absence of which is, as the song's title indicates, isolation. Each of Waters's personal losses, to which he refers repeatedly throughout his songs—Syd Barrett's catatonic dementia, Waters's father's death as a soldier in the war, and his increasingly distant relationship with his band mates, fans, first wife, and the rock business— are seen though this disconnection. The madness metaphor directly relates to a disconnection; Waters's major thematic can be summarized by the epigraph to E. M. Forster's great novel, *Howards End*: "Connect, only connect."

Conclusion

At the end of the day, Waters could not fully connect. He did not make his ideas understood, at least on a mass level. And that is why the Water-less Pink Floyd, with no pretensions to seriousness, is far more popular than the solo Waters.

Waters's solo albums have not sold in the meganumbers that Pink Floyd's—even their uninspired live album *Delicate Sound of Thunder*)—have achieved. Since the mid-1980s, Pink Floyd has consistently sold out huge stadiums, whereas Waters's concerts are held in more intimate venues for faithful audiences. Commenting about his 1987 tour, Waters recalled: "I will never forget being in Cincinnati playing to 1,500 people in an 8,000 seat arena and my ex-colleagues playing the next night in a sold-out football stadium."[46] And even at his intimate shows, the audience responds most avidly to the hit songs like "Money" and "Another Brick in the Wall, part 2." When Waters plays these familiar songs—and he is not foolish enough to omit them from his set list—the members of the audience stand and scream as soon as they recognize the opening bars, and sing along with him.

High culture, in whatever medium, has always required an educated (what José Ortega y Gasset termed a "select"[47]) audience. By *educated* I do not mean that one has had to have had formal schooling; rather, the select audience is the antithesis of a heterogeneous (mass) audience whose motto is "give me effortless pleasure or give me nothing." The mass audience has no clue that they are the "herd men" of Friedrich Nietzsche and Martin Heidegger, the "cultural dopes" who are addicted to "mass cult" described by mid-century thinkers like Herbert Blumer and Dwight MacDonald. In contrast, the select audience is knowledgeable about the objects that it appreciates: it is aware of genre standards and codes, and is able to apply comparative judgments.

The rock critics, for the most part, do not attempt to educate the mass audience (help it to become "select") but instead, pander to its prejudices. For more elevated analyses of rock music, one needs to seek out subcultural groups that informally, and in "zines" and online formats, educate one another.

If one carefully observes the audience at Waters's shows—and I have done so at three of them over the past fifteen years—one will see two distinct groups: the mass of greatest-hits fans, and the select fans who enunciate the words to songs that were never hits and who nod knowingly at significant phrases. Indeed, the '70s-era massively popular Pink Floyd was a double-coded confection with different appeals to their select and their mass fans. Like the animated sitcom *The Simpsons,* or the original Globe Theatre productions of William Shakespeare's plays, rock music can also have multiple appeals—and of course those who "get it" on the more sophisticated level can also appreciate it on the lower level.

Just as water reaches its own level, Roger Waters has reached a comprehending audience, even if it is only a subset of his fans and even a smaller subset of Pink Floyd's mass(ive) audience. Forster provided a credo for Waters: "Connect, only connect." Waters has done just that—for those who know how to listen.

Notes

1. Paul Stump, *The Music's All That Matters: A History of Progressive Rock* (London: Quartet Books, 1997), 73.
2. Edward L. Macan, *Rocking the Classics: English Progressive Rock and the Counterculture* (New York: Oxford University Press, 1997), 144–66.
3. See Lawrence W. Levine's description of how Shakespeare, whose works were appreciated by all classes at the beginning of the nineteenth century in the United States, was hijacked by the upper middle class in the latter part of that century as part of their effort to legitimate themselves and to separate themselves from the working class; Levine, "William Shakespeare and the American People: A Study in Cultural Transformation," *American Historical Review* 89 (1984): 34–66.
4. Macan, *Rocking*, 147.
5. Progressive rock and heavy metal came into being at the same time. Both are rooted, in part, in psychedelic music and both originated and crystallized in Britain. They can be seen as the claiming of countercultural music for two opposing classes.
6. See Macan, *Rocking*.
7. Stump, *All That Matters*, 9–10.
8. Simon Frith and Howard Horne, *Art into Pop* (London: Methuen, 1988), 73.
9. Stump, *All That Matters*, 9.
10. Keyboardist Richard Wright was thrown out of the band after the recording of *The Wall*, to which he contributed very little, and although he performed on the much abbreviated tour for that album, it was as a hired hand. He was not on *The Final Cut*.
11. Matt Resnicoff, "Roger and Me—The Other Side of the Pink Floyd Story," *Musician*, November 1992, http://www.ingsoc.com/waters/interviews/waters_nov_92.html.
12. Mick Brown and Kurt Loder, "Behind Pink Floyd's Wall," *Rolling Stone*, September 16, 1982, 14.
13. Ben Edmonds, "The Trippers Trapped: Pink Floyd in a Hum Bag," *Rolling Stone*, November 6, 1975, 64.
14. Kurt Loder, "Floyd's Artistic Epiphany: Review of *The Final Cut*," *Rolling Stone*, April 14, 1983, 65–66.

15. Lynn Van Matre, "Review of the Final Cut," *Chicago Tribune*, May 6, 1983, sec. 6, p. 25. When this critic reviewed Waters's solo work some years later she saw it as "decidedly optimistic in its belief that satellite communications can serve as a bridge between people and build a better world"; (Van Matre, "The Tide Turns: Roger Waters trades the 'Dark Side' for optimism," *Chicago Tribune*, August 23, 1987, sec. 13, p. 8.

16. Tom Hibbert, "Who the Hell Does Roger Waters Think He Is?" *Q*, November 12, 1992, http:www.mindspring.com/~ampfaq/Ash/1992 WatersATDHibbert.htm.

17. For a discussion of this, see the first section of chapter 7 in Deena Weinstein, *Heavy Metal: The Music and Its Culture* (New York: DaCapo Press, 2000).

18. Loder, "Review of *The Final Cut*," 65–66.

19. Paul Gallotta, "Pink Floyd Goes Beyond 'The Wall,'" *Good Times*, April 19–25, 1983, 13.

20. David Fricke, "Performance: Roger Waters Can't Top 'The Wall,'" *Rolling Stone*, August 30, 1984, 38.

21. Bill Wyman, "The Four Phases of Pink Floyd," *The Reader*, January 15, 1988, 12, 44.

22. Loder, "Review of *The Final Cut*," 65–66.

23. Nicholas Schaffner, *Saucerful of Secrets: The Pink Floyd Odyssey* (New York: Harmony Books, 1991), 216.

24. Cliff Jones, *Another Brick in the Wall: The Stories behind Every Pink Floyd Song* (New York: Broadway Books, 1996), 99.

25. Ibid., 125.

26. See, for example, Bruce Eder's on-line FAQ on progressive rock, in which he compares the lyrics of Genesis's *Foxtrot* and *Selling England by the Pound* to T. S. Eliot and Ezra Pound. "Art-Rock/Progressive Rock (Long Version)," at www.allmusic.com.

27. Stump, *All That Matters*, 52.

28. Pete Sinfield, quoted in ibid., 53.

29. Ibid., 26–27.

30. Ibid., 158.

31. For an examination of this discourse, see Deena Weinstein, "Art vs. Commerce: Deconstructing a (Useful) Romantic Illusion," in Karen Kelly and Evelyn McDonnell, eds., *Stars Don't Stand Still in the Sky: Music and Myth* (New York: New York University Press, 1999), 56–69.

32. See, for example, Adam Lacecky's "Why Roger Waters's Lyrics are Better than David Gilmour's," www.ingsoc.com/waters, for a discussion of slant, identical and internal rhyming, and Waters's penchant for lists. Lacecky sees the list at the end of "Dogs," in which each line starts with "who," as influenced by Allen Ginsberg's *Howl*.

33. Jones, *Another Brick*, 53.

34. Jim DeRogatis, "By the Way, This One's Pink; Waters Outdistances Ex-Mates," *Chicago Sun-Times*, July 23, 1999, Weekend Plus section, p. 5.

35. Schaffner, *Saucerful of Secrets*, 202.

36. Ibid., 214.

37. Jones, *Another Brick*, 53.

38. Ibid., 94.

39. "Pink Floyd and Company—Roger Waters Interview," *Penthouse*, September 1988. On-line at www.ingsoc.com/waters/interviews/ waters_pent88.html.

40. Jones, *Another Brick*, 106.

41. Nick Sedgewick, "A Rambling Conversation with Roger Waters Concerning All This and That," in *The Wish You Were Here Song Book* (London: Pink Floyd Music Publishers, 1982), 9–23.

42. Hipgnosis, *Walk Away Rene—The Work of Hipgnosis* (London: Paper Tiger, 1978), 148.

43. Perhaps long-time Pink Floyd producer Bob Ezrin, whose secretary became Waters's second wife, makes sense of both perspectives: "I think Roger is brilliant . . . a great artist. . . I *hate* the word *artist,* but I would definitely concede that Roger is a great artist—as well as a total obsessive and a psychiatrist's dream"; quoted in "Pink Floyd and Company."

44. Resnicoff, "Roger and Me," see note 11.

45. *John Lennon: Plastic Ono Band.* Capitol compact disc CDP 7467702, 1970.

46. Greg Kot, "The Different Shades of Roger Waters," *Chicago Tribune*, July 18, 1999, sec. 7, p. 8.

47. José Ortega y Gasset, *The Revolt of the Masses* (New York: W.W. Norton, 1957), 13–16.

A Promise Deferred

Multiply Directed Time and Thematic Transformation in Emerson Lake and Palmer's "Trilogy"

Kevin Holm-Hudson

The British group Emerson Lake and Palmer (ELP) became synonymous in the eyes of some critics with the worst excesses of progressive rock.[1] As only one example of their tendency toward grandiose presentation, their 1973–74 world tour involved 36 tons of equipment (including a quadraphonic sound system and lasers),[2] which led critic Lester Bangs to brand them as "war criminals" committing "energy atrocities" at the height of the energy crisis.[3] Keyboard player Keith Emerson's solos (which often emphasized virtuosity at the expense of restraint) attracted the most criticism, as well as the group's overly precious "arrangements" of classical repertoire such as Modest Mussorgsky's *Pictures at an Exhibition.* However, few critics have discussed ELP's original songs, the bulk of their recorded output.

The album *Trilogy* was released in 1972, a year that seems to have been the high point for progressive rock structuralism; Yes's *Close to the Edge* and Jethro Tull's *Thick As a Brick* were released in the same year.[4] *Trilogy* was one of Emerson Lake and Palmer's most commercially successful albums, reaching number 2 in the United Kingdom and number 5 in the United States.[5] Artistically it also comes closest to achieving the classical-rock fusion that was the group's aim. Several original songs on the album are formally (as opposed to stylistically) modeled after European art music. For example, a fugue is inserted between the two parts of the album's opening track "The Endless Enigma," and the closing track, "Abaddon's Bolero," is a nod to Maurice Ravel's 1928 orchestral composition "Bolero." The album's title track, "Trilogy," succeeds as a symphonic poem in a rock context and stands as one of ELP's most successful—and underrated—songs.

In this chapter, I examine the nature of thematic transformation in "Trilogy," and I show how the larger tonal areas of the piece constitute an interrupted (and finally satisfied) "harmonic macroprogression" of tonalities: an example of what Jonathan Kramer (1988) has called "multiply directed time."

The symphonic poem, or "tone poem," is generally attributed to Franz Liszt (1811–1886), who in turn was inspired by Hector Berlioz (1803–1869), especially Berlioz's *Symphonie Fantastique* (1830). In general, it is a type of programmatic orchestral work based on an extramusical idea (a historical figure or event, for example, or a literary source). Works in this genre, popular in the nineteenth and early twentieth centuries, generally consisted of one movement (although within a given piece there may be distinct sections). Standard classical forms were often abandoned in favor of a free rhapsodic structure, unity being maintained by a process of thematic development, which in turn followed the extramusical program.

Writing about Berlioz in 1855, Liszt explained how the symphonic poem differed from its classical counterparts regarding thematic treatment, and consequently form. "In the so-called classical music the return and development of themes is determined by formal rules which are regarded as inviolable," he noted. "In program music, in contrast, the return, change, variation and modulation of the motives is conditioned by their relation to a poetic idea. . . . All exclusively musical aspects, even though none are by any means left out of consideration, are subordinated to the treatment of the subject-idea. Thus the treatment and subject-matter in this type of symphony can claim an interest above the technical handling of the musical materials."[6]

Similarly, the theme of Emerson Lake and Palmer's "Trilogy" is developed according to the narrative advanced by Greg Lake's lyrics, which concern the dissolution of a love affair. This trajectory can be summarized as follows: bittersweet sadness expressed at the decay of a relationship; uncertainty and distress at that relationship's termination;

and optimism at the prospects of finding a new partner. Each of the piece's sections incorporate transformations of the theme, in the manner of a nineteenth-century symphonic poem.

The theme is stated at the outset by synthesizer, imitating the timbre of muted violins. Close examination of this theme's structure reveals important aspects of the piece as a whole. First, the tonality of B major is quickly undermined by accidentals (D-natural, C-natural, A-natural, G-natural) that suggest the inflection of B phrygian mode; this mixture of modes is found liberally throughout the first section (mm. 1–59 of the published score;[7] the first 2:24 of the CD recording), conveying the bittersweet mood through harmonic mode mixture.[8]

However, an alternate interpretation emerges when the structurally important pitches from the phrase's opening (mm. 1–2) are extracted. Omitting notes that reinforce the B major tonality through arpeggiation, an overall descent is revealed (see fig. 5.1). This descent is made up of pitches from an octatonic scale, consisting of alternating half and whole steps (see fig. 5.2). The scalar descent is momentarily interrupted by a descending C-major arpeggio (measure 3); in classical music theory, this arpeggio would function as a so-called Neapolitan, or ♭II, chord in B major. Both the octatonic scale and the half-step relation found between the tonic chord (B major) and its Neapolitan chord (C major) foreshadow later sections of the piece.

"Trilogy" also begins with a nod to Tin Pan Alley pop-song conventions. The form of the opening "song" proper (mm. 10–37; 0:30–1:41) is in standard AABA "song" form. The "A" phrases of the song—characterized by the aforementioned mode mixtures—also avoid any strong resolutions to the tonic or indeed to any conventional triad; cadences instead end on seventh chords or chords with suspended fourths (see, for example, mm. 13, 15, and 17; 0:35–0:51). These deceptive phrase endings help to portray the deceit inherent in the partners' relationship, where one "still pretends" with smiles that are "only there to hide" the couple's true feelings. The "B" phrase offers a contrasting brief modulation to D major accompanied by a circle-of-fifths harmonic progression of E minor, A, D, and G (m. 26; 1:13); this goal-oriented progression, contrasting the continually unresolved stasis of the "A" phrases, accompanies the singer's resolve to send his farewell letter. It becomes much more prominent in the last section of the song.

Fig. 5.1. Melodic reduction of "Trilogy" introduction, showing octatonic stepwise descent.

Fig. 5.2. Octatonic scale on B.

Once the song's protagonist has made the decision to leave, the music finally resolves to the tonic through a phrase elision at the return of the "A" phrase (1:21); the tonic arrival is confirmed by the music's first true point of repose, at measure 41 (1:49). The section is then extended, with some thematic development in the piano and repeated "goodbyes" (mm. 43–53; 1:53–2:16). A cadential flourish follows, oscillating between F-sharp minor and B major until a final surprise ending on F major (mm. 58–59; 2:21).

The appearance of F major is indeed striking; this moment marks its first appearance, and in the context of B major it is an improbable choice (♭V) for a cadence. The F major chord, however, points to the tonic of the last two-thirds of the piece (2:59 to end) as the dominant of B-flat major. The half-step relationship between the opening in B major and the conclusion in B-flat major was paralleled in the C-major arpeggio in measure 3; reinterpreting B as C-flat (♭II of B-flat), one finds—spanning the piece—a macroprogression of ♭II–V–I, audible at 1:49, 2:21, and 2:59 on the CD.

The fact that these three tonal centers—linked as a macro-progression—occur with interruptions of other developmental material makes it possible to listen to this piece as an example of "multiply directed time," as described by theorist Jonathan Kramer in his book *The Time of Music*. Kramer posits that music inhabits several temporal domains that are to be distinguished from chronological time; among these are *goal-directed linear time, vertical time,* and *multiply directed time*. Goal-directed linear time would describe music of the most predictable variety, and vertical time would imply a music of total stasis, without clearly articulated opening or closing gestures and with no progress implied (in such music one listens "vertically" to the interrelations among parts rather than to the direction of individual lines). Between these extremes Kramer also accounts for *nondirected linear time* (in which "the implied progression from one section to another is continually realized but the deeper-level implications arising from these middleground progressions fail to be fulfilled"[9]), *moment time* (in which there is no continuity from section to section in spite of internal consistency within a given section), and *multiply directed time.* Most pieces of music, in fact, exhibit a mixture of these temporal qualities.[10] However, Kramer does not apply his technique of temporal analysis to any examples of popular music.

In describing multiply directed time, Kramer refers to "pieces in which the direction of motion is so frequently interrupted by discontinuities, in which the piece goes so often to unexpected places, that the linearity, though still a potent structural force, seems reordered. I call the time sense in such music 'multiply-directed.'"[11]

Elsewhere Kramer clarifies this definition: "If the implication in every section is continually frustrated by the subsequent section but is often realized elsewhere, then the musical time is multiply-directed."[12] This description certainly fits the overall scheme of "Trilogy," where the implications of the F major chord are realized through a delayed resolution—in another key—some thirty seconds later. In fact, according to Kramer, the "implications" raised and delayed by multiply directed time often have a tonal basis. Tonal music, he notes, "is susceptible to multiply-directed listening for two reasons: (1) tonal processes are well-defined, so that their goal orientation can be understood even when the goal is not reached immediately; and (2) tonal music contains a wealth of gestural conventions such as beginnings, final cadences, transitions, climaxes, etc., which can be recognized even when they occur in the 'wrong' part of a piece."[13]

And what of the intervening music that delays the resolution of F major? Like the overall piece, it also is in three sections. The first section (2:25–2:38) prolongs the surprise I→♭V progression of measures 57–59 by emphasizing the polar opposition of F major and B major, in a passage reminiscent of the famous "Petrouchka chord" of Igor

Stravinsky (mm. 60–68). The second section (2:38–2:52) modulates once again to D major; this key was originally referred to in the "B" phrase of the opening song form (m. 26; 1:13), but here the modulation is much more decisive (mm. 71–77). The last section (2:53–3:04) is an aggressive cadential passage that again features an octatonic scale (this time the complement of the one at the opening) in the left hand, enharmonically spelled to alternate between B minor and F minor; the chords in the right hand, all major triads (B, G, B-flat, D-flat), have roots that belong to the same octatonic collection (see fig. 5.3). Measures 84–85, the final extended dominant of B-flat, similarly fit an F octatonic pitch collection.

Thus far we have focused on examples of harmonic foreshadowing in "Trilogy," as if numerous musical elements have pointed forward to the final section beginning at 2:59. These elements help to account for the emphatic sense of arrival at this point, dramatically underscored by the sudden timbral change to synthesizers and the entrance of drums a few measures later (at m. 90, or 3:04, the texture changes from solo acoustic piano to a full all-electronic sound). This is of course the main structural division in the piece, and from this point one can note several references to the earlier B major tonality. Kramer has noted that multiply directed time depends on "underlying linearity being perceptible even when not presented in linear order";[14] this implies that the nonlinearity may skip backward as well as forward. For example, the ostinato at m. 86 (2:59) is notated to emphasize the published score with alternating B-flat major and B major triads in the right hand; in the key of B-flat, the B major triad would normally be notated as a C-flat major triad. Indeed, when the synthesizers enter at measure 90 the bass line changes from B-flat—F, to B-flat–B–E–F-sharp, making it possible to hear only the first two beats of each measure in B-flat while the last three beats in the bass line suggest the tonic, subdominant, and dominant degrees of B major.

Two other retrospective references to B (or C-flat) should be noted.

Fig. 5.3. Octatonic pitch collection used in "Trilogy" piano cadenza.

First, the note is frequently used as an appoggiatura in the final section. For example, at the climax of his extended synthesizer solo (7:10–7:35), Keith Emerson twice emphasizes a C-flat[5] against the B-flat bass ostinato before "resolving" it to B-flat[5]. This C-flat to B-flat resolution also occurs just before the final trill of the solo, and C-flat makes one final appearance at the highest point of the final synthesizer cadenza (8:36), arguably resolved yet again to B-flat at the beginning of the final "blues coda" at 8:40. Second, the last two chords of the "blues coda" have as their respective bass notes B and B-flat. What appears to be yet another gratuitous ELP stylistic pastiche—the seemingly incongruous blues coda at the end of a song notably lacking any blues influence—nevertheless retains a subtle relationship to the structure of the song as a whole.

Against this larger background of tonalities as a delayed macroprogression, the opening theme also undergoes numerous changes in response to the changing emotional states of the song's narrative. The first phrase of the theme is isolated for development; most of the changes involve rhythmic alterations (to fit the different meters of the various sections), but notably the phrase endings are altered each time, usually in a way that denies resolution (for example, ending on the fifth or flatted-seventh scale degree instead of on the tonic). The descending arpeggio of the theme's second phrase is extensively developed throughout the piano transition (mm. 43–78; 1:53–2:52) but is absent thereafter. Timbre is also used to underscore changes in emotional quality; for example, the 5/4 appearance of the theme (the one time it is used in an asymmetrical metric context) is played on a Moog synthesizer with a shrieking timbre, contributing to the mood of distress. Table 5.1 summarizes these aspects of thematic development and their linkage to other musical elements.

The careful construction of "Trilogy" is indeed remarkable. Even at its most excessive moments (and ELP were notorious for their musical excesses), enough references are made to other sections of the piece to give it a coherence that may at least be intuited, if not consciously comprehended, by the casual listener. By deferring the "promise" of resolving the F major chord that concludes the first "song" section proper, Emerson (who wrote the music for "Trilogy") has not only managed to maintain a degree of musical suspense but has also ensured that the

Table 5.1. Textual/Musical Narrative in "Trilogy."

Measures:	CD Timing:	Key:	Narrative/Emotion:	Musical Devices:
Section 1:				
1–25	0:01–1:13	B	Regret over deception	Mode mixture; avoidance of expected chord resolutions; mostly 4/4 meter
26–29	1:14–1:21	D	Action— writing letter	Circle-of-fifths progression; faster harmonic rhythm; rubato; elision to next section
30–42	1:22–1:52	B	Decision to leave	As in mm. 1–25; development of descending arpeggio in mm. 38–39
43–59	1:53–2:24	B	"Goodbye" (ends on F)	augmentation of theme in mm. 43–48; development of descending arpeggio in mm. 50–53; minor v-I cadences; "Goodbye" a reference to melodic turn at end of first phrase of vocal theme
Section 2:				
60–70	2:25–2:38	B/F	Transition; uncertainty	B/F polarity emphasized; numerous references to descending arpeggio; mostly 2/4 (cut time)
71–77	2:38–2:52	D	Reflection; impulse	Bass enters; accelerando; circle-of-fifths reference to mm. 26–29; mostly 4/4
78–89	2:53–3:04	Trans.; ends in B-flat		Piano cadenza; Octatonicism (alternating B/F); fast harmonic rhythm; 3/4 meter changing to 5/4 ostinato (first quintuple meter)
Section 3:				
90–105	3:04–4:52	B-flat locrian? (refs. to B in beats 3–5)	Distress	Theme in synthesizer (3:04–3:45), rhythmically altered to fit asymmetrical meter (5/4) and melodically changed, first phrase lingering on flatted seventh scale degree
106–143	4:53–6:05	B-flat	Optimism	6/4 meter (frequent hemiola) "Introduction" 4:54–5:02 Alternation of circle-of-fifths synthesizer ritornello (5:08–5:33 ff.) with sung verses (diatonic-major alteration of theme, each phrase ending on fifth scale degree) (5:34–5:40ff.)
n/a*	6:06–7:41	B-flat (modal flux)		Synthesizer solo
144–156	7:42–8:15	B-flat	Optimism	As in mm. 106–143
157–169	8:15–8:53	B-flat		Circle-of-fifths synthesizer ritornello; continuation of circle-of-fifths pattern to ♭VI (enharmonic V of B) with synthesizer cadenza; "blues coda"

*Emerson's improvised synthesizer solo is not included as part of the published sheet music transcription.

appearance of B-flat will be expected and indeed welcomed. This concern with large-scale formal structure led Emerson to more ambitious experiments, including the three-movement (or three-"impression") "Karn Evil 9" from 1973's *Brain Salad Surgery* and his Piano Concerto, featured on 1977's *Works Volume 1*. The question of how to achieve large-scale coherence in the absence of conventional musical form is answered by the devices of thematic transformation and a large-scale harmonic design that embodies Kramer's concept of multiply directed time. Perhaps the disillusion of a dying love affair (with its broken promises) and the optimism of a new love (with promises anew) can be best conveyed using such temporal discontinuities.

Notes

1. The group consisted of Keith Emerson, Greg Lake, and Carl Palmer; on the album *Trilogy* the performance credits are as follows: Keith Emerson, Hammond C3 organ, Steinway piano, Moog synthesizer IIIC, Minimoog model D, and an Arabic reed instrument called a zoukra; Greg Lake, bass, guitars, and vocal; and Carl Palmer, percussion. N.A., liner notes to Emerson Lake and Palmer *Trilogy* (Cotillion SD-9903, 1972).

2. Patricia Romanowski and Holly George-Warren, eds. *The New Rolling Stone Encyclopedia of Rock and Roll* (New York: Rolling Stone Press, 1995), 306.

3. Lester Bangs, "Exposed: The Brutal Energy Atrocities of Emerson Lake and Palmer," *Creem*, March 1974, 40.

4. For a thorough analysis of Yes's title song "Close to the Edge," see John Covach, "Progressive Rock, 'Close to the Edge,' and the Boundaries of Style," in *Understanding Rock: Essays in Musical Analysis*, ed. John Covach and Graeme M. Boone (New York: Oxford University Press, 1997), 3–31.

5. Dafydd Rees and Luke Crampton, *Darling Kindersley Encyclopedia of Rock Stars* (New York: Dorling Kindersley, 1996), 298.

6. Quoted in F. E. Kirby, *Music in the Romantic Period: An Anthology with Commentary* (New York: Schirmer), 7.

7. All measure numbers refer to the score to "Trilogy" found in *Emerson Lake and Palmer* (New York: Warner Bros., 1977), 10–19. This edition is unfortunately out of print.

8. "Mode mixture" refers to the practice of borrowing chords from a parallel minor key and using them in a major context; here, chords diatonic to B minor (e.g., E minor, G major) are transferred to the major-key context of B major and used as inflected substitutions.

9. Jonathan Kramer, *The Time of Music* (New York: Schirmer, 1988), 58.
10. Ibid.
11. Ibid., 46.
12. Ibid., 58.
13. Ibid., 46.
14. Ibid.

References

Bangs, Lester. "Exposed: The Brutal Energy Atrocities of Emerson Lake and Palmer." *Creem*, March 1974, 40–44, 76–78.

Covach, John. "Progressive Rock, 'Close to the Edge,' and the Boundaries of Style." In John Covach and Graeme M. Boone, eds., *Understanding Rock: Essays in Musical Analysis.* New York: Oxford University Press, 1997, 3–31.

Emerson Lake and Palmer (sheet music). New York: Warner Bros., 1977.

Kirby, F. E. *Music in the Romantic Period: An Anthology with Commentary.* New York: Schirmer, 1986.

Kramer, Jonathan. *The Time of Music.* New York: Schirmer, 1988.

Rees, Dafydd, and Luke Crampton. *Dorling Kindersley Encyclopedia of Rock Stars.* New York: Dorling Kindersley, 1996.

Romanowski, Patricia, and Holly George-Warren, eds. *The New Rolling Stone Encyclopedia of Rock and Roll.* New York: Rolling Stone Press, 1995.

6

King Crimson's
Larks' Tongues in Aspic
A Case of Convergent Evolution

Gregory Karl

Parallels between the aesthetic concerns and formal procedures of progressive rock and Western art music of the romantic era have been broadly outlined in Edward Macan's *Rocking the Classics*. Macan notes that the two styles share "the same cosmic outlook, the same preoccupation with the infinite and otherworldly, the same fondness for monumental statement ... and the same concern with expressing epic conflicts,"[1] as well as a host of specific technical traits. More recently, John Covach has used a detailed analysis of Yes's "Close to the Edge" to inquire into the nature of these interstylistic links, taking pains to distinguish instances of superficial "stylistic reference" from deeper, structural parallels. Among the former one finds classical instrumentation (strings, pipe organ, etc.) used to coat traditional rock materials in a classical veneer, the imitation of classical textures and the borrowing of formal procedures such as fugato, and stylistic reference through traditional voice-leading and harmonic language. The deeper structural parallels in "Close to the Edge" are revealed by Covach as he shows how the work "unfolds a large-scale formal design reinforced by tonal, thematic, and rhythmic return and development."[2] Structural parallels notwithstanding, Covach resists claiming that "Close to the Edge" is a work of "art music in any traditional sense of the term"; rather, "it balances stylistically and structurally between the art-music and rock worlds . . . but ultimately does not cross over."[3]

Macan's list of aesthetic qualities, formal procedures, and stylistic traits linking the two styles could well have been generated by examining a single quintessential work of progressive rock, King Crimson's fifth studio album, *Larks' Tongues in Aspic* (*LTA*).[4] This study, however, is centrally concerned with stylistic links at once more esoteric and yet more fundamental than those Macan cites; links that, moreover, run deeper even than the structural parallels Covach finds in "Close to the Edge." This is not to say that the concrete structural parallels linking *LTA* to the art music tradition are not interesting in their own right. One might, for example, cite the album's overall arch form both in key structure and cyclic thematic relations, its tight motivic unity, its complex metric phasing effects, and its bold sonic experimentation. But these elements of high art style are, I maintain, merely the outward manifestations of a more fundamental affinity of aesthetic goals and narrative and philosophical content, which I call a neoromantic aesthetic stance. I suggest that *LTA*'s two title tracks ("Part One" and "Part Two") cogently dramatize the ebb, flow, tensions, crises, and resolutions of internal life in an abstract sense. Without the aid of words or programs, *LTA* exhibits a sophisticated form of narrative content and organization heretofore associated only with instrumental art music of the nineteenth and twentieth centuries.[5] Moreover, this is achieved primarily by transforming the materials of rock music from within, rather than by importing unassimilated material and procedures from a foreign realm.

In assessing *LTA*'s relation to the classical tradition, therefore, it is necessary to look beyond conventional models of stylistic fusion: to challenge the prevalent assumption that rock music sharing a suite of style traits with works of Western art music necessarily arises through the self-conscious emulation of classical models. *LTA*, at least, invites a more organic account of its genesis and its relationship to the classical tradition, one for which a concept from the field of biology, *convergent evolution*, is apt.

The term *convergent evolution* describes the processes by which different species develop morphologically and functionally similar adaptations in response to the same selective pressures in the environment, but in the absence of any direct genealogical relation. Eyes of remarkably similar morphology, for example, have evolved independently in different phyla of the animal kingdom because they are a particularly useful adaptation for any species moving in the presence of light through a transparent or semitransparent medium such as air or water.[6] Philosopher Daniel Dennett cites the case of octopi (phylum *mollusca*) and dolphins (phylum *chordata*) in this regard.[7] In a similar vein, Theodosius Dobzhansky and colleagues note that "dolphins (mammals), some sharks (fishes), and some ichthyosaurs (reptiles) resemble each other closely in form, despite belonging to separate classes."[8] Stephen Jay Gould elaborates this same example in illustrating the general truth that "converging lines begin from . . . different antecedents and must craft similarities from disparate starting points."[9]

I use the concept of convergent evolution in an extended, but not unprecedented, sense to describe the gradual transformation of features in a succession of related cultural artifacts: in this case, the works on King Crimson's early studio recordings. The "fossil record" of the structure of these songs illustrates a gradual convergence upon the formal processes and narrative paradigms of nineteenth- and twentieth-century art music, the resulting similarities crafted from the "disparate starting points" of popular song and sonata forms, respectively. The "selective pressure" driving this convergence, which reached its first major culmination with *LTA*, was, I argue, the group's neoromantic aesthetic stance.

In making a case for convergent evolution, it is prudent to bear in mind Dennett's cautionary remarks on the difficulties, where cultural artifacts are concerned, of distinguishing instances of convergence from those of direct descent (i.e., imitation, plagiarism). As Dennett points out, "We happen to know, because they told us, that the creators of *West Side Story* got the idea from *Romeo and Juliet*, but if they had been carefully secretive about this, we might well have thought they had simply reinvented a wheel, rediscovered a cultural 'universal' that will appear, on its own, in almost any cultural evolution."[10]

Are classical elements of *LTA*'s formal and narrative organization instances of rediscovered universals, or are they simple borrowings from classical models? Either answer would be simplistic, and, in any case, the question is moot. Given its composers' extensive familiarity with Western art music, it would be impossible—perhaps even for the composers themselves—to distinguish the roles of art music influence and individual attention in *LTA*'s construction. Thus, because one cannot rule out genealogical relationships among disparate "species," as one usually can in the animal kingdom, the analogy to convergent evolution is less than perfect in its application to musical style.

However, if one cannot use the analogy in establishing *LTA*'s aesthetic autonomy, it is nevertheless efficacious in arguing for the work's aesthetic integrity: to demonstrate that *LTA* is not a derivative product of stylistic borrowing and fusion, but an organic outgrowth of its roots in the forms and narratives of rock. The standards of evidence and the kinds of proof one might adopt in arguing such a position are, following Dennett once again, not unlike those required of a defendant in an industrial espionage case: "The interior of the defendant's new line of widgets looks suspiciously similar in design to that of the plaintiff's line of widgets—is this an innocent case of convergent evolution of design? Really the only way to prove your innocence in such a case is to show clear evidence of actually having done the necessary R&D work (old blueprints, rough drafts, early models and mockups, memos about the problems encountered, etc.)."[11]

In the next section I show that King Crimson did the necessary "R&D work," that all of the important elements of form and narrative content in *LTA* derive organically from the treatment of form and content in songs on the preceding albums. Two steps are required to make this case: (1) establishing the "fossil record" by showing how the extended instrumental forms of *LTA* Parts One and Two derive from song forms used on earlier albums; and (2) showing that King Crimson's early vocal and programmatic works consistently enact plots in which a persona or subject is beset by and usually devastated by external forces—a narrative paradigm that is then adapted to purely instrumental structures on later recordings.

Form

The first step is readily accomplished with the help of the formal diagrams in fig. 6.1. Here the opening songs on three albums, "21st

Century Schizoid Man" (*In the Court of the Crimson King*, 1969), "Pictures of a City" (*In the Wake of Poseidon*, 1970), and "LTA, Part One" are graphed. The first two, songs with lyrics by Peter Sinfield, are in modified popular song forms, beginning with the standard alternation of an instrumental theme and vocal verse. Two distinctive formal features of these songs are critical to the genesis of *LTA:* (1) the relative length of the developmental sections, which in each case account for at least half of the playing time; and (2) a contrasting section, with its own subtitle ("Mirrors" and "42nd and Treadmill," respectively) interpolated as or shortly before the retransition to a reprise of the first instrumental theme or final verse.

The diagram of "*LTA*, Part One" illustrates how its structure derives from the modified song forms of these earlier examples. The section I have labeled *exposition* corresponds to the alternation of instrumental theme and verse in traditional song forms. In *LTA*, however, there are simply two contrasting instrumental themes (A and B). The development and recapitulation are straightforward, except that H in the latter is rather distantly related to B. The most striking departures from song form are the relative durations of the introduction and interlude, the latter like a small, self-contained suite. Once one makes allowances for the relative durations of these sections, however, the structure of "LTA, Part One" can be seen to be virtually identical to that of "Pictures of a City."

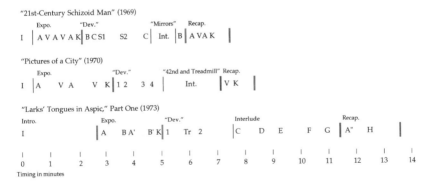

Fig. 6.1. Part of the fossil record.

Content

In an entry of his *King Crimson Journal*, dated October 29, 1969, Robert Fripp records his impressions of the band's first U.S. gig, at Goddard College, Vermont, where they played "to an audience with a high proportion tripping and expecting a happy soul band. We began with "Schizoid Man." The audience never recovered from the first shock, their condition being delicate anyway. I had the impression of the crowd being squashed."[12]

The hint of pride in this statement befits a band whose members, in the words of Jamie Muir (percussionist on *LTA*) "were interested in creating monstrous power in music."[13] Apparently, this very power could be disconcerting for the players themselves. Violinist David Cross, for example, stated: "It sometimes worries me, what we do—we stretch so far and our music is often a frightening expression of certain aspects of the world and people. . . . Most of the time our improvisation comes out of horror and panic."[14]

On the first album, *In the Court of the Crimson King*, this power was, in a specific aesthetic-theoretical sense, focused outward: the songs communicated a view of reality directly to the listener without the intermediary of a projected persona or subject fictionally inhabiting the world of the work.[15] "Schizoid Man," for example, portrays humankind in psychopathological terms, and "Epitaph" evokes the collective dread of the Cold War era, the suspicion that "the fate of all mankind . . . is in the hands of fools." In both cases the expressive qualities of the music are appropriate to the subject matter, but one need not ascribe them to a character or persona in the songs themselves. With the second album, *In the Wake of Poseidon*, comes the first hint of the inward turn that I have characterized as a neoromantic aesthetic stance. The experience embodied in the music is that of a fictional subject or persona, and the dynamic and expressive qualities of the music are to be understood as dramatically characterizing this experience in some central sense.

Perhaps the first example of this phenomenon in King Crimson's work is "42nd and Treadmill," the retransitional interlude in the opening track, "Pictures of a City," which runs from 5:00 to 7:09. Over a repeated bass pattern following a modified blues progression in

G minor, guitar and drum parts gradually grow more elaborate. At the beginning of the third and final cycle of the bass, the guitar begins to cut against the prevailing meter (alternating measures of 5/4 and 3/4) with repeated figuration in groups of three eighth-notes, later further subdivided, growing steadily more agitated and distorted. This rhythmic effect perfectly captures an image suggested by the title: running in place, ever faster, to stay on a treadmill. A screeching upward glissando by the guitar a second before the recapitulation vividly illustrates the failure to do so.

In the context of a song on the madness of modern city life, the image of the treadmill has a rather obvious significance: it is a metaphor for the urban rat race. That the interlude's expressive qualities of panic and desperation should be ascribed to a fictional persona within the music is suggested by the last two lines of the lyric ("Lost soul, lost trace / Lost in hell . . ."), which indicate a unitary persona, a single lost soul whose experience is expressed through the music. Moreover, the original title of the song, "A Man, A City," argues for interpreting it as the experience of a single (male) persona.[16]

If there is doubt about this hint of a nascent neoromantic stance on *The Wake of Poseidon*, "Cirkus," the first track on the next album, *Lizard* (1971), dispels it once and for all. A setting of an apocalyptic allegorical poem about an unidentified speaker's initial encounter with, and later submersion in, a society on the brink of chaos, the song begins by concisely capturing this speaker's relationship to the outside world in musical terms. The opening, accompanied by the music-box sonority of electric piano in a high register, recounts his emergence into existence and consciousness, setting a tone of wonder and expectation. The last syllable of the opening stanza, reached by a steadily rising vocal line, is left hanging on the leading tone, D-sharp. After a brief tonic (E minor) resolution on the third beat of the next measure, the definitive answer to the wonder and expectancy of the opening stanza comes on the succeeding downbeat—and the answer is bitter disillusionment. Here a sinister theme outlining an inverted A-sharp diminished seventh-chord enters loudly on the mellotron (brass), ushered in by drums and cymbals. Its even eighth notes oscillate mechanically between A-sharp and G like a broken spring, although it later rises to E and eventually replaces the A-sharp with B. This theme acts as an antagonistic force in the structure, inimical to the speaker of the poem, finally becoming the symbolic object of his terror after anarchy descends in the last stanza.

"Cirkus" and "Pictures of a City" are just two examples of a broader category of King Crimson's early works in which the persona or subject whose experience is represented falls prey to antagonistic forces. For example, in "Sailor's Tale" (*Islands*, 1972), a programmatic instrumental work after episodes from Homer's *Odyssey*, the subject, Odysseus, encounters an array of hostile entities and phenomena, including the Sirens, Scylla, Charybdis, and a maelstrom unleashed by the god Helios. "Lizard" recounts the adventures of one Prince Rupert who, after dazzling victories, is in the end left on a corpse-littered battlefield, wracked with remorse. The social climbers lampooned in "Indoor Games" (*Lizard*, 1971) are driven mad by their own perverted machinations—amply illustrated in some labyrinthine group improvisation.

More telling to the interpretation of *LTA,* however, are works following the specific narrative pattern noted in "Cirkus"; that is, opening with an opposition between a theme associated with the persona (in each case a vocal verse) and a contrasting one linked to an antagonistic force. Two songs on the succeeding album *Islands* are the clearest cases. Like "Cirkus," "The Letters"—a melodrama about a wife who receives a poison pen letter and responds with a suicide note—introduces the persona whose experience the music dramatizes (the wife) within the first eight lines of the lyric. These tense, hushed verses quoting the poison-pen letter are followed by a sudden loud attack and a change in texture. A new theme for saxophones with a searing counterpoint on guitar captures the wife's initial psychological shock. Free group improvisation follows, exploring her grief, rage, and finally, suicidal frenzy. "Ladies of the Road" also begins with vocal verses, pianissimo, introducing its female subjects, in this case, groupies. The initial instrumental section then begins loudly, unleashing an external force against one of them. In this case, however, it is a perversely squirming baritone sax solo representing the sexual advances of a band member. Later, a lewd guitar solo serves the same function.[17] One further example of this pattern might be found, if one allows for a collective persona: the lyric beginning "The Battle of Glass Tears" (*Lizard*, 1971) introduces the armies that are soon annihilated in the instrumental continuation, once again with the usual extreme dynamic contrast.

These eight examples establish a common narrative practice or paradigm: King Crimson's early works routinely embody the experience of a fictional subject who is put through dangerous or deadly trials and overwhelmed with extremes of negative affect. The very prevalence of this pattern and the fact that the formal architecture of *LTA* clearly derives from that of the early songs are the two most obvious reasons for interpreting *LTA* according to this paradigm.

Analysis

"LTA, Part One" begins with an introduction of nearly three minutes. In the foreground one hears an improvised set of variations for thumb piano on a short melodic figure in A pentatonic minor, which reaches a subtle climax at 1:35 and then gradually fades to nothing (by 2:43). Its hypnotic permutations work a conjuring spell: as they unfold, the surrounding darkness gradually fills with the sound of tiny bells and wind chimes whose numbers multiply to an impossible legion, filling space with a dense, scintillating sheet of sound.

Against this icy backdrop, the warm tones of the violin enter with a tense, quiet pulsation in double stops on C and E-flat (2:53), beginning the exposition and establishing a clear quintuple meter. The suggestion of C minor tonality, however, proves illusory. A distorted guitar line twists out of the silence (3:03), bending down from C to A to define the violin's pitches as part of a diminished sonority. Subsequently, the violin's upper line rises fitfully, and chromatically, over twelve measures of 5/4, the lower voice maintaining a C pedal, while the guitar line falls away in contrary motion before rising by a diminished octave to end on E-flat. Harmonically, this first phrase, in the shape of an opening wedge, merely prolongs vii^7 in the tonic key, G minor. The violin then begins the phrase again an octave higher. This time, however, the guitar line bends from C down to A-flat as the violin winds around F-sharp, creating an even more unstable sonority defined by an augmented sixth. The soul of the passage, however, is in the percussion. As the wedge opens anew, an impressive battery— beginning with triangle, cymbals, and miniature drums and ending with floor toms, gongs, and metal sheets—is used to build a huge descending crescendo culminating during the theme's last three measures, the harmony having returned by linear motions to vii.

At 3:40, after nearly a minute in which tonic harmony is conspicuously absent, the second theme begins in G minor with deafening power chords supported by bass, drum kit and prepared drum kit, and soon, a shrieking treble line on guitar. The basic riff in this passage, which always peaks on the tritone, D-flat, is in units of seven beats. When the A theme returns quietly fifteen seconds later (3:55), the treble guitar sustains over its first measure a wailing descending bend (G to F) at the dynamic level of the louder second theme, like a baleful cry of pain or terror, underscoring the dynamic and expressive contrasts.

Both themes are then repeated in varied form with reinforced textures. The guitar's descending line in the first theme, for example, is doubled an octave lower by a growling fuzz-wah bass. The most remarkable change, however, is the use of phasing effects. At 4:17 the violin in double stops is echoed by bicycle horns at a lower dynamic level and slightly slower. This slower part gradually goes out of phase and then back into phase with the violin as another huge crescendo builds on vii. The moment of its reconvergence coincides with the explosive return of the second theme. The exposition then concludes with a virtuosic, upward-clawing cadenza for guitar using buzz-saw distortion. Special note should be taken of the cadenza's opening (and pervasive) three note motive, G–D–A-flat, comprising a rising fifth and tritone (later appearances of the motive are found in figure 6.2a). This motive, henceforth X, is not only the basis of the cadenza, but also of much of the development, the beginning of the interlude, and even the principal theme of Part Two.

With the exception of its last thirty seconds, most of the development derives from the preceding guitar cadenza. Section 1 (29 bars of fast 7/8; 5:00–5:51) spins out motives from the cadenza in two-part counterpoint (guitar with buzz-saw distortion and bass), accompanied by drum kit and a fantastic palette of percussion instruments. It comprises a series of passages (roughly, a, a', b, a"), each beginning with a variation on the sequence quoted in figure 6.2. The second of these centers around A-flat, all of the rest around G. A great deal of rhythmic tension in this section derives from the fact that the guitar's irregular

Two motives from Part One:

Two related motives from Part Two:

Fig. 6.2. Cyclic motivic relationships in *Larks' Tongues in Aspic*.

phrases only line up with the even phrases of the bass at the beginnings of larger divisions. Moreover, if we interpret this section as describing the embattled persona—an interpretation following from the role of its source material in the guitar cadenza—then we see that the precise way the guitar and bass fail to line up is sometimes used to great dramatic effect. The section's final passage (a"; 5:38), for example, begins like the first, but soon adds three extra sixteenth notes (5:43), thus displacing the now familiar motivic material by a beat and a half. Because of the "change of phase," notes formerly sounding on beats shift to off beats. The passage therefore seems to get behind, to bog down and to lose its rhythmic energy, ultimately dissolving into a transition in simpler 6/8 meter at 5:51. The transition itself then bogs down at 5:57 when the drums cut against the prevailing 6/8 meter with duple patterns (implying 2/4), precipitating a tight bottleneck effect (6:03–6:13).

The struggle is then reengaged at a more intense level in section 2 of the development (6:14–7:40). Though in simple 4/4 meter and, until the very end, unrelenting G minor tonality, this section outdoes the first both in ferocity and in rhythmic complexity. Fuzz-wah bass, prepared drum kit, and the guitar grinding out chordal textures join in what would seem to be free improvisation, were it not for a few moments of uncanny rhythmic convergence. Most of the harmonies of this section are built from the notes of G pentatonic minor, some of them arranged as stacked fourths. Thirty seconds from the end, however, a sonority built on X, that is, a tritone atop a perfect fifth, is sequenced upward by minor thirds in a blur of harsh tremolo, resulting in the following three chords: A–E–B-flat, C–G–C-sharp, E-flat–B-flat–E. All three call for a resolution on D, and the lowest voice of this chordal sequence, A–C–E-flat, quotes an unconventional cadential move from the exposition. Specifically, it is a transposition of B's final riff, G–B-flat–D-flat, by which a return to the illusory key of C minor is effected at 3:55. After a crescendo of near metric dissolution toward the end of the development, this chordal sequence—whose bottom line transposes the riff by a whole step—is indeed resolved as one would expect: in an exhausted collapse on D (7:38). However, the guitar's E-flat is not resolved in register, so that when it is revived in the first bar of the succeeding interlude it has the effect of a suspension.

The interlude begins in the aftermath of this collapse with a rhythmically free lament for violin against a shimmering harmonic backdrop. The heart of the texture is a series of upward slipping three-note chords on guitar, all inversions of the X chord; that is tritones under perfect fourths. The first of these, spelled E-flat–A–D, resolves the last chord of the development (E-flat–B-flat–E) while leaving its E-flat suspended. Moreover, the bass line of the four inverted X chords fills in the minor third from E-flat up to G-flat, completing a sequence by minor thirds underlying the X chords in the end of the development (A–C–E-flat). The unsettled and destabilizing effect of this bass line, which shadows the soprano a major seventh lower, perfectly complements the violin melody's creeping chromatic motion and tremulous dynamic fluctuations. The passage is seasoned throughout with near-subliminal bird calls.

The second of the interlude's five parts (8:34), a gentle soliloquy for unaccompanied violin, begins somberly. After the statement and reiteration of a three-note descending motive (A-flat–G–D), however, the mood suddenly lightens. The motive is freely inverted and chained through a circle of fifths. Starting on each of the open strings (i.e., G–A-flat–C, D–E-flat–G, etc.), it flowers irresistibly in three upward flourishes, each rising higher and more fluidly than the last. The third reaches high E and then flutters down a descending diatonic sequence into a mysterious suggestion of D minor, ending on a low A, pianissimo. Without warning we are on the threshold of a magical realm.

The sound of an autoharp, played tremolando, begins and then dominates the third section (9:10), which is notable as the work's first passage in the major mode. The autoharp's delicate, bell-like sonorities, restricted to a narrow range, accompany simple figures in G pentatonic major on the violin. Having begun as a whisper, the violin grows quieter still at 9:52, circling repeatedly around the tonic pitch. As the violin fades to nothing, the ringing of the autoharp grows louder, becoming a whirling cascade as it moves from the high to the low register before zinging off of the low strings.

An exuberant violin solo in double stops, emphasizing perfect intervals and centering around D, begins the fourth section, the cycle's only moment of unalloyed joy. The violin is joined at its climax by sweeping ascending glissandi from the autoharp, which dissolve into a surprisingly intricate concluding figure in E minor. The fifth section is a simple unison melody for violin and autoharp in the same key. Its effect is elusive; it is, on one hand, vaguely exotic, and perhaps also overprecious; but somehow, for these very reasons, it is ominous. The final cadence omits the tonic pitch.

The path back to C minor (iv of the tonic key, G minor) is through two common tone modulations, comprising a cycle of major thirds. After the final E minor cadence of the interlude, the guitar, with edgy distortion and staccato articulation, winds up out of the depths pianissimo at 11:23, playing the violin's double stops from the A theme in the key of A-flat minor. Nine measures later (at 11:41), while the guitar repeats the pitch A-flat, the violin enters on C, preparing the next modulation, this time to the tonic key though its subdominant, C minor (11:44). The A theme is then recapitulated measure for measure, the guitar taking the violin's double stops and the violin playing a new melody. The descending line in contrary motion originally taken by guitar is omitted, so that rather than a two-part opening wedge the contour is now simply a two-part ascent. Throughout this ascent, the sound of the human voice is heard for the first time, though there is no singing and the spoken words are largely unintelligible. Nevertheless, they suggest a vague sort of programmaticism. During the first part one hears the thin, wind-blown, and increasingly agitated voice of a woman, perhaps a companion of the persona. At the beginning of the second part of the ascent, it is replaced by a snarling, threatening male voice that grows louder as the inevitable climax approaches.

With an explosion on G minor (12:26), the angry and quasi-hal-lucinatory assault of this stranger seems to be absorbed into an instru-mental voice, that of fuzz-wah bass playing a new melody. Its thick, growling tone as it ascends by glissando to high D and its subsequent sliding trill between C and B natural are excoriation incarnate. It is accompanied by a simple lament in the violin, arpeggiated figures from guitar, and the muttering of male voices in a monotone on the tonic G. Bells make a late entry as the other elements fade to nothing. Their gentle ringing in parallel thirds recalls the introduction, like a return to an infantile state after the trauma of a psychotic break.

The content of "LTA, Part Two," both formal and narrative, is more readily accessible than that of "Part One." The finale to the album, it begins loudly and angrily with a theme derived from the A theme and the guitar cadenza of "Part One." The guitar, playing stacked perfect fourths, borrows the opening rhythm in 5/4 from the former; from the latter comes the unison continuation, an augmenta-tion of the cadenza's first motive (see fig. 6.2c). The motive's progres-sion through a cycle of major thirds (G, E-flat, B, G) is accompanied by drums and heavy percussion, including metal sheets and pipes struck with hammers and chains. The second theme, built from a motive of A" (Part One, 11:23ff.; see figs. 6.2c and 6.2d), begins in a moment of welcome serenity. Soon, however, the melody is sequenced by minor thirds, the theme slogging upward in the manner of a labored march with the drums pulling "backward" against the beat. After it halts on the dominant (D) at 1:48, both themes are repeated, the first truncated, the second expanded with additional ascending sequences. As a crescendo builds on the second theme, percussionist Jamie Muir uses balloon noises—rubbing them, squeezing air out slowly, and so on—prominently, often (especially at 3:40), it seems, to simulate the inflections of human laughter. At the top of the sequential ascent the dominant is pounded out twenty-five times as the squeals and squeaks of the balloons cling to and twist among the reiterated chords, like slime that refuses to be shaken from one's foot. The final confrontation is at hand.

An ostinato in power chords (on G, A-flat, and F) cuts in at 3:42, recalling the cycle's only other passage in power chords: the antagonistic B theme of "Part One" (which also centers around G). In a cycle dominated by quintuple and septuple meter, it is surprising that this ostinato in 8/4, albeit an irregularly divided 8/4, is the most jarring and angular figure of all. Because of its irregular subdivisions (3–3–2), it sounds as though it is cut a beat short, like a mechanism with a missing cog, slipping violently on every cycle. After an interruption by the quintuple motive of the principal theme, the guitar is joined on the ostinato by the rhythm section. At 4:00 the final struggle is engaged: a hair-raising ascending figure from the violin shivers upward and then falls back, beginning an extended "solo" in which this contour is repeated several times. It is as though the violin line embodies a desperate desire to escape the mechanized violence of the ostinato. Indeed, its sense of desperation derives in part from the fact that it initially is caught in lockstep with the very mechanism it would escape.

After six cycles, however, the persona exerts a great effort of will; the quintuple second theme enters against the ostinato (4:25), setting in motion a passage of metric phasing in which eight measures of the quintuple theme cut against five repetitions of the eight-beat ostinato. For the first two of its five subsequent cycles, the ostinato seems to retain control; against it the phrases of the second theme sound strained and unnatural, and it is to the ostinato's phrasing that the violin solo remains tied. At 4:35, however, there is a breakthrough. The quintuple meter begins to take control, probably as a natural effect of the phasing cycle, and the violin switches allegiance to it, suddenly accelerating its rhythmic activity. Its bowed sixteenth-note triplets spit upward like sparks, cutting a path for the ascending quintuple theme. At 4:46 the metric cycle closes with the persona's quintuple theme in full control. The violin's line, freed of all restraints, takes flight; a sliding glissando over the next five measures, first natural and then in harmonics, whistling upward, its frequency at the end seemingly escaping the range of human perception. After this flight of transcendence, the quintuple theme climbs through further ascending sequences, the rhythm section no longer dragging backward, but instead pushing it forward in an orgy of percussive abandon. It reaches D once again, reiterating the D major sonority until a long coda arpeggiating this triad explodes at 5:58.

Interpretation

The exposition of "LTA, Part One" is readily interpreted according to the plot motif underlying the openings of "Cirkus" and "The Letters." Like these songs, its first theme finds the persona poised on the verge of disaster, just before the unleashing of a dangerous force inhabiting the second. In LTA, because the second theme completes the first harmonically, supplying the tonic that is so painfully absent in the first, the sequence of two themes takes on the character of continuous action, of being pulled inexorably into a vortex and then thrashed helplessly about by its internal currents. The cadenza is perhaps best understood as the beginning of a counteraction to the events of the exposition; an attempt to claw one's way out of the chaos of a destructive cycle. Although its dynamic and expressive qualities are consistent with such an interpretation, the principal rationale for hearing the cadenza in this way is the role of its material, especially X, in the work as a whole. Most obviously, X is the basis of the principal theme of "Part Two," the victorious finale that reverses the catastrophe of "Part One." That X is also an essential element in both sections of the development of "Part One" is consistent with this interpretation as well. Whether one hears it as a fight or a flight reaction, the struggle played out here does win a reprieve, clearing the way for the calm of the interlude, with its fleeting moments of wonder. Moreover, the tonal goal reached at the beginning of the interlude, D, is the same as that on which the finale concludes. Thus the development might well be heard as a rehearsal for the more successful counteraction of "Part Two."

The E-flat suspended from its last sonority undercuts the tranquillity of C, the first section of the interlude. That this perturbation results from the inversion of the X chords of the development is an example of the subtle way in which formal and expressive logic converge in the work. The transition from the development to the interlude is arguably the most extreme disjunction in the progress of "Part One." The inversional harmonic relation not only provides a hidden formal link bridging this disjunction, but defines a "psychologically true" expressive relation between the sections as well; that is, the trauma of the development is not easily forgotten, so its echoes, embodied in the inverted X chords, live on in the restless and shell-shocked brooding of C.

One would be hard pressed to find any obvious formal logic behind the subsequent, rhapsodically unfolding episodes of the interlude. Nevertheless, the expressive coherence of the whole is straightforward. In the most general terms, it moves steadily from dark affect to light, a natural progression for the work's persona as the terror of the exposition and the turmoil of the development fade into the past. The lulling effect of this gradual and gentle progress toward the light leads to complacency, so that when one is immersed in the E minor tonality of the interlude's final section, the antipode of the piece's tonal journey, one has no indication that the persona is once more standing on the brink of disaster. Nevertheless, there is something disconcerting in the E minor passage, and one knows that its rootless cadence on G and B cannot be the end of the story. It is not, for in the recapitulation the persona is plunged into madness.

In addition to the derivation of the principal themes of "Part Two" from material aligned with the interests of the beleaguered persona of "Part One," there are further and less obvious ties between the two parts that might be described as procedural rather than thematic. One is the use of phasing effects; that is, the rudimentary form of the procedure based on incommensurate tempi in "Part One" and the more sophisticated metric phasing cycle in "Part Two." The former precipitates a crisis in "Part One," the crescendo leading to the second onslaught of the B theme in the exposition; the latter is integral to conflict and resolution at the climax of "Part Two." Now, it might be making too much of this parallel to say that the second example seals a rift opened by the first. Nevertheless, there is a further parallel in compositional procedure that admits just such a cogent dramatic interpretation: the quasi-hallucinatory use or simulation (using squeak toys) of the human voice. In both parts this human factor emerges at the beginning of a long crescendo built on a theme in quintuple meter, and in both cases it takes the form of an external element impinging on the experience of the persona. Yet whereas the hallucinations are a harbinger of madness in the catastrophe of "Part One," in "Part Two" they are squeals of ineffectual, rodent-like laughter that the persona drives before it and crushes underfoot; a perfect metaphor for the growing power of the persona with respect to the antagonistic forces it confronts and finally overcomes.

Conclusion

By any standard, the classical leanings of *LTA* are less conspicuous than those of King Crimson's two preceding albums, *Lizard* and *Islands*. The level of superficial "stylistic reference," to use Covach's term, is undoubtedly critical here, particularly with respect to instrumentation. On the earlier albums, standard rock instrumentation is supplemented by soprano voice, flute, bass flute, oboe, English horn, cornet, trombone, timpani, crash cymbals, strings, solo double bass, and harmonium. On *LTA,* by contrast—aside from the pervasive use of violin—there is little reference to classical instrumentation.[18] Even mellotron is used sparingly (on two tracks, "Exiles" and "Easy Money"), and then not primarily for orchestral weight, as it usually was on *Lizard* and *Islands,* but rather for the sake of timbral transparency.[19] Similarly, the evocation of classical textures, harmonic language, and voice leading, everywhere in evidence on *Lizard* and *Islands,* is on *LTA* largely confined to two songs, "Book of Saturday," and "Exiles." Finally, and in sharp contrast to *LTA*'s formal structures, the most ambitious works on *Lizard* and *Islands* are sprawling, multimovement affairs with only tenuous connections to popular song forms.

With respect to all of these elements of style, *LTA,* it would seem, is a decided move back in the direction of rock basics. It may seem paradoxical, therefore, that it is on the instrumental tracks of this album that King Crimson made a critical breakthrough—the convergence on classical narrative paradigms and constructive principles detailed above. In fact, however, there is no paradox; I would argue that this convergence took place not *in spite of* the move toward rock basics, but *because of it.* Popular song forms as modified on King Crimson's early albums were already uniquely well adapted to embodying dramatic content of the kind required for the traditional struggle-to-victory narrative paradigm. Once the guiding idea that instrumental music has the potential to dramatize internal life in an abstract sense was in place, all that was required to refit the form was a little tweaking.

This case of convergent evolution holds several lessons for our understanding of Western-classical traditions. Most important, it prods us to reevaluate some of our habitual thinking about the relation of form and content. For example, because narrative organization and narrative interpretive criticism grew up in symbiosis with the dramatic sonata style of Beethoven, we all too readily assume that there is something privileged or inevitable about this relationship. We tend to assume that the normative tonal polarities, thematic contrasts, and dialectical developmental processes of sonata forms are an indispensible substrate for this sort of dramatic content, simply because in the only relevant cultural evolution we know, these features happen to have been exploited in the majority of works actually exhibiting such content. *LTA* is an instructive counterexample. Its existence suggests that we should listen more closely to the numerous critics who have argued that the sonata form is at best a flawed medium for conveying dramatized internal experience. Scott Burnham, for example, in addressing the fact that many narrative interpretations of the first movement of Ludwig van Beethoven's *Eroica* Symphony skip over the recapitulation, offers as a likely rationale "the embarrassment of trying to fit a large-scale repetition into a dramatic narrative."[20] Nor is extensive obligatory repetition the only feature of sonata form that has, historically, been at odds with a dramatic conception of first-movement form. Equally problematic is the form's traditional *climax profile*,[21] defined by the normative occurrence of the principal climax at the point of retransition. When, with middle-period Beethoven and increasingly thereafter, the opening movement of a sonata or symphonic cycle came to be understood as the first chapter in a unified multimovement drama, it became necessary to sustain the main tension of the movement until later in the structure, and even to leave some of it unresolved to be projected forward to a resolution in the finale. One solution was to revisit and extend the conflicts of the development in a lengthy coda, an adaptation that often contributed to unwieldy length in sonata structures of the nineteenth century and beyond.

"LTA, Part One" fulfills all of the essential narrative functions associated with the first movement of an instrumental cycle following the struggle-to-victory plot type: it presents a cogent thematic opposition that is developed throughout the movement; creates a sense of imbalance by alternating sections embodying irreconcilable contrasts; and culminates in a catastrophe which must be reversed in the finale through the reinterpretation of its themes. How well adapted to these narrative functions is the modified popular song form underlying "LTA, Part One"? Very well indeed. First, there is virtually no literal repetition to explain away. The modified repetition of the exposition—which in any case incorporates not only marked variations in timbre and doubling, but new countermelodies as well—takes only one minute out of thirteen and a half. The recapitulation, on the other hand, is so thoroughly modified as to nearly obscure its formal function. All in all, "LTA, Part One" is remarkable for its psychological naturalness and the unity of its effect in the nearly complete absence of literal repetition. Its climax profile is also ideal for the first chapter of a multimovement drama; the final peripety and the principal catastrophe are reserved for the last minute and a half, so that the listener has no time to come to terms with the persona's shocking reversal of fortunes in the recapitulation. Indeed, the listener is assimilating new material until the final seconds, so that the sense of resolution created by its formal rounding and tonal resolution is counteracted by its unsettled psychological and dramatic progress.

Perhaps the most far-reaching lesson to be taken from this case of convergent evolution is the sheer power of aesthetic ideas in the face of the inertia of musical institutions and traditions. It is hard to imagine a musical form and performance venue more poorly suited to classical instrumental development and narrative organization than the rock song in its setting of arena-style concerts. Nevertheless, under the influence of a fleeting change in aesthetic climate, this form became a medium in which it was possible to reinterpret the narrative paradigms of art music in a distinctly contemporary voice.

Notes

1. Edward Macan, *Rocking the Classics: English Progressive Rock and the Counterculture* (New York: Oxford University Press, 1997), 41.
2. John Covach, "Progressive Rock, 'Close to the Edge,' and the Boundaries of Style," in John Covach and Graeme M. Boone, eds., *Understanding Rock: Essays in Musical Analysis* (New York: Oxford University Press, 1997), 22.
3. Ibid.

4. King Crimson, *Larks' Tongues in Aspic,* Editions EG compact disc EG CD7, 1973.

5. A few among many recent studies of classical works addressing this kind of narrative content are Anthony Newcomb's essays on symphonies of Schumann and Mahler ("Once More 'Between Absolute and Program Music': Schumann's Second Symphony," *Nineteenth-Century Music* 7 [1984], 233–50; "Action and Agency in Mahler's Ninth Symphony, Second Movement," in Jenefer Robinson, ed., *Music and Meaning* [Ithaca NY: Cornell University Press, 1997], 131–53); a number of analyses in Robert Hatten's *Musical Meaning in Beethoven* (Bloomington: Indiana University Press, 1994); William Kindermann's "Beethoven's Piano Sonata in A-flat Major, Opus 110," *Beethoven Forum* 1 (Lincoln: University of Nebraska Press [1992]: 111–45); Richard Taruskin's "Public Lies and Unspeakable Truth: Interpreting Shostakovich's Fifth Symphony," in David Fanning, ed., *Shostakovich Studies* (Cambridge: Cambridge University Press, 1995), 17–56; James Webster's "Brahms's *Tragic Overture*: The Form of Tragedy," in Robert Pascal, ed., *Brahms* (Cambridge: Cambridge University Press, 1983), 99–124; in Charles Fisk's "What Schubert's Last Sonata Might Hold" in Robinson, ed., *Music and Meaning*, 179–200; and my analysis of the first movement of Beethoven's Sonata *Appassionata* ("Structuralism and Musical Plot," *Music Theory Spectrum* 19 [1997]: 13–34).

6. Daniel C. Dennett, *Darwin's Dangerous Idea* (New York: Simon and Schuster, 1995), 356.

7. Ibid.

8. Theodosius Dobzhansky et al., *Evolution* (San Francisco: W. H. Freeman, 1977), 327.

9. Stephen Jay Gould, *Dinosaur in a Haystack* (New York: Harmony Books, 1995), 118.

10. Dennett, *Darwin's Dangerous Idea*, 356–57.

11. Ibid., 72.

12. *The Young Person's Guide to King Crimson*, booklet accompanying the recording of the same name (1976), 16. Published at http://www.elephant-talk.com/articles/fripp-yp.htp.

13. David Teledu, "The Talking Drum—A Jamie Muir Interview," *Ptolemaic Terrascope* 8 (1991); on-line at http://www.elephant-talk.com/intervws/muir.htp.

14. Interview, *Sounds*, February 1974. Quoted from *King Crimson Journal*, February 9, 1974 (see *Young Person's Guide*, 32; full citation in note 12).

15. Edward T. Cone is largely responsible for making the term *persona* familiar in music critical theory. See *The Composer's Voice* (Berkeley and Los Angeles: University of California Press, 1974).

16. The song is so titled on *Epitaph*, a collection of live 1969 performances by the band (Discipline Global Mobile compact disc DGM 9607A/B, 1997).

17. My acknowledgment to James Crary for this observation.

18. The discreet use of flute on "Exiles" is the only obvious example. Moreover, even the use of violin may have more to do with the influence of jazz fusion than with stylistic reference to classical music: If there is a model for King Crimson's instrumentation on *LTA*, it is the Mahavishnu Orchestra, which included Jerry Goodman on violin.

19. The only exception here is the first theme of "Exiles."

20. Scott Burnham, *Beethoven Hero* (Princeton, N.J.: Princeton University Press, 1995), 18. James Webster and Charles Fisk, to cite just two among many authors, acknowledge this problem in interpretations of Brahms's *Tragic Overture* and Schubert's Sonata in B-flat, respectively (see note 5 for citations).

21. This is William S. Newman's term, used throughout *The Sonata since Beethoven* (Chapel Hill: University of North Carolina Press, 1969).

7

Tales of Change within the Sound

Form, Lyrics, and Philosophy in the Music of Yes

Jennifer Rycenga

As he spoke my spirit climbed into the sky.
I bid it to return to hear your wondrous stories.
　　　　　—Jon Anderson, "Wondrous Stories"

Similar to this becoming is temporal experience. It is when things in being are read as a text of their becoming that idealistic and materialistic dialects touch.
　　　　　—Theodor Adorno, *Negative Dialectics*

"Take water from the ocean and hold it in a jar," the carpenter said. "It is chemically-defined ocean only; all the essential ocean attributes of movement and white noise and meaning are lost."
　　　　　—June Arnold, *The Cook and the Carpenter*

Literal interpretation—whether of a sacred text or of music—is, by definition, a reductive process, craving to fix meaning into a single hermetically sealed frame. Literalism chokes whatever language it seizes, snapping off resonances and relations between words and between ideas: like clear-cutting, it creates a universe that is easily and immediately comprehensible, but only because pathetically denuded.

In their majestic sea of musical resonance, "The Revealing Science of God" (the first side of *Tales from*

Topographic Oceans, released in 1973), the British progressive rock group Yes demonstrated that they understood this dynamic of literalism (given how it was applied to them so often by their critics). In one of the thorniest lines in the composition, the nobility and the quietism of lead singer Jon Anderson's cosmology apparently converge:

> Getting over overhanging trees
> Let them rape the forest,
> They might stand and leave them
> clearly to be home

I will return to nobility and quietism after posing the usual questions provoked by Anderson's lyrics: What does such a line mean? Who are "they"? Are "they" multiple? Who is going home? Why this terrifyingly accurate image of, and apparent permission for, environmental rape?

Questions such as these have been raised about every cell of Jon Anderson's lyrics by a wide spectrum of listeners, from cynical critics to adoring fans. During Yes's most creative output—what Bill Martin has dubbed the "main sequence" of six studio albums from *The Yes Album* in 1971 through *Going for the One* in 1977—Anderson's lyrics were often savaged as incomprehensible gibberish. "Quasi-mystical lyrics produced in alien falsetto" intones the ever-hostile editorial staff at *Rolling Stone*,[1] but even sympathetic listeners have found them "opaque" and inflated with self-importance.[2]

I would argue, however, that all such critiques have fallen into an error of logocentric literalism, in which words are presumed to have primarily denotative linguistic meanings. Anderson's lyrics should at least receive the connotative license given to poetry. In his case, though, trying to establish *any* linguistic meaning for the lyrics, independent of the music, is frustrating at best and counterproductive at worst.

The sympathetic explanations proffered—that Anderson was being intentionally ambiguous (Thomas Mosbø), or that he was choosing words for their sonic value as well as their poetic resonances (John Covach), or that the words are inextricable from the music (Bill Martin)—are correct but incomplete. In their defiance of grammar, syntax, and common meaning, Anderson's lyrics radically negate any presumed narrative and linear logic of language. Yet the words chosen retain their connotative tinges, thus invoking overall cosmological themes: archetypal beings and settings connected with things of the earth and nature (rivers, seas, mountains, valleys, flying, birds, generations and teachers) and, even more centrally, with time and sound themselves (motion, song, music, eons, vibrations, waves, tempi, and the dynamism of change). In other words, the lyrics actively point the listener to the intended locus of spiritual experience in the music, and in material existence in general. In so doing, the lyrics give rise to a panentheistic neopagan immanent cosmology, inviting the listener into the temporal experience of this cosmology in music.

Pantheism, which literally means "all god," is the religious worldview that holds that everything is sacred, or that everything is a manifestation of divinity. Pan*en*theism is a philosophic expansion of pantheism. Like pantheism, pan*en*theism suggests that all we know and experience is sacred. But panentheism goes beyond the simple identification of the sacred with the human world by saying that the sacred also goes beyond what we (can) know: we (and the world) are "part or parcel of God."[3] Thus, panentheism retains both transcendence and immanence spiritually (and in fact sees them as unified).[4]

Given the bias toward transcendence in Western culture (shaped by Judaism, Christianity, and Islam), immanence has been belittled as precluding depth, complexity, and ethics.[5] But such critiques are best seen as another example of the dualistic devaluing of matter that feminists have so trenchantly analyzed. To take the possibility of immanence seriously—without therefore simply endorsing all claims of it—is part of the challenge to radically rethink the world. Music—a medium that includes both intensely physical sensations and, in the Euro-American world, extensive transcendent baggage—is a most interesting location for consideration of such questions.[6]

One enunciation of this comes from a rather nonmystical thinker, philosopher Susanne Langer. Her discussion of "presentational knowledge" suggests that symbolic forms such as music and visual art open "unexplored possibilit(ies) of genuine semantic [*sic*] beyond the limits of discursive language,"[7] on "matters which require to be conceived through some symbolizing schema other than discursive language."[8] As Emily Culpepper has noted, this means that the forms of "presentational symbolisms (e.g., art and music, ritual, poetry) are not only emotionally expressive, but elaborate complex *ideas* as well."[9] Presentational forms are appropriate to the expression of panentheistic concepts, because of their ability to portray relation in its interactions.

When Langer turns to discuss music in particular, the inherent likeness between her ideas and the function of Anderson's lyrics is evident. She writes, "Music is revealing, where words are obscuring, because it can have not only a content, but a **transient play** of contents. . . . The assignment of meanings is **a shifting kaleidoscopic play**. . . . The imagination that responds to music is personal and associative and logical, tinged with affect, tinged with bodily rhythm, tinged with dream, but *concerned* with a wealth of formulations for its wealth of wordless knowledge, its whole knowledge of emotional and organic experience, of vital impulse, balance, conflict, the *ways* of living and dying and feeling. Because no assignment of meaning is conventional, none is permanent beyond the sound that passes; yet the brief association was a flash of understanding."[10] While I doubt Jon Anderson read Langer, I think he would recognize a lyric kin in her prose. Her description of music fits what he is doing *with words*: a transient, shifting kaleidoscopic play of meanings, tinged with physical and dreamt affect, but concerned with vital meanings, creating flashes of understanding but nothing denotative enough to be static or permanent.

Using simultaneous presentational forms in their lyrics and music, Yes created a body of work that models panentheism as an enacted spiritual practice. Two large-scale experimental works stand as exemplars of studio-based composition as a philosophy *with* music: "The Revealing Science of God" which forms the opening movement of *Tales from Topographic Oceans* (1973), and "Sound Chaser" (*Relayer*, 1974).

Jon Anderson's spirituality, given his emphasis on the positive (as in the very affirmative name, *Yes*), the mythic, and the speculative, is highly eclectic and syncretic. Specific religious references in his songs and interviews cover a wide range of traditions, from Buddhist to Mayan, Native North American to Hawaiian, Christian to Celtic. He is a self-proclaimed visionary, who told me in a 1988 interview, "I'm singing for God, I'm not singing for myself, I'm singing for God, no question about it in my mind." The main sequence albums between *The Yes Album* and *Going for the One* suggest that he was then a devout pagan sun worshipper (over 60 percent of the songs written or cowritten by Anderson on those albums prominently feature the sun); since the early 1980s, he has adopted the language of the New Age unreservedly, and to an extent this has modified his previous mythology.[11]

During the 1970s Anderson developed a self-image as priest of this sun-worshipping faith.[12] The centrality of this persona emerges on the epic double-album *Tales from Topographic Oceans*. On "The Ancient," subtitled "Giants Under the Sun," Anderson shouts out the name of the sun in a variety of archaic languages:

> Sol. Dhoop. Sun. Ilios. Naytheet. Ah Kin. Saule.
> Tonatiuh. Qurax. Gunes. Grian. Surje. Ir. Samse.

He follows this with the story of the defeat of paganism, using one of the ancient solar names as a sighing pun:

> Saw the flowering creativity of life, wove its web face to face with
> the shallow. And their gods sought out and conquered: Ah Kin!

The pre-Christian religion comes face to face with the shallow new religions of dominance. The result is that the new gods, who practiced warfare, conquered the old religion.

In "Ritual" (the fourth movement of *Tales*), Anderson has recourse to a foreign language for his statement of faith: "Nous sommes du soleil." While French is hardly in the same ritual league as Sanskrit, Hebrew, or Latin, the impact is similar—the declaration has the sense of being "heightened" speech where the meaning is not immediately transparent or mundane to an English speaker.

I cite these examples of his neopaganism for two reasons. First, Anderson's religious profile meshes perfectly with the growing neopaganism of the 1970s, especially in its relation to English romanticism, and what Raymond Williams called "the green language" linking "radical social critique" with a spirituality about earth and the natural world. As Bill Martin summarizes this, "the essence of the green language is the idea of living human minds and bodies immersed in a world that is itself living."[13] Margot Adler's sketch of neopagan beliefs certainly embraces Anderson's worldview. She writes, "Most neopagans sense an aliveness and 'presence' in nature. They are usually polytheists or animists or pantheists, or two or three of these things at once. They share the goal of trying to live in harmony with nature and they tend to view humanity's 'advancement' and separation from nature as the prime source of alienation. Most Neo-Pagans . . . gravitate to ancient symbols and ancient myths. . . . They are reclaiming these sources, transforming them into something new, and adding to them the visions of . . . writers of science fiction and fantasy."[14]

The second reason is that the composition of *Tales from Topographic Oceans* will always be connected to Swami Paramahansa Yogananda's *Autobiography of a Yogi*.[15] Anderson relates, on the album cover liner notes, the genesis of *Tales*, writing, "We were in Tokyo on tour, and I had a few minutes to myself in the hotel room before the evening's concert. Leafing through Paramhansa [*sic*] Yoganada's [*sic*] 'Autobiography of a Yogi' I got caught up in the lengthy footnote on page 83. It described the four part shastric scriptures which cover all aspects of religion and social life as well as fields like medicine and music, art and architecture. For some time, I had been searching for a theme for a large scale composition. So positive in character were the shastras that I could visualise there and then four interlocking pieces of music being structured around them." The liner notes proceed to give each of the four movements of *Tales* the names corresponding to the divisions of Hindu shastric scripture. But aside from the names, the compositions bear almost no relation to any Hindu concepts.

Furthermore, it is embarrassing how little Anderson knows about Hinduism. He misspells both parts of Paramahansa Yogananda's name, in ways that would be impossible for anyone versed in Hindu thought (i.e. breaking up the internal units *maha* "great" and *ananda* "bliss"). He then refers to the second division of the shastras as "suritis" instead of "smritis," as if the conjunction of three consonants in a row had appeared to him as an apparent misprint!

But the really important difference is that the spiritual elitism and transcendent bias of the *kriya yoga* method that Paramahansa Yogananda advocated is miles away from the physically embodied musical thought of Jon Anderson. "The contemplative mind, attempting its return to divinity," writes Paramahansa Yogananda, "is constantly dragged back toward the senses by the life currents. *Kriya*, controlling the mind *directly* through the life force, is the easiest, most effective, and most scientific avenue of approach to the Infinite."[16]

From the sensory impact of their highly amplified music to the connotative images of the lyrics, Yes's music could hardly be construed as disdaining the senses. While they eschewed much of the sexual/sexist hedonism of other rock bands, their music did not reinforce a spirit/body dualism, either. Even the very passage that leads to the famous footnote suggests a spiritual hierarchy; Paramahansa Yogananda's guru said "I never eat on trains, filled with the heterogeneous vibrations of worldly people."[17]

While Anderson's eclectic spiritual search probably gained something from reading Paramahansa Yogananda's book, the content of that book has minimal impact on *Tales* other than providing ideas for titles. Anderson took the footnote, and read it with his own cosmological presuppositions, remarkably unmoored from anything Hindu. I give below an annotated version of Yogananda's footnote; Sanskrit words are retained in italics, as in the original, while I have emphasized those words and phrases that stood out for Anderson as he conceived of *Tales*:

> Pertaining to the *shastras*, literally, 'sacred books,' comprising **four classes of scripture:** the *shruti, smriti, purana,* and *tantra.* These **comprehensive treatises** cover every aspect of religious and social life, and the fields of law, medicine, architecture, art, etc. [note: Anderson adds ***music***]. The *shrutis* are the **'directly heard'** or **'revealed'** scriptures, the *Vedas.* The *smritis* or **'remembered' lore** were finally written down in a remote past as the world's longest epic poems, the *Mahabharata* and the *Ramayana. Puranas*, eighteen in number, are **literally 'ancient' allegories;** *tantras* **literally mean 'rites' or 'rituals': these treatises convey profound truths under a veil of detailed symbolism.**[18]

What Anderson wanted thematically was something comprehensive about time (both expansive eons and discreet moments, such as rituals), and something that would involve sound (that which is "directly heard").

I am not raising Anderson's ignorance about Hinduism as a snide intellectual critique; like many countercultural aspirants of the time, he was on an honest search, and allowances should be made for honest beginner's errors. But in this case Yes's actualized cosmology in the music is so much more interesting than searching for esoteric clues in Hindu thought that it is worth exposing Anderson's ignorance to lead listeners back to his more original contributions. Many commentators have been led astray by taking the presence of Paramahansa Yogananda in *Tales* literally: it, too, is part of the kaleidoscopic play of meaning.

Take, for instance, Anderson's liner note description of "The Revealing Science of God":

> 1st Movement: Shrutis. The Revealing Science of God can be seen as an ever-opening flower in which simple truths emerge examining the complexities and magic of the past and how we should not forget the song that has been left to us to hear. The knowledge of God is a search. Constant and clear.

The idea of a constant but clear search, one that has no final closure, is the aim of the composition. It manifests in the form of the piece being like an ever-opening flower. The simple examines the complex, and vice versa, through the interplay of form and detail.

Is the piece successful in achieving these goals? The resulting musical composition is encumbered with quite a few disadvantages. The intragroup battles over the album are legendary;[19] Anderson and guitarist Steve Howe had formed the conception, and the other band members were dubious about it. The result is that some performances, especially those of keyboardist Rick Wakeman (who was never spiritually in sync with the band), were often uninspired.[20] In contrast to the breathtaking virtuosity of "Sound Chaser" (see below), there are sections in "The Revealing Science of God" that sound stagnant; again, this can be largely laid at the feet of Wakeman, whose choice of synthesizer sounds dooms any dynamism in sustained chords. (Patrick Moraz's playing on the middle instrumental section of "To Be Over" on *Relayer* provides a convincing contrast.) But despite these flaws, the music does succeed because of the openness of the formal structure and the enormous range of musical details in the guitar, bass, and vocal lines.

To unfold the particularities of how a panentheistic philosophy *with* music performs, consider the use of the word *moment* in "The Revealing Science of God." Here the text is describing (and pointing back to) a temporal phenomenon taking place in the music. There are three times in the piece when the word *moment* is emphasized by a rhythmically suspended point (4:56, 6:32, and 19:36), preceded by the words "I must have waited all my life for this . . ." (later pluralized as "We must have waited all our lives for this . . ."). The first two times this pause comes as the climax point of an extended 4/4 song-like section, and is heralded by a descending bass line, which also slows as the drums drop out. The meter is suspended (and for longer times with each occurrence of this "moment"), and the polyphonic voices that sing out the next words take one back to the beginning of the entire piece, which was a metrically irregular pulsating chant.

All of this musical and structural highlighting calls attention to what has been awaited: this *moment.* But the moment is no blip in linear time, as we learn when the word is enunciated contrapuntally by different voices.[21] The moment of "moment" is suspended in time, as a duration. This is made even more explicit across the three times this event occurs. The first time, the word is repeated four times, and gives a triumphant cadence in E major, the primary key of the entire work (the chanted sections that open the piece are built on a modally inflected relationship of B minor–E major), leading to a second verse of the song-like form.[22] The second time, the word is repeated six times, the suspension of the drums lasts for a longer period, and although we get a similar cadence on E major, it leads rather quickly to a new section. The third time the "moment" occurs is as the final transition to a pulsating chant section that forms a condensed mirror image of the opening. But now the word *moment* is not even clearly heard—instead, all sorts of vocal lines are compressed and superimposed in the suspension of drummed meter, with the phrase "all our lives" assuming some prominence in the hazy mix. From this linguistically and musically undefined moment arises the ending of the composition; it is no surprise that a chanted version of the word *moment* emerges at the pivot point in the overlapped mix at the beginning of the final chanted section. Thus, the "moment" can now be seen as extended, including both itself and the chanted section, in anticipation of the final, delayed gentle cadence on E major.

The moment refers to itself, but it also contains the entire piece: recalling the chanted opening, both climaxing and suspending the song-like section, and engaging the words "all our lives." This musical concept of moment has more in common with philosophic notions of moment as logically necessary (but temporally simultaneous) steps in the process of becoming (as in G. W. F. Hegel) or *durée* (as in Henri-Louis Bergson) than it does with clock time. It can also connect such moments to large expanses of time, such as a lifespan, or even geological eons (the piece commences with a series of dawns: "dawn of light," "dawn of thought," "dawn of our power," and "dawn of love"). The boundaries of any given "moment" are fluid and expandable; yet formal divisions clearly exist within the piece without thereby negating the fluidity. The moments point us back to the form and the details of "The Revealing Science of God," thus showing the panentheistic principle of the unity of the one and the many. The moment encapsulates hearing an immanent panentheism in the material details of music: sound, time, form, texture, line, voice, and so on.

By the early 1970s, advances in studio technique had made the possibilities of directly "sculpting in sound" a presumed part of rock compositional strategies, though few bands exploited this as much as Yes. Their recording sessions would last from twelve to eighteen hours, often ending with just a few minutes worth of music.[23] By 1973, as they went to record *Tales,* Yes had achieved a very high degree of popularity, and so they were given vast amounts of studio time, and almost free rein from their record company. Serendipitously, this happened to be the Atlantic label, which had been associated with black American jazz musicians, including noted figures of the avant-garde such as John Coltrane and Ornette Coleman; as a result they were willing to trust the rock band members as artists.[24] The kind of studio composition situation that produced this album—that a band at the height of its popularity would be allowed to dictate its next move with the blessing of a hands-off approach from a record company—seems doubtful in today's market.[25]

The comparison to Coltrane is quite revealing. As his compositions became longer and more imbued with a syncretic spirituality, Coltrane's music became more difficult for the average jazz listener (on the albums *A Love Supreme* and *Om,* for instance). This is because

Coltrane had begun to view the process of musical creation—in his case, improvisation—as a spiritual practice. As Brian Priestly notes in his Coltrane biography, "The continual looking which may be described as the spiritual aspects of improvisation, from the point of view of the player, was obviously also an ideal metaphor for the spiritual searching of mankind."[26] Improvisation is seen here as a kind of focused attention that can serve as a metaphor for the search for God, for attention and interrelation to the Ultimate. Yes seems to have asked the same question of studio-based rock composition: How can a similar sense of search, attention, and relation be achieved?

Yes's answer on "The Revealing Science of God" is to constantly pour attention back into embodied musical details. There is no transcendent escape, no separation from the body; the final lines refer to

> You seekers of the truth accepting that reasons will relive
> and breath [*sic*] and hope and chase and love
> for you and you and you.

"Seekers" here includes musicians and listeners, and "the truth" is an additive, cumulative, moving, breathing, ever-expanding whole: it is not static.

Panentheism, like any philosophy of immanence, elaborates itself through particularity and emphasis. *Emphasis* is quite naturally a panentheistic term, because it is derived from the Greek and Latin *enphainein*, meaning "to show within/in"; as used in common language, it is a heightening that draws or focuses attention on some particularity. Emphasis is not a peremptory exclusion of what is not chosen, but a dedication and intensity toward what *is* chosen.

The largest scope of emphasis involves form. Like much of Yes's music, "The Revealing Science of God" has definite sections with clear formal divisions. But there is no existing formal grid on which these sections are placed. Despite attempts to read various pieces by Yes in symphonic or sonata form, they do not finally fit any given Western art music template, nor do they fit standard rock song forms, although hints of both can be discerned (see Mosbø, Covach, Martin, Josephson). Studio composition, with its blend of improvisation and working out details in real time and in real sound (as opposed to the more alienated form of musical notation), tends to create unique forms, especially with a visionary composer like Anderson who was unconstrained by schooled ideas of form. (It is significant that the more technically oriented Chris Squire was less involved with the composition of *Tales* than any other Yes albums.)

The result is a composition where form and organization are clearly present—there are repeated and developed motifs, ideas, textures, and sections—yet that form is very difficult to hear as an external abstraction while the music is progressing. There is a basic arch structure, in that the beginning and ending sections are both pulsating, vocally driven chants (0:00 and 19:43). There are two large song-like structures that make two appearances each, again in arch form—one that begins "called out a tune" (at 3:55, and a shortened version at 18:58), the other that opens with "they move fast" (at 9:44 and a shortened return at 17:29). But just when it appears that an arch form is revealing itself, there are other sections, such as the more angular "Starlight movement" (at 7:47, 11:07, and, in an instrumental version at 16:39), that don't fit. The piece is hardly in an easily intuited structure: section changes are aurally obvious enough, but their interrelationship remains multivalent.

Here Yes achieves a one-to-one correspondence between form and content in which the two are hardly separable; the form remains definitively *formal* without becoming a *closed system*. But, as is true of the lyrics, the form does not play out a standard narrative pattern. The uncoupling of form from both lyric narrative and formal expectations establishes open temporal space, wherein the trajectory of a section is driven only by the music. Linear time is replaced with a modular (or moment) form, which turns attention back to musical details without sacrificing interest in larger stretches of time. Climactic moments in Yes compositions, therefore, are not predictable or consistent. In "The Revealing Science of God" it is most easily placed at the opening of the ever-opening flower—the first three minutes of the piece covering the chant, the transition between the chant and the first theme in E major, and the entrance of the vocals inviting us to "talk to the sunlight caller."[27] It is then recapitulated and compressed near the end, particularly at the transition point of the third "moment." This unpredictability of form and climax turns attention back to the music, to the "tales of change within the sound" rather than to externals. Finally, Yes chooses to end the composition with a quiet indwelling rather than with ostentation: another sign of the locus of meaning, and sacred immanence, being within the music.[28]

In these *Topographic Oceans* the listener is awash in an ocean of sound;[29] the thick textures contrast with the clean, sharp lines of Yes's other albums. Some critics have seen this as part of the failure of the album (it became "largely horizontal" says Dan Hedges),[30] but to my ears, it moves the stress from linear counterpoint to a counterpoint that includes elements of instrumental timbre as well as line. The emphasis moves to details of articulation and counterpoint. A fine example of this is how Chris Squire, using the standard technique of octave jumping in the bass to build tension at the final return of the section "Getting over overhanging trees," then stretches them to leaps of ninths and tenths on the line "we need love," before the surprising vocal, guitar, and bass unison on the line "is our only (freedom)." Even more striking, because it is extended in time, is the compendium of guitar sounds Steve Howe uses in the first song-like section "Called out a tune" (3:35–6:52). We hear quickly strummed chords producing a percussive attack, slower arpeggiated chords, running legato passages, almost organ-like thirds and sixths between the sung sections, articulated single notes, slides, and styles that range from rock standards to country to classical. But all of these guitar articulations occur without disrupting the sonic environment; their variety reflects that environment even as it creates its range.

But, as always with Yes, and especially on *Tales*, where the conception emanated from Howe and Anderson, it is the guitar and vocal counterpoint that best functions as an "ever-opening flower." Counterpoint concerns the actual fabric of relationship (whether human/human, or human/divine), rather than the mediation of relationship through social forms (i.e. marriage, state, family, and so on).[31] This does not mean that counterpoint does not reflect social relations, as it can model hierarchy, dominance, equality, or any other quality. As with relationships of any kind—whether tepid or passionate, queer or straight, easy or tension-filled—contrapuntal textures can be illuminating or boring, but multiple voices are always present. Like Langer's description of presentational knowledge, contrapuntal textures combine feeling and intellect, both unfolding in time and grasped "through their whole form, which constructs an 'integral presentation.'"[32] The guitar and vocal duet in the "Called out a tune" section has such qualities. When Anderson sings the lyrics of this section's verses, Howe's single-note counterpoints weave in and out of the mix, emerging sometimes with almost no attack, at other times with a definitive articulation. His notes generally take the form of a staccato glissando eighth note on the first beat of a new chord, followed by a sustained pitch on the second beat. As each verse nears its end (on the lines "I ventured to see" and "to feast on the treasure"), Howe's playing becomes more melodic, with an ascending arpeggiated line, which then collapses into a reverberating chord (Anderson is quite fond of the image of rebounding vibrations). The guitar lines in these verses exemplify a careful, attentive exuberance, bursting with ideas yet holding back from a kind of awe at the surroundings.

The composition "Sound Chaser," from *Relayer* emphasizes even more directly music's immanent sacredness. At times dismissed as mere virtuostic noise, its form seems indecipherable even to many dedicated Yes fans; Martin refers to it as "lunatic," "bizarre," and "crazy."[33] The piece was conceived by Anderson as reveling in fractional tempo changes, but this was not merely an idle amusement with the material of sounds, or a serialistic formulation. The title gives us the first clue—chasing sound is, for Anderson, exactly what a panentheistic musical seeker does. The song begins with an electric piano and a bell tree chasing each other up and down a lightning-fast jazzy scale. A melange of sounds grows to include filtered drums, bird sounds, mellotron, bass, and synthesizer; the drums are soloing at an incredibly fast unmetered pace, until a bass and guitar unison proclaim the principal 5/4 theme, leading with its chromatic tail into the brief (a mere fifty-six seconds) and highly syncopated vocal section. The furious tempo is only slightly tamed when the vocals start declaiming a sonically saturated set of notions, such as "Faster moment spent spread tales of change within the sound, counting form through rhythm" and "Our bodies balance out the waves / As we accelerate our days to the look in your eyes." As with most Yes songs, the "you" is not gender specified; nor it it improbable as a cosmic force rather than another human being.[34]

As with "The Revealing Science of God," the lyrics of "Sound

Chaser" support the music and are self-reflexive: linguistic content is important to the extent that it reflects the music, not in its ability to stand on its own. Furthermore, the sheer virtuosic exuberance (unlike the thick textures of *Tales,* "Sound Chaser" is crisp and sharp, even at its most timbrally crowded) and the content of the lyrics indicates that the materials of music themselves carry ontological, embodied importance for musician and listener. Howe's solo bursts forth after the brief verses, another compendium of guitar techniques, but this time with the volume and the treble turned up. The tempo of the meter changes constantly in this cadenza-like tour de force. It only resolves into something like quiet when Anderson returns for another brief vocal moment—in effect, a recitative. It begins with the cosmogonic line "From the moment I reached out to hold, I felt a sound," and proceeds to describe the effect of fractional tempo changes "to know that tempo will continue / Lost in trance of dances as rhythm takes another turn." He concludes with the goal of the seeker/chaser "as is my want, I only reach to look in your eyes." In the remainder of the song, metric modulations and small tempo changes abound as the instrumentalists return to the blinding speed of the opening, interrupted only by the 5/4 theme being wordlessly sung.

We hear in this song the materials of music—waves, time, rhythm, speed, sound, and motion—as immediately present, and as objects/beings to pursue in a spiritual quest. A focused attention on meter and tempo marks the particularity of this piece; as the lyrics broadly hint, this chase is for and with a vital energy that is immanently present in the music.

Perhaps the examples provided are still frustratingly slippery; perhaps they have to be so. Panentheism, by positing a monistic immanent spiritual unity within matter, renounces the easy path of pointing outside of ourselves to name the sacred. When everything can be the occasion for a manifestation of the sacred, perhaps nothing stands out.[35] Furthermore, using words to explicate the presence of anything in music involves one in a logical puzzle; if words were sufficient to the thought, music would be superfluous (and vice versa, which is why great poetry often makes for poor lyrics).

The principles of emphasis and particularity dovetail with the (ironic) imperative to oppose the forces of dualism. This effectively *does* establish some parameters for what is expressed in a panentheistic worldview. This brings me to an e-mail conversation, concerning sexuality and the music of Yes, that launched this particular essay. How could it be that Yes—a group that has always consisted of heterosexual men (at least as far as I know) who are not particularly politically radical—has functioned as a rich source of thought to me as a lesbian-feminist, Marxist-humanist revolutionary? I took solace in the fact that other revolutionaries had tapped into what I would call the dialectics of Yes: their refusal of stasis (as both antilife and antimusic), their appreciation of the material world (including their environmental consciousness), and their Gramscian positing of themselves as part of the contradictions between a critique of the contemporary world and their ability as contemporary popular musicians to reach people via their "electric freedom."[36] However, to answer a question I've left suspended from the beginning, political quietism *is* a risk involved in all panentheistic systems: withdrawal can be easier than engagement because there is a safe place of retreat. In Yes's lyrics, this is expressed as a journey home.

There is a nobility in seeing injustice, but why is Anderson ready to allow "them" to "rape the forest"? This is an immobile nobility; Hegel called this romantic-era type, with its exceptionalism and aloofness, the "Beautiful Soul," which "lacks force to externalize itself, the power to make itself a thing, and endure existence. It lives in dread of staining the radiance of its inner being by action and existence. And to preserve the purity of its heart, it flees from contact with actuality."[37]

Here the potential ahistoricity of a monistic perspective becomes clear. Upset by an imperfect world filled with content, specificities, contradictions, and particularities, panentheism can attempt to flee to the safety of its own internally constructed, humming, monistic home. Given that reality is sacred, there are internal resources and reasons to remain engaged with the struggles of the world; some of this emerges in Yes songs such as "Ritual" or "Gates of Delirium," yet these same pieces often end in cocoons of individual insight rather than transformative change (social or individual). While I am not prepared to consign the "main sequence" Yes albums to the level of Hegelian incompleteness that the Beautiful Soul represents, there are broad hints it belongs there.

Pondering questions of sexuality elicits another perspective on the immanence in sound. First, those who critique Anderson's lyrics, stage appearance, and vocal tessitura ("alien falsetto") are often (implicitly and/or explicitly) hurling gendered insults, perceiving Anderson as not "macho" enough to "really rock." In a related and much debated theme among Yes fans, I considered again the alienating effect when Trevor Rabin was brought into the group in the early 1980s. Rabin's guitar showmanship, tight pants, and "marketing" as a star, his predictable song structures, and even more predictable song themes about heterosexual love, all seemed uncharacteristic for this band. When I discovered that before becoming a member of Yes, Rabin had written a song portraying himself as Jack the Ripper, then it came through loud and clear: Rabin was imbued with sexism in a deep way that the 1970s band never was.[38] And this was exemplified in the music, in a loss of formal openness, and lyric openness.

While Yes of the 1970s was not explicitly queer, it was never heteronormative. Given Anderson's Tolkien-like emphasis on generations and continuity across generations, it easily could have slipped into heteronormativity (not unlike, say, the gendered archetypes of Led Zeppelin's "Battle of Evermore"). Instead, Yes always opened up more possibilities, never restricting the field of human relations. Consider the love song, "And You and I," which never uses gendered references; or "Wondrous Stories" which names a deity/superior being as male, but not the interlocutor whose "wondrous stories" draw the narrator back from the brink of transcendence into the material world.

In an intense e-mail discussion of Yes and sexuality, the perspective of a queer student was raised, one who had "treasured" Yes due to "the total absence of the typical themes of straight romance" and the way "the fantastical, image rich lyrics, along with the excessive stretches of formally ambiguous music, seemed to him a totally open field for identification."[39] Of course, it was *not* a totally open field for identification that he was hearing, but a field that was not precluding him, or closing possibilities. This feature is reflexively true: Yes does not foreclose the ontological or spiritual possibilities for music. Though I dispute the political/philosophical direction inherent in their panentheism that leads to their apolitical solutions, Yes, too, was derailed by commercialism and the streamlined demands of the recording industry.

Creating an audible immanence in rock music by opening up form, and by using lyrics as a map back into the music, was a noble experiment,[40] too quickly abandoned because of market imperatives and the disdain of those who mistook music for something that lets "the ears lie back in an easy chair."[41]

Notes

All notes refer to the Works Consulted list that immediately follows. I would like here to graciously acknowledge an interview I had with Jon Anderson, February 27, 1988 San Francisco.

1. Quoted in Jan Overduin and James Overduin, "The Pipe Organ in Rock Music of the 1970s," 19.
2. Ibid., 20.
3. Ralph Waldo Emerson, *Selected Essays*, 39.
4. I have developed a feminist concept of *panenphysicality* in other writings; see Jennifer Rycenga, "Lesbian Compositional Process: One Lover-Composer's Perspective." While Yes's music can be interpreted as a manifestation of panenphysicality, it fits more comfortably into the category of panentheism because they still name the sacred as deity. Yet overcoming "the pseudodichotomy between transcendence and immanence, between otherworldliness and worldliness"—a hallmark of pan-en-*anything*—is consistent throughout Yes's work. See Daly with Caputi, *Wickedary*, 83. "Immanence" is the opposite of "transcendence;" it refers to those forms of spirit that dwell within or are internal.
5. The standard arguments against immanence and pantheism are that they (1) erase distinctions between the divinity and humans, and (2) by erasing such distinctions invalidate notions of good and evil (primarily by removing the deity's external judgment). But the language of the debate is hopelessly polemical—here are two examples: "Pantheism is materialism grown sentimental, and by its very nature makes for the isolation of the soul in individual religion, and its indifference in social manifestations" (Fulton J. Sheen, *Philosophy of Religion*, 123), and, from the 1929 *Encyclopedia Brittanica*, "The common religious objections to Pantheism are based on the fear that it must obliterate moral distinctions; or that it must destroy faith in a God with whom man can hold converse" (vol. 17, 191). However, it seems obvious to me that this is nonsense, since the only morality ruled out by immanence is that which must be mediated by external judgment. There is no compelling reason to deny immanent philosophies' ability to ascribe value, emphasis, respect, and response.

Yet saying that immanent philosophies can sustain ethics is not equivalent to saying they will all be equally accomplished at it. And immanence does have its own special pitfalls (as does transcendence; its ethical pitfalls are centered around authoritarianism, oppression, legalism, etc.). Immanence without an analysis of power can become self-serving, can transform itself into a subjectivity that does not recognize the subjectivity of others and ignores social context and responsibility. And when immanence is based on being awake to one's divinity but remains blissfully detached from "sordid" folks, a dualism based in elitism easily emerges, often called *gnosticism*.

6. For a fuller discussion of taking immanence seriously in music, see Rycenga, "The Composer." For the extensive transcendent baggage in Western art music, see Susan McClary, *Feminine Endings*.

7. Susanne K. Langer, *Philosophy in a New Key*, 81.

8. Ibid., 83.

9. Emily Erwin Culpepper, "Simone de Beauvoir and the Revolt of the Symbols," 10; emphasis in the original.

10. Langer, *Philosophy in a New Key*, 206–7; boldface emphasis added.

11. This adoption of the New Age, I would maintain, has resulted in music and lyrics of a generally lower quality. Having an available set of tropes, image, and narratives for reference has circumscribed Anderson's kaleidoscopic play of meaning and made his lyrics inescapably specific.

12. See Chris Welch, "Keep 'Em Yessing," 9.

13. Bill Martin, *Music of Yes*, 86.

14. Margot Adler, *Drawing Down the Moon*, 4.

15. Swami Paramahansa Yogananda (1893–1952) came to the United States in 1920 to attend the International Congress of Religious Liberals. His Self-Realization Fellowship was established as a result of this trip, reaching a peak of over 150 centers in the U.S. before his death (see Tweed and Prothero, *Asian Religions*, 162). His method of *kriya yoga* (a technique of breath control), his syncretic inclusion of Christ and Paul among yogis, and his readable *Autobiography of a Yogi*, first published in 1946, led to his becoming one of the pioneers of Hinduism in North America and a posthumous countercultural phenomenon in the 1970s.

16. Swami Paramahansa Yogananda, *Autobiography of a Yogi*, 282; emphasis in the original.

17. Ibid., 104.

18. Ibid. The discrepancy with Anderson's page citation given in the *Tales* liner notes is due to a difference in editions.

19. See Bill Martin, *Music of Yes*, 157–58, and Dan Hedges, *The Authorised Biography*, 88–90.

20. Martin, *Music of Yes*, 148.

21. I remain eternally grateful to Dan Plonsey for pointing this *moment* out to me, even though he found it amusing. I also wish to acknowledge Mira Zussman, Fred Maus, Dirk von der Horst, Kevin Holm-Hudson, Julie Stege, and Jane Caputi, who each sparked key moments of resonance as I worked on this paper.

22. As Kevin Holm-Hudson points out, the keys of B major and B minor are avoided in the larger formal structure of "The Revealing Science of God," as is the relative minor of C-sharp. This may be another example of how Anderson is opening the formal elements of large-scale composition, in a way that creates internal sections without creating a formal narrative.

23. Steve Turner, "The Great Yes Technique Debate," 10; see also the accounts in Hedges.

24. Hedges, Ibid., 88–89.

25. With the democratization and affordability of certain kinds of computer and studio techniques, however, there are certainly opportunities for "sound sculpting" today. It is simply the combination of commercial success and compositional freedom that seems impossible. See Martin, *Music of Yes*," on the "audacity" of *Tales* (146) and Covach, "Progressive Rock," on the progressive rock underground of the 1980s and early 1990s (5ff).

26. Brian Priestley, *John Coltrane*, 52.

27. Other examples of interestingly placed climaxes in Yes include the traditional finales of "The Remembering" on *Tales* and "Awaken" on *Going for the One,* the double moments on *Tales'* "Ritual"—one at the repetition of "at all" at the end of the song section, and another when the guitar, Brahms-like, pulls us from the percussion solo with its heroic notes for "Nous Sommes du Soleil;" and the most unusual, best heard in live performances: the instrumental cascading near the end of section 2 of "And You and I."

28. Other pertinent examples of this include "And You and I," "To Be Over," and, most crucially, the immanent ending of "Awaken," where the climactic mystic union—reached in an instrumental moment (Anderson often lets music itself take the songs to their highest point)—dissipates to the opening search, with the assurance that even if I try to "run away," I will "turn around" and find what I am looking for "standing close to me." The panentheism of combining their most explicitly transcendent musical composition with this exquisite expression of immanence cinches the case, even without the fact that Anderson indicated to me that "Awaken" was the pinnacle of his work with Yes (interview). It is also interesting to note that in the reunion tour of 1991, Anderson sacrificed having a solo number in favor of the entire band performing "Awaken" as the conclusion of the concert. This demonstrates the intentionality of

Anderson's spirituality, since "Awaken" is not one of the better-known Yes songs; many people in the audience were under the impression that it was a new work (personal observations, Inglewood, California, May 1991).

29. The title of the album, *Tales from Topographic Oceans,* is a miniature example of how Anderson's words lead nowhere but to the phenomenon in which they participate. *Topographic* is not really a modifier for *oceans*; in common language, *topographic* is applied not to an area itself, but to the representation of an area, as in a map, chart, or drawing. Anderson seemed to have in mind here two obscure dictionary definitions that relate to his word association with Yogananda's footnote: "(4) the features, relations, or configurations of a structural entity. (5) a schema of a structural entity, as of the mind, a field of study, or society, reflecting a division into distinct areas having a specific position relative to one another." See "topography," Random House Dictionary of the English Language, 2nd ed., Unabridged).

30. Hedges, *The Authorized Biography*, 90.

31. Audre Lorde makes a similar point in distinguishing the erotic from social forms: "That self-connection shared is a measure of the joy which I know myself to be capable of feeling, a reminder of my capacity for feeling. And that deep and irreplaceable knowledge of my capacity for joy comes to demand from all my life that it be lived within the knowledge that such satisfaction is possible, and does not have to be called *marriage,* nor *god,* nor *an afterlife.*"

32. Emily Culpepper, "The Politics of Metaphor: A Feminist Philosophy." Unpublished paper, delivered at the American Academy of Religion, 1986.

33. Martin, *The Music of Yes*, 159, 160, 32.

34. In this respect, of course, Yes is part of a long line of mystics who use the analogy of human love to illustrate the divine/human relationship.

35. Walt Whitman gives classic expression to the ubiquity of the sacred in panentheism in section 48 of "Song of Myself": "I hear and behold God in every object, yet understand God not the least / . . . I find letters from God dropt in the street, and every one is sign'd by God's name, / And I leave them where they are, for I know that wheresoe'er I go, / Others will punctually come for ever and ever" (71).

36. I have written more on the relation of Yes to a revolutionary aesthetic in an unpublished paper, "A Noisy Century: Revolutionary Creativity and its Feedback Loop," delivered at the Unnatural Acts Conference, University of California at Riverside, April 1997. The full quote from Antonio Gramsci, the Italian Marxist, reads "The philosophy of praxis is consciousness full of contradictions in which the philosopher himself, understood both as an individual and as an entire social group, not merely grasps the contradictions, but posits himself as an element of the con-

tradities and elevates this element to a principle of knowledge and therefore of action" (quoted in Raya Dunayevskaya, *Rosa Luxemburg*, 197, n. 27).

37. G. W. F. Hegel, *The Phenomenology of Mind*, 666.
38. Rabin's song "The Ripper" was on his 1980 *Face to Face* album, when the Yorkshire Ripper was still on the loose. As Jane Caputi points out, Rabin's song "is basically a singing version" of a tape that the murderer had sent to police, and Rabin sings it "in the first person—the performer identifies himself with the ripper"; see Caputin, *Sex Crime*, 48.
39. Judith Peraino, e-mail communication, May 11, 1999.
40. Martin, in *Music of Yes*, points out that with progressive rock "there was the possibility of a 'popular' avant-garde.... this was not a time of cultural or political 'business as usual.' I worry that formulations such as Adorno's are not sufficiently attuned to the possibility that such a moment may erupt" (248, n. 52).
41. Charles Ives, *Essays before a Sonata*, 97.

References

Adler, Margot. *Drawing Down the Moon: Witches, Druids, Goddess-Worshippers, and Other Pagans in America Today.* Revised and Expanded Edition. Boston: Beacon Press, 1986.

Adorno, Theodor W. *Negative Dialectics.* Trans. by E. B. Ashton. New York: Continuum, 1973.

Arnold, June. *The Cook and the Carpenter: A Novel by the Carpenter.* Plainfield, VT: Daughters, 1973.

Caputi, Jane. *The Age of Sex Crime.* Bowling Green, OH: Bowling Green State University Popular Press, 1987.

Covach, John. "Progressive Rock, 'Close to the Edge,' and the Boundaries of Style." In John Covach and Graeme M. Boone, eds., *Understanding Rock: Essays in Musical Analysis.* New York: Oxford University Press, 1997.

Culpepper, Emily Erwin. "Simone de Beauvoir and the Revolt of the Symbols." *Trivia* 6 (1984–85): 6–32.

———. "The Politics of Metaphor: A Feminist Philosophy." Unpublished paper, delivered at the American Academy of Religion, 1986.

Daly, Mary, with Jane Caputi. *Websters' First New Intergalactic Wickedary of the English Language.* Boston: Beacon Press, 1987.

Dunayevskaya, Raya. *Rosa Luxemburg, Women's Liberation, and Marx's Philosophy of Revolution*, 2nd ed. Champaign: University of Illinois Press, 1991.

Emerson, Ralph Waldo. *Selected Essays.* Edited by Larzer Ziff. New York: Penguin, 1982.

Hedges, Dan. *Yes: The Authorised Biography.* London: Sidgwick and Jackson, 1981.

Hegel, G.W.F. *The Phenomenology of Mind.* Translated by J. B. Baillie. New York: Harper and Row, 1967.

Ives, Charles. *Essays Before a Sonata.* Edited by Howard Boatwright. New York: Norton, 1961.

Josephson, Nors S. "Bach Meets Liszt: Traditional Formal Structures and Performance Practices in Progressive Rock." *Musical Quarterly* 76, no. 1 (1992): 67–92.

Langer, Susanne K. *Philosophy in a New Key: A Study in the Symbolism of Reason, Rite, and Art,* 2nd ed. New York: New American Library, 1951.

Lorde, Audre. *Sister/Outsider: Essays and Speeches.* Freedom, CA: Crossing Press, 1984.

Martin, Bill. *Music of Yes: Structure and Vision in Progressive Rock.* Chicago: Open Court, 1996.

McClary, Susan. *Feminine Endings: Music, Gender and Sexuality.* Minneapolis: University of Minnesota Press, 1991.

Mosbø, Thomas J. *Yes, But What Does It Mean? Exploring the Music of Yes.* Milton, WI: Wyndstar Books, 1994.

Overduin, Jan, and James Overduin. "The Pipe Organ in Rock Music of the 1970s." *Diapason* 87 (1996): 18–21.

Peraino, Judith. E-mail communication, May 11, 1999.

Priestley, Brian. *John Coltrane.* Jazz Masters Series. London: Apollo Press, 1987.

Rycenga, Jennifer. "The Composer as a Religious Person in the Context of Pluralism." Ph.D. Diss. Graduate Theological Union, Berkeley, California, 1992.

———. "Lesbian Compositional Process: One Lover-Composer's Perspective." In Philip Brett, Elizabeth Wood, and Gary C. Thomas, eds. *Queering the Pitch: The New Gay and Lesbian Musicology.* 275–96. New York: Routledge, 1994.

———. "A Noisy Century: Revolutionary Creativity and its Feedback Loop." Unpublished paper, delivered at the Unnatural Acts Conference, University of California at Riverside, April 1997.

Sheen, Fulton J. *Philosophy of Religion: The Impact of Modern Knowledge on Religion.* New York: Appleton-Century-Crofts, 1948.

Turner, Steve. "The Great Yes Technique Debate." *Rolling Stone,* March 30, 1972, 10.

Tweed, Thomas A. and Stephen Prothero, eds. *Asian Religions in America: A Documentary History.* New York: Oxford University Press, 1999.

Welch, Chris. "Keep 'Em Yessing." *Melody Maker,* August 3, 1973.

Whitman, Walt. "Song of Myself," in *Leaves of Grass.* 1892 Edition. New York: Bantam Books, 1983.

Yogananda, Swami Paramahansa. *Autobiography of a Yogi.* Los Angeles: Self-Realization Fellowship, 1973.

Discography

Led Zeppelin. 1971. *Led Zeppelin IV*. Atlantic 7208.

Rabin, Trevor. 1980. *Face to Face*. Chrysalis 1221.

Yes. 1972. *Close to the Edge*. Atlantic SD 7244.

Yes. 1973. *Tales from Topographic Oceans*. Atlantic SD 2–908.

Yes. 1974. *Relayer*. Atlantic SD 18122.

Yes. 1977. *Going for the One*. Atlantic 19106.

Precarious Pleasures

Situating "Close to the Edge" in Conflicting Male Desires

Dirk von der Horst

The thing about "Close to the Edge" is the form,
I think. The shape of it is perfect.
—Bill Bruford,
quoted in Tim Morse, *Yes Stories*

I can't tell whether Jon Anderson is queer, or just
back from a Robert Bly "Iron John" camp.
—Martin Kavka,
personal communication

I do not understand my own actions. For I do not
do what I want, but I do the very thing that I hate.
—Romans 7:15

Yes's "Close to the Edge" models masculinity in a manner similar to many examples of sonata form by purging feminine elements to achieve closure and by using form as a primary locus of musical pleasure.[1] I experience this construction of masculinity as a negotiation of contrasting relations to the closet: the body-denying nature of formal listening was a component of my closeted adolescence, while the purging of femininity evokes pleasures of bonding with straight men as an openly gay person. This understanding differs from readings of "Close to the Edge" that focus on long sections of formal ambiguity and the absence of heterosexual romantic lyrics as a basis for queer identification.[2] In rare moods, I myself hear the song on these terms. However, I temporarily took an intensified pleasure in the song after noticing a troublesome masculinity. This pleasure contradicted my queer identity informed primarily by feminism and cross-identification with lesbians. The tension between a queer identity marginalized by traditional masculinity and taking pleasure in that very masculinity raises the question of how musical pleasure can be sites of disidentification, as much as identification.[3]

A wide range of feminist scholarship notes an intimate intertwining of the construction of gender and the logic of identity.[4] According to the logic of identity, a sense of self is predicated upon devaluing an "other." Historically, men have tended to adhere more closely to the logic of identity than women have. Male gender identity often rests on a notion of autonomy that requires extensive surveillance of the boundary between self and other. A consequence of this boundary maintenance is that patriarchal thought works with binary oppositions. Patriarchal logic arbitrarily maps distinctions such as reason/emotion or mind/body onto a masculine/feminine binary.[5] This binary mapping contributes to the perpetuation of gender complementarity, a construct that asymmetrically limits both women and men. Furthermore, gender complementarity posits love, affection, and desire between people of the same sex as anomalous, unnatural, or perverted. Therefore, according to feminist and queer theorists, a sense of identity that does not contribute to oppressive relations must acknowledge internal differentiation and fluid boundaries. In the interests of such fluid boundaries, queer musicology devotes attention to the relation between music and listener, rather than simply describing music "on its own terms."[6] The confessional mode of narrating a relation between self and music aims to take the role of desire in musical perception into account, while honoring the power of music to shape subjectivity. For these reasons, this chapter analyzes the split within myself that "Close to the Edge" produces.

I initially approached "Close to the Edge" with formalist presuppositions that made for a somewhat odd listening experience. I was curious about the song for over a decade before I heard it. I became intrigued by the song in high school while leafing through the *New Harvard Dictionary of Music*, where under "art rock," it is described as using sonata form.[7] I remembered this entry sporadically for several years until my curiosity was piqued to the point that I went to the store and bought the CD. I just had to know what a rock song would do with sonata form.

My experience of locating sonata form in the song was one of initial frustration, followed by a sense of satisfaction and mastery. At the store, I noticed that the song was divided into four titled sections: "The Solid Time of Change"; "Total Mass Retain"; "I Get Up I Get Down"; and "Seasons of Man." I thought, "Hmm, so there are four movements just like in a classical sonata." This observation displaced my expectation for a five- to eight-minute song in sonata form proper. Upon arriving home, I eagerly popped the CD into the player and waited for the clarity of "Eine Kleine Nachtmusik" to unfold before my ears. I had the words right in front of me, so I would know when one movement ended and the next began. By the time I was following the words to "Total Mass Retain," I was completely lost. Wasn't I supposed to have gone through two themes, a development, and a nice stable return? Here I was in what sounded perhaps like the scherzo, but I was right back at the music from the middle of the first movement before I'd gotten to the opening material again. I was enjoying, even intensely wrapped up in the sounds, but was annoyed with not being able to find my way around the form. Had they perhaps printed the words wrong? I hadn't lost my place in the liner notes, at least; the words coming from the speakers matched the ones on the page. With "I Get Up I Get Down" I figured I had reached the slow movement and felt a little better. Then there was the fast last movement, as expected, but I felt cheated by my *New Harvard Dictionary of Music*. That just wasn't the sonata form I had bargained for.

I listened to it again, was still confused at the end, and was more annoyed with myself and with my *New Harvard Dictionary of Music*. I even went back to the entry for "art rock" to see if I had purchased the right album. I had. What was my problem? I'd been taught how to recognize sonata form in high school, for crying out loud. After pausing for dinner and a phone conversation, I returned to it a third time and realized, "Oh! Those four sections don't correspond to movements!" The first section consisted of a lengthy introduction and the presentation of two themes. These two *themes* were repeated in "Total Mass

Retain"—the *exposition* was thus repeated; "I Get Up I Get Down" was something like a *development*; "Seasons of Man" was the *recapitulation*. I was pleased; I could sleep at night.

This was a very different encounter with a rock song than my first hearing of Patti Smith, for example, in which my awareness of structure helped articulate some of the pleasure the music provided but was not my primary concern. While identifying the large-scale formal design of "Close to the Edge" was pleasant enough, my satisfaction quickly gave way to puzzlement. What exactly had I achieved? Why was I looking at a version of myself I had long since retired? My exercise in approaching a rock song first and foremost through formal concerns echoed performing the same activity in a different context.[8]

Formal listening was a coping mechanism of mine as a closeted adolescent because it gave concretion to the notion of platonic forms through which I attempted to escape sexual desire. In high school I discovered Saint Augustine's *Confessions* and Dante's *La Vita Nuova*. These neo-platonic writings articulated a clear solution to my problem of homoerotic panic: flee the body. Turning to a realm of platonic forms proved to be an effective, if illusory, method of achieving my goal of transcending the merely physical world. Exactly *how* I made the leap from platonic forms to musical form fifteen years ago is unclear to me. In any case, after my exposure to Neoplatonism, paying attention to formal aspects of primarily nineteenth- and twentieth-century music became a daily exercise in attempting to forget my body.[9] Like private prayer, these exercises felt like an unmediated connection to the universal or absolute, unencumbered by messy bodily particularities. Because I enjoyed formal listening immensely, choosing for or against my body manifested a conflict within musical pleasure, rather than a strict choice between pleasure and displeasure.[10]

By choosing to listen to "Close to the Edge" primarily to find a classical form, I engaged a mode of listening I had laid aside upon coming out. After I came out, I continued to listen to Brahms and friends. However, because I had so tightly yoked music with sexual repression, I was at a complete loss as to what music might mean to me for a couple of years. Slowly, I learned ways of putting my body back into my listening practices. One of the major sources of this shift was dancing to disco regularly at gay clubs, where I was able to synchronize my movements and desires with like-minded men.[11] A bass-player friend introduced me to ways of hearing that were refreshingly anti-intellectual. I discovered in feminist musicology explicit parallels to concerns of feminist theology, through which I made sense of my life after I came out.[12] So, my deliberately seeking to experience a rock song on the terms of absolute music struck me as a retreat from listening practices gained in gay male clubs, in a semierotic friendship, and through feminist theories, to a listening practice rooted in a strangely disembodied pleasure.

The formal listening strategy I associate with a quest for asexual purity reinforces a masculine subjectivity in other contexts. Pleasure in the "free play of form" is gendered masculine in its marginalization, or even suppression, of bodily and affective responses to music. By maintaining a controlling awareness over the music, structural listening prevents music from seducing the listener into a softening of the firm boundary between self and other. For example, a close reading of Eduard Hanslick's influential 1854 treatise, *Vom musikalisch-Schönen*, shows large-scale formal awareness to be a conceptual prophylactic against the sensual and irrational aspects of music. Furthermore, Hanslick explicitly distances the perceiver of unfolding musical forms from the body and women, concretizing the gendering of the binary oppositions at work in his text.[13] The prophylactic function of formal listening continues to structure the agenda of music theorists, as Fred Maus shows through his teasing out of gendered implications of mainstream music theory.[14] Maus convincingly argues that emphasis on distant, technical, and nonexperiential language enables theorists to stay "on top" of music, thus compensating for the passive, feminized role of listener. Taking the issue from another angle, Marion Guck explores the relation between the marginalization of affect in music theory and the social and academic constraints that feminize affect and detail.[15] So, by returning to a listening strategy that privileged large-scale formal concerns to the detriment of sensual enjoyment of musical moments, I found myself participating in an ideology that pushes feminist concerns to the side.

But I distort Yes by dwelling on my initial attempt to find sonata form at all costs. Surely subjecting "Close to the Edge" to a way of hearing designed for nineteenth-century German instrumental music destroys the pull of eclectic elements that make progressive rock what it is.[16] The interplay of formal coherence and ambient sounds in the song creates ambivalence regarding listening strategies that aim for a controlling awareness over the music. The very opening of the song brings out this conflict. A fifteen-second silence followed by a soft murmuring sound and bird song usually causes me to get out of my chair and check the volume. This uncertainty immediately disrupts one of the main pleasures I expect from the song: nearly twenty minutes of music that pulls me through a variety of events, but leaves me with a feeling of integration at the end. I want the music to "pull me through"—to control me. However, the failure to recognize whether the music is playing makes me anxious about whether or not *I* am in control of *it*. The song both defuses and heightens this anxiety to various degrees as it runs its course.

The use of "environmental" sounds to disrupt a large-scale structure brings out a tension between two modes of musical organicism. On the one hand, notions of musical structure often rely on organicist metaphors, relating pieces to the growth of a plant.[17] On the other hand, the very elements that disrupt the self-contained feeling of a coherent structure are "nature sounds," creating a binary between the obviously culturally and technologically produced song and the remaining natural world. At the closing of the song, the dissolving of a triumphal ending into the opening "nature sounds" reinforces this tension. This tension reflects contradictory notions of the relation of sound to the body, as organicist metaphors generally refer to idealized (i.e., nonexistent) bodies, while the "nature sounds" suggest an environmentalist ethic that upholds a sense of responsibility to the physical world.[18] By splitting organicism into incompatible components, "Close to the Edge" pushes Baconian ideology, in which a masculine knower dominates feminine natural objects, to a breaking point.[19]

Shortly after my initial puzzlement, I encountered an alternate masculine identity related to "Close to the Edge." During the year in which I discovered the song, I spent many evenings after work with a group of straight men drinking beer, smoking weed, playing euchre, or just hanging out. In short, I went to enjoy male bonding. I first processed my reactions to Yes with these friends. A series of animated, if sometimes superficial, conversations about the music established a link between the song and "the Hermosa St. guys." For the first couple of years I listened to "Close to the Edge" it would inevitably trigger images of my friends' apartment, complete with the hazy glow from their red chili Christmas light chain. The mental space the song created for me had considerable overlap with their living room. Listening to the song was a way of securing a sense of self that was nurtured in that community of straight men.

While listening as a dutiful observer of formal components brought back memories of being a closet case, the association of the song with "my buddies" called forth a radically different sense of self. This link evoked a pleasurable tension between being assertively open about my sexual orientation and participating in a sort of male bonding often predicated on the suppression of homoeroticism.[20] While not passing as straight, I tacitly legitimated the social experience of male bonding. For example, I never questioned why those friends who had girlfriends generally visited them on separate occasions, rather than creating a gender-integrated social network. Thus, "being gay" suddenly meant something very different to me than it had previously, as I had formed friendships with women, moved in women's circles, and explicitly positioned male homosexuality as an antipatriarchal stance. Queer theorist Eve Kosofsky Sedgwick suggests that blurring the divide between male homosocial bonds and male homosexual desire is an important antipatriarchal strategy;[21] in my case, exploring that fuzzy area seemed to bring me closer to patriarchal privilege.

Turning again to sonata form will illuminate some reasons why I experience "Close to the Edge" as a simulacrum of a male social context. Sonata form can be heard through several grids. Peter Rabinowitz notes that different (even irreconcilable) narratives can emerge through focusing on tonal schemes as opposed to thematic ones.[22] A recent strategy is a feminist account of the subordination of the thematic material to the tyranny of the tonal plan. Susan McClary and Marcia Citron, drawing mostly from the terminology of A. B. Marx, note that the thematic layout of an exposition is generally mapped along gendered lines.[23] Thus, the first theme group is gendered as masculine while the second is understood as feminine. While the "feminine" theme group is presented in a new key in the exposition, the tonal demands of the form force it to submit to the primary key in the recapitulation. According to these theorists, then, sonata form possesses an intrinsic violence: "the masculine protagonist makes contact with but must eventually subjugate (domesticate or purge) the designated [feminine] Other in order for identity to be consolidated, for the sake of satisfactory narrative closure."[24]

While some pieces might correspond more closely than others to this interpretation, "Close to the Edge" offers a good model of this understanding of sonata form. However, dispute exists as to whether "Close to the Edge" *is* in sonata form. If sonata form is understood primarily in thematic terms, "Close to the Edge" works. However, given the lack of motivic development and tonal instability within the development, and the fact that the *second theme* maintains tonal independence in the *recapitulation,* the song departs from a sonata form model. This ambiguity allows one to interpret Yes's crossover techniques with various ideological emphases. Ascriptions of sonata form to "Close to the Edge" push progressive rock closer to the notion of classical-rock fusion, while other readings secure the rock context of the song by linking the formal components with traditional chorus-verse structures.[25] Rather than resolve the ambiguity, my discussion will use a feminist account of sonata form heuristically to tease out a violent, if confused, logic of identity at work in the song. My reading of "Close to the Edge" thus differs from that of Edward Macan, who previously read it through a gendered model of sonata form.[26] In his cultural analysis of progressive rock, he asserts that the song, and progressive rock generally, reconciles masculine and feminine elements in the interests of masculine identity. This reconciliation reproduces, rather than challenges, gender inequity insofar as femininity is absorbed into a masculine identity.

"Close to the Edge" conforms to the feminist account of sonata form mainly in that the "recapitulation" provides the clearest instance of violence to a feminine "other." However, this violence does not occur through the accommodation of the second theme to the primary tonal area. In fact, the *exposition* in "The Solid Time of Change" and "Total Mass Retain" creates an indeterminate sense of whether the first or second theme area has a primary claim on identity. After a lengthy instrumental introduction, Jon Anderson enters, singing a somewhat tense melody (3:54). The melody of the second theme (4:54) undoes the tension of the first melody. The accompaniment becomes rhythmically clearer and the melody moves around more, relaxing the sense of motion; it has a feeling of contentment. Such contentment does not elicit a sense of threat, despite the fact that the melody introduces large-scale tonal difference. The jubilant statement "now that you're whole" at the end of the melody establishes this "second theme" as a proper goal. When the first melody returns, it seems unsettled in comparison to the contentment of the second melody. Thus, one interpretation might assert that "Close to the Edge" reverses the usual position of identity in an exposition.

However, of all the material in the song, I am most invested in the melody Anderson first sings. To disrupt a mechanistic sense that the first theme must create a sense of identity for a listener, I describe here specific ways in which I identify with the first theme. Though I am aware that the tonal movement of the introduction sets up Anderson's entrance as an obvious point for feeling secure, the feeling of hitting tonal bedrock is not what I most closely cherish. Nor am I particularly thrilled with the quality of Anderson's voice, because he sings from his throat in a register that would sound prettier in "head voice." Furthermore, in contrast to my hearings of Dave Matthews or Bruce Cockburn, I am not erotically invested in blurring the persona and the person of the singer; I experience Anderson as an anonymous narrator. Rather, the music draws me to identify with a complex texture. Anderson's simple melody circles around two notes, expanding slightly only at cadences. While the melody feels slightly contained, receiving a sense of motion mainly from the lilting rhythm, the surrounding texture doesn't stay put at all, creating a driving, somewhat prismatic groove that I happily click into. Anderson is singing something about a witch,[27] but I lose track of most of the words, focusing rather on the overall texture and irregular rhythms of the bass. This is the moment I wait for; this is why I play the song repeatedly.

Though the musical material of "The Solid Time of Change" and "Total Mass Retain" does not perform an obviously gendered distinction, "I Get Up I Get Down" presents *Otherness* with a capital *O*. At the end of "Total Mass Retain," the music leads to a radically different space. At 8:30, one figure within a polyphonic texture lands on a low note that pivots into the slow section. The low note has the effect of releasing freon, quickly "cooling" the sonic environment. Long tones played on the mellotron, sounding like a string section, especially contribute to this "cooled" sense. Relatively quick, harmonically static arpeggiations anchor a sense of "not going anywhere." Distant blips of guitar and low sounds that fade in and out add textural interest to the long string sounds and arpeggiations. But even to describe that much, I have had to violate my own listening habits in this section. Usually I drift away from attention to musical detail at this point. The effects of this "drifting away" are astonishingly diverse. The section can evoke boredom, listlessness, a dreamy clarity, or a momentary serenity. Thus, in contrast to the faster sections, the music does not control me. Rather, the music allows emotions to rise to the surface that relate to particular and ephemeral situations.[28]

Bearing in mind that patriarchal logic works with a binary understanding of gender, this slow section sets a number of oppositions in motion that evoke a masculine/feminine polarity.[29] The focus of the text shifts from the listener's journey to an invitation to cast one's gaze upon a woman. Various musical devices support the textual shift; for instance, impressionistic textures replace driving rhythms. The use of this opposition to signal gender differences has long-standing historical precedents, for example in Claudio Monteverdi's contrast of *stile molle* and *stile concitato*.[30] The impressionistic textures include prominent "environmental sounds," such as water dripping, that create an illusion of it being somehow "closer to nature." The fictive relation of these devices to anything having to do with actual women needs to be kept in mind.

While the section presents problematic stereotypes of "femininity," another factor distinguishes the section along the lines of sexuality. The interaction of voices becomes significantly more intimate in this section. While Anderson's voice remains relatively isolated from the other voices in the outer sections, in this section the voices overlap and move apart frequently, often confusing the distinction between foreground and background singers. This drawing close and pulling away of voices has clear analogs in the movement of bodies during lovemaking. The interchange of background and foreground positions also suggests the interchange of "top" and "bottom" positions characteristic of queer sexuality/subjectivity.[31] Thus, in contrast to the rest of the song, the singers interact in a manner that invites a straightforwardly homoerotic identification with the flow of sounds.

This slow section, however, is shoved aside rather violently. Initially the music moves into a pipe organ solo, connecting this "feminized" space to ecclesiastical or redemptive discourses. However, the organ music then takes off and—with a bubbling, burping eruption from the low register—transforms into a fanfare. A synthesizer suggestive of a cowbell announces the imminent arrival of the "Close to the Edge" theme from the opening of the song, played now over driving rhythms. Some particularly flashy Hammond organ playing leads to the return of Anderson's first melody, which resolves the harmonic tension this section creates. Anderson describes the motivation for this violence, noting "There are several lines that relate to the church. . . . So at the end of the middle section there's a majestic church organ. We destroy the church organ through the Moog. This leads to another organ solo rejoicing in the fact that you can turn your back on churches and find it within yourself to be your own church."[32]

Aside from the fact that Anderson presents a highly individualist ethic here, the flow of the music suggests that Yes has achieved more than indicated in Anderson's statement, for the smooth transitions between Anderson's voice and the organ solos integrate the solos into the overall section rather than setting them apart. Thus, rather than simply destroying the church organ, the transition back to Anderson's melody destroys the entire slow section.

For the first year I heard this song, the slow section did not elicit a variety of responses. It bored me. Furthermore, the lack of instrumental activity and harmonic motion brought the lyrics into greater relief, so I was not able to ignore a text I, with many others, found pretentious. Thus, the return to Anderson's initial melody, with which I closely identified, always brought on a sense of elation. Furthermore, the rhythmic dissonance of the melody is "straightened out" when it returns.[33] This move from instability to stability is an example of an identity consolidating effect in rhythmic, rather than tonal, terms. Though overall I prefer the unstable renditions of this melody, the clearer rhythms contribute to a sense of successful triumph over chaos, as represented by the amorphous slow section and the struggle of the transition. This procedure corresponds precisely to the logic of identity McClary and Citron discern at the heart of sonata form. The lyrics in "The Solid Time of Change" foreshadow this masculine understanding of identity: "We relieve the tension only to find out the master's name."

Disturbingly, when I first made the connection between the elation I experienced at the return of the first theme and the violence done to the slow section, I found myself more drawn to the music than ever. Suddenly, my pleasures were guilty ones because I was aware of the way they were tied to an exclusionary setting of male bonding. I began to question what I found pleasurable about such exclusions. Over time, as I began to hear the slow section as pleasurable in and of itself, the return to Anderson's first melody no longer brought on pleasure, but a sense of loss. I was painfully aware that two distinct pleasures the song afforded me could not coexist in a healthy way in this song.

Yes's music is not the only music from the 1970s that I love, and I could now turn to examples of women's music or disco that engender me in ways I find more appealing than the ways in which progressive rock does. However, turning to explicitly queer music might reinforce a binary understanding of sexual identity that my willingness to identify with a song on the very terms that make it seem "straight" calls into question.[34] Thus, I will turn to a song by a quintessentially "masculine" band that, to my mind, queers "Close to the Edge"—namely, "No Quarter" by Led Zeppelin.[35] Paradoxically, "No Quarter" resolves the fraught tensions in "Close to the Edge" by offering a sonic experience of nonresolution. The textures that compete with each other in the Yes song coexist in "No Quarter" as "ambient" and "aggressive" elements ebb and flow in and out of each other, each allowing the other to exist at any given moment. And that ebbing and flowing invites a variety of unpredictable responses. In the continually shifting relations between the differing elements it offers, it still allows for the enjoyment of complexity. In "No Quarter" complexity evokes the ambiguities of living, rather than a quest for mastery and control. This is what I want from music; this is what I want from a man.

Notes

I would like to express my gratitude to the following people. The genesis of this paper was an assignment in Fred Maus's graduate seminar in analysis at the

University of Virginia, Fall 1998. His encouragement and critical feedback is greatly appreciated. Bob Reeder endured more drafts than I care to admit. Jessica Courtier kept me honest. This essay is for Winston Berger, with whom I once shared many a precarious pleasure.

1. Yes, "Close to the Edge." On *Close to the Edge*, Atlantic compact disc 82666–2, 1972.

2. I would like to thank Judith Peraino and Jennifer Rycenga for sharing examples of queer identification with "Close to the Edge."

3. David Schwarz addresses dis/identification with musical constructions of masculinity from a Lacanian perspective in "Peter Gabriel's 'Intruder,' a Cover, and the Gaze," chapter 5 of his *Listening Subjects: Music, Psychoanalysis, Culture* (Durham: Duke University Press, 1997). See Jennifer Rycenga's "Sisterhood: A Loving Lesbian Ear Listens to Progressive Heterosexual Women's Rock Music" in David Schwarz, Anahid Kassabian, and Lawrence Siegel, eds., *Keeping Score: Music, Disciplinarity, Culture* (Charlottesville: University of Virginia Press, 1997), for a rather different exploration of queer identification with "straight music."

4. The literature is extensive. See Allison Weir, *Sacrificial Logics: Feminist Theory and the Critique of Identity* (New York: Routledge, 1996), for a summary of feminist critiques of the logic of identity and how traces of it continue to inform various feminist positions.

5. The gendering of the mind/body distinction is a central issue in feminist theory. For a classic formulation of this problem, see Sherry B. Ortner, "Is Female to Male as Nature is to Culture?" in Michelle Zimbalist Rosaldo and Louise Lamphere, eds., *Woman, Culture, and Society* (Stanford: Stanford University Press, 1974).

6. One might take, as paradigmatic of this approach, Wayne Koestenbaum's *The Queen's Throat: Opera, Homosexuality, and the Mystery of Desire* (New York: Vintage Books, 1993).

7. Patrick T. Will, "Art Rock," in Don Randel, ed., *The New Harvard Dictionary of Music* (Cambridge: Belknap Press, 1986), 56.

8. I had by this time read Rose Rosengard Subotnik's "Toward a Deconstruction of Structural Listening: A Critique of Schoenberg, Adorno, and Stravinsky," chapter 3 of her *Deconstructive Variations: Music and Reason in Western Society* (Minneapolis: University of Minnesota Press, 1996). While Subotnik does not lay out the sexual politics of structural listening, her argument clarified, and probably informed, some of my puzzlement.

9. Years later I made the connection between the private endeavor of structural listening and the historical ramifications of the practice. See Carl Dahlhaus, *The Idea of Absolute Music*, trans. Robert Lustig (Chicago: University of Chicago Press, 1989).

10. Another repertory that served the same purpose was the Tallis Scholars' recordings of renaissance polyphony. I explored this relation in "Queer and Modern Aspects of Listening to Recordings of the Tallis Scholars," unpublished paper, University of Virginia, 1998.

11. For studies of ways disco structures gay male subjectivity, see Walter Hughes, "In the Empire of the Beat: Discipline and Disco" in Andrew Ross and Trisha Rose, eds., *Microphone Fiends: Youth Music and Youth Culture* (New York: Routledge, 1994); and Gregory W. Bredbeck, "Troping the Light Fantastic: Representing Disco Then and Now" *GLQ* 3 (1996): 71–107.

12. Feminist theology arose out of religious reflection on the women's movement of the 1970s. Crossing institutional religious divides, it interprets religious traditions with emphasis on women's experience, integration of mind and body, and a "this-worldly" understanding of spirituality. See the two anthologies edited by Carol P. Christ and Judith Plaskow: *Womanspirit Rising: A Feminist Reader in Religion* (San Francisco: Harper and Row, 1979); and *Weaving the Visions: New Patterns in Feminist Spirituality* (San Francisco: Harper and Row, 1989). Musicological texts that resonate with feminist theology are Susan McClary, *Feminine Endings: Music, Gender, and Sexuality* (Minneapolis: University of Minnesota Press, 1991) and Suzanne G. Cusick, "Feminist Theory, Music Theory, and the Mind/Body Problem," *Perspectives of New Music* 32, no. 1 (1994): 8–27.

13. Fred Everett Maus, "Hanslick's Animism," *Journal of Musicology* 10, no. 3 (1992): 273–92.

14. Fred Everett Maus, "Masculine Discourse in Music Theory," *Perspectives of New Music* 31, no. 2 (1993): 264–93.

15. Marion Guck, "A Woman's (Theoretical) Work," *Perspectives of New Music* 32, no. 1 (1994): 28–43.

16. Durrell Bowman makes a similar point in assessing music theorists' analyses of progressive rock; see his essay on the music of Rush in this volume.

17. Ruth Solie, "The Living Work: Organicism and Musical Analysis," *Nineteenth-Century Music* 4, no. 2 (1980): 147–56.

18. For a reading of Yes that elides this crucial difference, see Bill Martin, *Music of Yes: Structure and Vision in Progressive Rock* (Chicago: Open Court Press, 1996).

19. See Evelyn Fox Keller, *Reflections on Gender and Science* (New Haven: Yale University Press, 1985).

20. Beverly Wildung Harrison, "Misogyny and Homophobia: The Unexplored Connections" in Carol S. Robb, ed., *Making the Connections: Essays in Feminist Social Ethics* (Boston: Beacon Press, 1985).

21. Eve Kosofsky Sedgwick, *Between Men: English Literature and Male Homosocial Desire* (New York: Columbia University Press, 1985).

22. Peter Rabinowitz, "Chord and Discourse: Listening through the Written Word" in Steven Paul Sher, ed., *Music and Text: Critical Inquiries* (Cambridge: Cambridge University Press, 1992), 49–52.

23. McClary, *Feminine Endings*, 13–16, and Marcia Citron, *Gender and the Musical Canon* (Cambridge: Cambridge University Press, 1993), 132–41. See Scott Burnham, "A. B. Marx and the Gendering of Sonata Form" in Ian Bent, ed., *Music Theory in the Age of Romanticism* (Cambridge: Cambridge University Press, 1996), for a critique of McClary and Citron's use of Marx. Burnham fails to recognize that most feminists find the ideology of gender complementarity he discerns in Marx to be part of the problem of male dominance, rather than an alternative to it.

24. McClary, *Feminine Endings*, 14.

25. On the former, see Will, "Art Rock"; Thomas J. Mosbø, *Yes, But What Does It Mean? Exploring the Music of Yes* (Milton, WI: Wyndstar, 1994); and Edward Macan, *Rocking the Classics: English Progressive Rock and the Counterculture* (New York: Oxford University Press, 1997). For the latter, see John Covach, "Progressive Rock, 'Close to the Edge,' and the Boundaries of Style" in John Covach and Graeme M. Boone, eds., *Understanding Rock: Essays in Musical Analysis* (New York: Oxford University Press, 1997). This distinction does not hold absolutely. See Brian Robison's discussion of "Close to the Edge" in primarily "classical" terms that does not use the sonata form model; Robison, "Classical Music and Rock in the 1970s: Synthetic and Syncretic Combinations," paper delivered at the "Cross(over) Relations" conference, Eastman School of Music, Rochester, NY, September 27, 1996.

26. Macan, *Rocking*, 99–103.

27. Anderson's reference to a "seasoned witch" is a punning reference to Donovan's 1966 song "Season of the Witch." The melody here may be a musical pun as well, as Donovan's song also oscillates between two pitches.

28. On noncoercion as central to a lesbian-feminist musical aesthetic, see Suzanne G. Cusick, "On a Lesbian Relation with Music: A Serious Effort Not to Think Straight" in Philip Brett, Elizabeth Wood, and Gary C. Thomas, eds., *Queering the Pitch: The New Gay and Lesbian Musicology* (New York: Routledge, 1994).

29. See also Macan, *Rocking*, 102.

30. See McClary, "Constructions of Gender in Monteverdi's Dramatic Music," chapter 2 of her *Feminine Endings;* and Barbara Russano Hanning, "Monteverdi's Three Genera: A Study in Meaning" in Nancy Kovaleff Baker and Barbara Russano Hanning, eds., *Musical Humanism and its Legacy: Essays in Honor of Claude V. Palisca* (Stuyvesant, NY: Pendragon Press, 1992).

31. See Cusick, "On a Lesbian Relation with Music," 74–77; and Earl Jackson Jr., *Strategies of Deviance: Studies in Gay Male Representation* (Bloomington: Indiana University Press, 1994).

32. Jon Anderson, quoted in Morse, *Yes Stories,* 36.

33. Covach, "Progressive Rock," 13–14.

34. Judith Peraino criticizes women's music for such a binary and essentialist understanding of lesbianism in her "'Rip Her to Shreds': Women's Music According to a Butch-Femme Aesthetic" *Repercussions* 1, no. 1 (1992): 19–47. Peraino's articulation of the sexual politics of the form content offers an interesting and important tension with the one I lay out here. I do not, however, endorse her wholesale rejection of women's music. See also Martha Nell Smith, "Sexual Mobilities in Bruce Springsteen: Performance as Commentary" in Anthony DeCurtis, ed., *Present Tense: Rock and Roll and Culture* (Durham: Duke University Press, 1992), on Springsteen's challenge to binary conceptions of sexual identity.

35. Led Zeppelin, "No Quarter." On *Houses of the Holy*, Atlantic compact disc 19130-2, 1973.

"Let Them All Make Their Own Music"

Individualism, Rush, and the Progressive/Hard Rock Alloy, 1976–77

Durrell S. Bowman

> I think. . . . Everything I do has Howard Roark [Ayn Rand's fictional individualist architect] in it, you know, as much as anything. The person I write for is Howard Roark.
>
> —Rush's Neil Peart, interview in *Creem*, 1981

> Neil Peart's rugged individualism makes Metallica's James Hetfield seem like a Commie by comparison.
>
> —Bob Mack, "Confessions of a Rush Fan"

This chapter discusses the emergence of progressive rock in the half decade following the late 1960s counter-culture (1969–74), in part engaging with issues of genre designation and cultural hierarchy. It then explores Rush's "2112," "Xanadu," and "Cygnus X-1" (all from 1976 or '77) as case studies of the band's peculiar, late 1970s brand of individualism. These three extended compositions use not only lyrics but also varied stylistic features, alternating textures, specific musical gestures, and contrasting tonal areas to inscribe a skeptical point of view concerning the possibility of individual agency, both within an existing society and even in the absence of such a structure.

Progressive Rock and the Postcounterculture Era

In the late 1960s, the term *progressive rock* first appeared, referring to numerous coexisting aspects of diversity and eclecticism within rock music. This music combined roots in "British Invasion" manifestations of rhythm and blues (R and B) and eclectic pop with psychedelic, avant-garde, and/or "classical" tendencies. Examples of these stylistic currents include much of the late-60s music of the Beatles, the Moody Blues, and Procol Harum.

As Edward Macan has argued, aspects of residual spiritualism and mysticism from the late-60s counterculture provided certain elements of much early progressive rock music.[1] However, the communalism central to the counterculture—including unprecedented racial, gender, and class integration among antiestablishment activists, student protesters, and rock music fans—was beginning to fracture into separate agendas, including the black power and women's movements, by 1969. At precisely the same historical moment, a new genre of rock music emerged: progressive rock or "art rock." Its overwhelmingly white, predominantly male subculture became increasingly negative about the attempted sociopolitical "revolution" of the late 1960s. Furthermore, although certain features of late-60s rock music continued into the 1970s (including the extemporizations of blues-rock guitar solos and the hedonistic excesses of psychedelic rock), many rock musicians found it more appropriate to counter these residual elements by including in their music large-scale formal design, metrical complexities, virtuosity, and similar elements from art music. Thus, I find it difficult to agree with Macan's central premise that British progressive rock was primarily an extension of the counterculture's spiritualism and mysticism.

Indeed, in addition to its formal musical aspects (virtuosity, etc.) and in substantial contrast to the psychedelic rock aesthetic of the late 1960s (centered in the San Francisco Bay Area in the U.S.), the new progressive rock style of the early 1970s consisted almost entirely of British bands. In its most memorable work, it involved science-fiction narratives and technological/sociopolitical themes rather than spiritual/mystical ones.

In addition, early-70s progressive rock often prominently featured highly virtuosic, "over-the-top" keyboard playing (including piano and synthesizer) instead of the more integrated, timbre- and texture-oriented keyboard (especially organ) contributions of much late-60s rock.[2] Progressive rock keyboardists include notoriously "flashy" players, such as Emerson Lake and Palmer's Keith Emerson and Yes's Rick Wakeman, both of whom had studied and performed classical music before pursuing rock music, and whose aesthetic arguably derived from the flamboyant style of Franz Liszt over a century earlier. The excess of such performers has, for better or worse, marked progressive rock as being obsessed with art music to the virtual exclusion of all else. In fact, the bourgeois origins and formal "classical" proclivities of progressive rock were (and are) considerably overstated. With a few notable exceptions (the members of Genesis, for example) most progressive rock musicians came from the same small town and working-class British origins where hard rock and heavy metal originated. Furthermore, improvisational skills from other forms of popular music were an essential component of progressive rock, but generally only up until a piece of music began to resemble its permanent formal design.

The dominance in rock music of blues-based electric guitars was also challenged in progressive rock by a more eclectic aesthetic, so that blues-rock guitar heroes such as Eric Clapton were joined by much more "technical" players, such as King Crimson's Robert Fripp and Yes's Steve Howe. Thus, the continuing electric guitar style of the 1960s counterculture—emotive, blues-rock stylings (either virtuosic or slow and sustained, as in Eric Clapton and Jimi Hendrix)—was joined by a more eccentric, "busy," compositionally intricate style inspired largely by jazz and classical chamber music.

Important progressive rock bands to release debut albums in 1969 or '70 included Genesis, Yes, King Crimson, and Emerson Lake and Palmer (ELP). Within two or three years, these groups were among the top-selling album-oriented rock (AOR) bands in North America and the U.K.[3] This was partly due to the fact that numerous leading artists of the late 1960s—including the Beatles, Cream, Jimi Hendrix, and the Doors—had ceased to create music (some for more obvious reasons than others) by 1970 or '71. In addition, a number of the surviving 60s-era rock groups consciously reorganized as progressive rock ensembles in order to continue commercially into the 1970s. For example, the Moody Blues and Procol Harum somewhat abandoned their lushly

orchestrated, post–R and B psychedelic/classical fusion in favor of guitar-based, heavier-sounding, progressive rock music. Pink Floyd
remained the hugely successful exception to the progressive rock rule
by continuing its nonvirtuosic, psychedelic, spacey, mystical, emotive,
and sustained sound into the 1970s and beyond.[4] Clearly, though, the
late-60s fascination with psychedelic music was declining, at least for
mainstream rock musicians and fans.

Progressive rock drummer Bill Bruford (of Yes, King Crimson, and
other groups) said, "Psychedelia? I couldn't have given a monkey's
about it. I'm sure I went to Kensington Market and bought my purple
flared trousers but all I was interested in was being [jazz drummer]
Elvin Jones, like Mitch Mitchell was [in the Jimi Hendrix Experience].
I wanted to be Elvin Jones with Yes."[5] Jazz also influenced progressive
rock in the flute playing of British band Jethro Tull's frontman Ian
Anderson, which was clearly modeled after that of the American jazz
wind player Roland Kirk.[6]

Although progressive rock "purists" would like to believe that all
true fans of the genre understood its references to art music, in fact the
vast majority of such references (with the notable exception of certain
famous examples by ELP) went largely undetected—or at least under-
appreciated—by fans. As I know from experience, those of us (young,
white, North American suburban males) who became enthusiastic
about early-70s British progressive rock in the early 1980s associated
the genre more with our own growing inclinations toward mathematics, science, computers, and structure. (Indeed, a number of my closest
friends from that period are now professionals in fields such as computer programming, astrophysics, and architecture.)

For us, progressive rock functioned as a kind of escapist art-music
substitute, and some progressive rock musicians had already voiced this
assessment about a decade earlier. For example, Yes's lead singer Jon
Anderson said, in 1971, "We are beginning to think in terms of whole
sides of albums and not just tracks, and making music with more
depth. We're not trying to get *into* classical music, but get what classical music *does* to you."[7]

Anderson means that progressive rock translated the formal complexities (extended constructions and "depth") of European art music
into a rock music context, but he certainly also implies that actual

"classical" music *itself* was much less important than the stylistic fusion. John Covach argues that "these musicians [he lists members of Yes, ELP, King Crimson, and Genesis] set new performance standards on their respective instruments while incorporating some aspect of 'classical' playing into their personal styles."[8] Certainly there are many art music elements in progressive rock, but there are probably *more* elements from other styles (jazz, psychedelia, blues-rock, pop, R and B, soul, hard rock, and heavy metal) and a wide variety of ideological and musical factors (even among Yes bandmates Bruford and Anderson).

Music theorists such as Covach, Walter Everett, and Lori Burns tend not to incorporate historical/interpretive arguments directly into their analyses, preferring to start with brief examples of the former as prologues to long examples of the latter. Thus, progressive rock "engag[es] ... art music practices ... [and] grappl[es] ... with the problems of form, harmonic and melodic language, contrapuntal textures, instrumentation, and virtuosity." Such statements are then "proven" in the analyses that follow. This strategy has led to an emphasis on early-70s progressive rock and on younger, underground (i.e., relatively obscure or "cult") progressive rock bands that emerged after the 1970s and self-consciously modeled themselves after the earlier bands.[9]

Jon Anderson says that Yes only "*sometimes* emulate[d] the structural form [of classical music]," reminding us that this did not happen all of the time.[10] Covach, after quoting Anderson on this point, goes on to say that "borrowings [from] baroque-era counterpoint, romantic-era virtuosity, and modernist rhythmic syncopations and sectional juxtaposition [are] of the same kind: 'classical.'" He may not mean that broadly understood elements of "classical" music do not appear in other kinds of popular music, but he certainly does imply it.[11] In any case, an emphasis on "classical" music, music theory, and limited historical/interpretive arguments provides a fairly direct method for arguing that other music—progressive hard rock, progressive heavy metal, and so on—is not really progressive rock. In fact, progressive rock—whatever its boundaries—is at least as eclectic as any other subgenre of rock music, and even Yes's "Close to the Edge" includes numerous stylistic features that have nothing to do with "classical" music.[12]

In addition to the "seriousness" of its lyrics (which also include adventure-fantasy and science-fiction narratives), the considerable visual spectacle often involved in its live shows (e.g., lasers, films, and flashpots), and the elaborate design of much of its album art, progressive rock often involved a specific type of musical-social collaboration involving several musicians, each of whom, including the drummer and bass player, made substantial, individual contributions to the whole.[13] This is not terribly different from the activities of hard rock and heavy metal artists, and, in fact, the existence of a large, overlapping "hard/metal/prog" audience was already recognized by the early 1970s through the creation of specialized rock music record labels such as Harvest and Charisma. The audience still overlapped during my early teen years (1979–81) and was only theorized otherwise (as distinct) in the 1990s.

Of course, there are some differences among the three "genres." Hard rock mainly features an ambivalence between control and freedom, elements of volume and power (through amplification), and is riff-based, rhythmically regularized (especially when compared to the early Delta blues riffs of Robert Johnson, for example), and blues-influenced (although specific instances, including songs by Johnson, often went uncredited). It was initially exemplified, around 1966–68, by British bands such as the Yardbirds, Cream, and the Jeff Beck Group, by the American rock guitarist Jimi Hendrix (active 1967–70), and then, around 1969–72, by their slightly younger British colleagues Led Zeppelin, Black Sabbath, and Deep Purple. These latter three groups (which also featured acoustic music, vestigial "psychedelia," and, in the case of Deep Purple, prominent keyboards) also produced—in certain distorted/overdriven guitar-based songs—the basic sound of early heavy metal. Hard rock—which also included, by 1973–74, groups such as Bad Company and the American bands Aerosmith and Kiss— also featured powerful, high-tenor lead vocalists (Robert Plant, Ian Gillan, Paul Rodgers, et al.) who often extended their contributions well into the falsetto range.

Progressive rock music (although this is often conveniently overlooked today) was actually highly eclectic and included pop, avant-garde, folk, and even pedal-steel and other country music elements. Early-70s progressive rock was arguably *more* eclectic than either hard rock or heavy metal and, depending on the artist and the period, incorporated elements of both of those genres. On the other hand, progressive rock musicians were certainly also interested in the possibility of extended forms (derived from European art music), and this is what differentiates the borrowed aesthetic of art music in progressive rock from the specific gestural appropriations of art music by hard rock and heavy metal guitarists (Ritchie Blackmore, Eddie Van Halen, et al.).[14]

A small amount of twentieth-century art music has explored metrical complexities and/or musical-social collaborations of the type that progressive rock would later explore. Although some 1970s progressive rock *musicians* were familiar with twentieth-century art music, such music would have been largely unknown among progressive rock *listeners*.

For many rural, small-town, and suburban working-class and lower middle-class young men born at the end of the baby boom (1955–65), progressive rock was fanciful, escapist music, especially in its formal complexities, its virtuosity, and its elaborate instrumentation and stage shows. For the same audience, a shift in ideology away from New Left communalism at the end of the 1960s made it possible for the emerging genre of "progressive" rock to avoid being revolutionary (or even political) in a Marxist kind of way.[15] Instead, in the aftermath of the counterculture (around 1969–71), individualism and libertarianism emerged as ideological options and came to be aligned with progressive rock and hard rock so that even comparatively cynical, individual-squelched-by-society songs from the early 1990s by the eclectic American hard rock and heavy metal band Metallica—such as "The Unforgiven" and "My Friend of Misery"—are consistently dark and defeatist within each song compared to the elaborate, multisectional "individual struggle, defeated" narratives of certain Rush songs from the late 1970s.[16]

Rush's Style in Relation to Hard Rock and Progressive Rock

On the whole, Rush's music is best termed "progressive hard rock." More specifically, the trajectory from the band's first album (recorded in late 1973 and early 1974) to its fourth and fifth studio albums (1976–77) demonstrates that the band no longer desired to pursue solely the riff-oriented, blues-rock, "Led Zeppelin Lite" tendencies of its origins (1968–74). Instead, it turned to extended structures, complex rhythms, and other features of progressive rock. (In some cases, the earlier Rush style is still used, but as an important delineator within extended narrative structures.) Rush's mid-70s style included a number of softer, commercially oriented rock songs (such as "Fly By Night," "Lakeside Park," and "Closer To The Heart") as well as early examples of "progressive heavy metal" (such as "Anthem," "Bastille Day," and "Something For Nothing"). However, it also included a number of extended works that were clearly inspired by early-70s British progressive rock (including "By-Tor and the Snow Dog," "The Necromancer," "The Fountain Of Lamneth," and, especially, "2112," "Xanadu," and "Cygnus X-1").

"Progressive hard rock" also evokes the second incarnation (ca. 1973–74) of the British rock band King Crimson, with drummer-percussionist Bill Bruford, bassist-singer John Wetton, and (sometimes) violinist David Cross joining founder-guitarist Robert Fripp.[17] A progressive/hard genre mixing is especially true of King Crimson's 1973–74 studio albums *Larks' Tongues In Aspic, Starless and Bible Black*, and *Red*, each of which—like certain Rush songs from 1976–77—contains a number of extended instrumental passages comprising timbrally distorted and rhythmically complex music. For example, King Crimson songs such as "Fracture," "Red," "One More Red Nightmare," and "Starless" explore the harder side of progressive rock.[18] Indeed, shortly after King Crimson's *Starless* and *Red* period (featuring the jazz-influenced, former Yes drummer, Bill Bruford), Neil Peart (who was also influenced by jazz and by Bruford) replaced Rush's original, blues-rock drummer, John Rutsey. Peart, who was also from southern Ontario, joined his fellow Canadians, bassist/singer Geddy Lee and guitarist Alex Lifeson, and became the catalyst for what Rush (and many of its fans) considered a more complex kind of music than seemed possible after the band's first album. Peart also began a new career as a lyricist upon joining the band in the late summer of 1974, and he took the band into an ideologically individualist, libertarian, and semiobjectivist direction for several years.

Rush's genre and ideology experiments after 1974 made it possible for the band to establish a constantly regenerating audience numbering in the millions while, at the same time, being despised by nearly every rock critic. In 1976, Alex Lifeson explained that "We don't want to change what people think about rock and roll. We just want to show them what we think about it."[19] Similarly, in explaining the band's attitude toward its music and fans in 1977, Rush's bassist-singer Geddy Lee said, "We took a risk. . . . individualism, concepts of thought and morality are causes that we believe in. We've tried to transcend [attitudes of only being in it for the money] by having something for everyone. We don't ask that everyone believe in what we do. Let them take our stuff on any level they want."[20]

However, despite the band's self-effacing openness to interpretation, most rock critics found it very difficult to explain the appeal of Rush's style or of its strongly stated individualism. For example, journalist Roy MacGregor suggested that Rush, "held no kindred love for the social conscience of a Bob Dylan . . . not even [for] the street justice of a Mick Jagger. They found themselves speaking for a large group of young rockers without spokesmen—a group who, despite their love of loud, violent music, were themselves nonrevolutionary [and] certainly self-centred."[21] Actually, MacGregor's statement pigeonholes Bob Dylan and Mick Jagger at least as much as it pigeonholes Rush, because—even in the 1960s—Bob Dylan was certainly not always socially conscious and Mick Jagger (of the Rolling Stones) only sometimes called for street justice.

In any case, for certain rock fans in the postcounterculture of the 1970s and '80s, these artists seemed musically and ideologically old-fashioned and thus were no longer considered suitable role models. Indeed, the "large group of young rockers without spokesmen" was—in addition to being large and young—also specifically white, suburban, and male, and it *did* have spokespersons, including Rush's unique fusion of hard rock, progressive rock, and individualist/libertarian ideology.

"2112" (from *2112*, 1976)

Rush first began to advance a libertarian social critique in certain songs from 1975, including "Anthem" and "Bastille Day." However, the band then took up issues of individualism much more fully—and in a science-fiction context—in the title work of its 1976 album *2112*. The LP-side-length suite "2112" pursues a proindividualist/antiauthoritarian subject matter, but many rock critics nonetheless associated Rush with fascism in the years following the album's release. This has partly to do with Rush's affinity for the objectivist political philosophy and (related to this) highly individualist literary characters of the Russian-born American writer Ayn Rand (1905–82). Rush's 1975 song "Anthem"—in its title and in certain elements of its lyrics (especially selfishness as a virtue)—had already evoked Rand's early novella *Anthem* (1938) to a certain degree. However, it is in "2112" that the band makes its most extensive use of her ideas, "transliterating" them for the postcounterculture rock generation. The influence is most obvious in drummer/lyricist Neil Peart's lyrics, but it is also true of the music *itself*, which follows a large-scale, progressive rock narrative.

Ayn Rand detested rock music, but she only wrote about it in relation to the counterculture (the late 1960s), a time when collectivist ideas were highly visible in mainstream society. It is impossible to know what she would have thought of Rush's very sympathetic applications of her ideas in rock music a decade later. Rand's ideas have been called a "revers[al of] the traditional Judeo-Christian aesthetic," espousing "laissez-faire capitalism [as] most congenial to the exercise of talent," and "deeply conservative."[22] The traditional western concepts of "brotherly love" and "do unto others as you would have them do unto you" are anathema to Rand's work and she certainly favors laissez-faire capitalism, but to call this "deeply conservative" necessarily posits a revisionist reading of what it means to be conservative.

Conservatism originally had to do with community and tradition, and—at the turn of the twentieth century—it was *liberalism* that espoused free trade along with individual rights and freedoms. Howard Roark—the central character of Rand's later novel *The Fountainhead* (1943)—has been called a "highly romanticized architect-hero, a superior individual whose egoism and genius prevail over timid traditionalism and social conformism."[23] This would otherwise appear to be a perfect definition of nineteenth-century romantic social liberalism, and thus if it is "deeply conservative," one would have to include Beethoven and most of his legions of followers in the same category.

The problem with Rand is that her ideas first circulated on the periphery of the mainstream (especially among college students) during the decade—the late 1950s through the late 1960s—when civil rights, social progress, and Americanist/technological pride (through NASA, etc.) all began to transform the Western definition of "liberalism." By the mid-1980s the transition was complete, and anyone who favored individualism, laissez-faire capitalism, and smaller government (or at least a lesser amount of government interference in the lives of individuals) was considered "conservative." It made no difference if such a person—like me—was also against capital punishment, abhorred censorship, favored gun control and abortion rights, and supported increased immigration and the rights of homosexuals and other minorities. Anyone, like Neil Peart, who wrote lyrics espousing individualism was considered conservative, when, in fact, "libertarian" would seem the more suitable term. Scott Bullock tells us that in reality, Neil Peart considers himself to be a "'left-wing libertarian,' noting that he could never be a conservative due to the right's intolerance and support of censorship. Moreover, the rise of religious fundamentalism in America and throughout the globe 'terrifies' him. But he also sees rising intolerance coming from the left, exemplified by a Toronto law 'forbidding smoking in any bar, restaurant, coffee shop, doughnut shop, anywhere.' Thus, though he believes that economic freedom is generally increasing, Peart also observes that 'socially it seems to be the opposite—there is actually more oppression.'"[24]

Like Rand's, Peart's views do not fit with generally accepted definitions of "conservative" or "liberal." Like literary critics and philosophers (who are generally embarrassed by Rand's "contributions" to their areas of study), nearly all rock critics and many musicians have assigned convenient and easy labels to Rush's music, largely in order to justify their ridiculing or ignoring it.

On the other hand, Rand's strongly stated principles of rational self-interest were out of step (and interpreted by some as dogmatic, cultist, or even fascist) in the context of civil rights and other social movements of the 1960s and '70s, whereas Rush made numerous modifications in its lyrics and musical style (especially in the 1980s and '90s) in recognition of the contributions of others, and certainly also quickly tempered its emphasis on Randian individualism. Moreover, quite apart from Rand's influence, the hazy reception of Rush's "2112" also resulted from the band's inversion of the conventional Western metanarrative (as often seen in normative sonata form in classical music) in which a hero establishes order, undergoes some kind of conflict with a disturbing force, and then emphatically reestablishes the initial order.

In "2112," Rush establishes an administrative priest "collective" as the antihero of a futuristic totalitarian world called Syrinx. However, the work actually begins with an instrumental "Overture" (0:00–4:32), similar to an operatic overture, that presents four or five important later themes. The overture also incorporates a brief quotation from Pyotr Ilich Tchaikovsky's *1812 Overture* (1869) and—as in the Tchaikovsky—the sounds of explosions, as though a battle is underway.[25] Out of the din of the end of the overture comes Geddy Lee's natural voice (around Middle C, at 4:25) on the only words in the otherwise instrumental section: the strangely Christian-overtoned, although probably intended as ironic (considering the chant-like nature of the melody and the narrative's eventual outcome), "and the meek shall inherit the earth" (see fig. 9.1).

In the following section, "The Temples of Syrinx" (4:32–6:43), the band uses heavy metal (largely in B minor) and Lee's shrieking vocal style to portray the undesirable collective of authoritarian priests. Lee sings extremely high and tensely in this section—near the top of the treble clef—and the listener is thereby to infer that the priests are unnatural, dogmatic, and perhaps even insane.[26] Indeed, the narrative effect of Lee's vocal style in this section lies somewhere between heightened shouting and shrill, irrational "preaching" (see fig. 9.2).

The limited pitch range and nearly continuous nature of the first eight measures (the verse section) evoke the priests' pride in themselves for some of the things that they control: literature, music, and art. The rhythmic anticipations and shorter phrases of the latter eight measures (the chorus section) further suggest a swaggering pride in their "accomplishments." The priests here are akin to the controlling forces in

Fig. 9.1. Excerpt from "2112—Overture," 4:25–4:32.

Fig. 9.2. Excerpt from "2112—The Temples of Syrinx," at 4:48.

various episodes of the original *Star Trek* television series (1966–69) and in the mid-70s science fiction film *Logan's Run*.[27]

A section entitled "Discovery" (6:43–10:15) then follows. In it, the actual hero of the narrative—an individual man—explores his musically creative side, something that is not allowed under the restrictions of his totalitarian society. However, the accompanying music for this section is rather tentative and gentle, thus subverting the expectation that a main hero's music should be forceful and determined. This "protagonist"—if that is not too strong a word in such a narrative inversion—parallels Ayn Rand's discover-hero ("Unity 5–3000") in her antiauthoritarian novella *Anthem* (1938). Rand's book is about a man who rediscovers the principles of electric light and the idea of individual identity, but ends up battling a totalitarian state that will have none of it.[28] In "2112," Rush more firmly transplants the same ideological viewpoint.

In the "Discovery" section, the hero rediscovers not the electric light, but the electric *guitar,* and he similarly "threatens" society with his individualist predilections. By means of controlled and "scientific" experimentation, he learns how to tune the guitar (including the voicing of string harmonics) and eventually to play it, the latter by means of increasingly rhythmic and metrical sequential figurations. Indeed, he finds his way from open strings to D major and its relative minor and, finally, to its dominant, A major. Essentially, on a distant planet, the protagonist (rediscovers the sum total of Western major-minor tonality in about thirty seconds. Also, in order to differentiate this individualist hero from the authoritarian priests, Lee sings in a much more "normal," high-baritone vocal range when portraying him. The music is also gentler and more reflective, especially compared to the onslaught we have just encountered in the "voices" of the priests. The lyrics refer to a "strange device [that] gives forth sound" (the guitar) and to how the hero "can't wait to share his new wonder" so that others will be able to "make their own music."

In the following section, "Presentation" (10:15–13:57), the hero attempts to convince the priests of the merits of his discovery ("an ancient miracle") by presenting his argument in a kind of jazz-inflected R and B style.[29] However, precisely as in the rejection of Unity 5–3000s rediscovery in Ayn Rand's *Anthem,* the priests here chastise the well-meaning protagonist for obviously wishing to incite an individualist social revolution with his new "toy" (as they call it), the electric guitar. They inform him that the device is "just a waste of time, [a] silly whim [that] doesn't fit the plan." To add to their argument, the priests' violent, B-minor, heavy metal music (from the "Temples of Syrinx" section) reappears (at 13:00), but at a much faster tempo and in a guitar solo that frenetically elaborates or "develops" the earlier music. The effect is one of a insistent, impenetrable worldview, one in which the individual's counterarguments will not be tolerated (see table 9.1).

The narrative here is subtly different from the typical counter-culture scenario of radicals marching, protesting, or otherwise going up against the establishment. In fact, the hero of "2112" is not interested in *dropping out* of society (living communally, experimenting with drugs, etc.) but instead wishes to find a way to contribute to the *improvement of* society. This is very similar to the idealistic concerns about social and moral contributions expressed by Victoria Anne Steinitz and Ellen Rachel Solomon's early-70s informants in *Starting Out: Class and Community in the Lives of Working-Class Youth.*[30]

Table 9.1. Large-Scale Structure of "2112."

1. Overture (0:00)	• introduces 4–5 later themes and all subsequent tonal areas except the last • tonal areas: A minor, D, B minor, A, B, and E • ends with battle explosions, then the texture dissipates with Geddy Lee entering on "and the meek shall inherit the earth" (natural voice, at 4:25)
2. The Temples of Syrinx (4:32)	• "theme 1," introduces the authoritarian antihero priests • uses A minor and B minor in verse-chorus form and violent heavy metal • creates a B minor refrain from material also in the overture • ends with a dissipating texture for guitar only (B minor)
3. Discovery (6:43)	• "theme 2," introduces the individual hero "protagonist" • he discovers and explores an "ancient wonder": an electric guitar • he modulates from D major/B minor to A major (his subsequent tonal area) • gentle and tentative music, but gradually becomes rhythmic and recalls music from later sections of the overture
4. Presentation (10:15)	• the hero attempts to convince the priests of the merits of his discovery (in a pleasant, jazzy, pop/R and B kind of style, A major) • they dismiss his arguments and explode into a violent, B minor guitar solo (at 13:00)
5. Oracle: The Dream (13:57)	• the hero dreams of exiled individualists on a distant planet • gentle "dream" music at first, then recalls more animated (and previously unrecalled) overture material; B minor, D, A minor, B minor "frame"
6. Soliloquy (15:58)	• the hero despairs about his "cold and empty" life, D/esp. A minor; ends on E
7. Grand Finale (18:18)	• violent, progressive heavy metal style, recalls especially part 2, then material from the end of the overture (including explosions); control "announcement," E/B modes/F-sharp major (at 19:58)

In the fifth section, "Oracle: The Dream" (13:57–15:58), the protagonist-hero dreams of a "strange and wondrous land," a planet of exiled individualists, the works of whose "gifted hands" are actually fostered, encouraged, and allowed to contribute to society. The initial waking moment after the dream, called "Soliloquy" (15:58–18:18), centers mainly around D major, then A minor, tonalities. Its intensity rises in a loud, three-part section (16:54–18:18) that brings closure to the hero's portion of the "2112" narrative, first as he verbally recognizes the "cold and empty life" of his totalitarian planet and then as his despair deepens in Alex Lifeson's angry, frustrated blues-rock guitar solo in A minor. This newly established stylistic mode (blues rock) and tonality (A minor) completely subverts the hero's initial "jazzy" optimism and A major tonality of the earlier "Discovery" and "Presentation" sections. However, this "Soliloquy" section actually ends in E major, the dominant of the hero's resigned A minor. The individual is not allowed to have the final word. (This also continues the strategy of tonal segues between major sections of the work.)

The composition is not yet over, however. Indeed, the seventh (and final) section, "Grand Finale" (18:18–20:32), further subverts the conventional heroism metanarrative, in part by reprising the totalitarian/priest-associated heavy metal style of several earlier sections. The music becomes ever more violent, including chaotic and densely layered ("collective") guitar melodies. This music largely reprises B major, B minor, and B-based modal themes that have not been heard since the latter parts of the overture. The close proximity of these different "shades" of B serves to emphasize the irrational, collective nature of the priests. The work then ends extremely forcefully in an unanticipated tonality, F-sharp major (at 19:58), the dominant of the priests' B-based thematic material. This surprising tonal shift—and an initial unison rhythmic insistence in all instruments (evoking Morse Code for V/Victory: short-short-short-long)—would be quite sufficient to establish the hegemony of the priests and of totalitarianism within the narrative. Certainly, the protagonist-hero's D major, A major, and A minor—as well as his gentler, exploratory, "lighter" music—are no longer allowed, or even possible. However, the battle explosions of the end of the overture are also reprised, and a spoken voice—"Attention all planets of the solar federation . . . We have assumed control" (each phrase repeated twice and treated by studio effects to sound disembodied and "multiple")—joins the din, drastically contrasting the ironically texted individual voice that had briefly presented a very thin musical texture (about the "meek") at the end of the overture.

The layered guitar elements in the penultimate section of the finale, the simultaneous rhythmic insistence (in all instruments) on the resultant, dominant tonality of the priests, and the multiple voice (plural) of the final proclamation—"*We* have assumed control"—all definitively establish that the antiauthoritarian point of view, once explored by the individual guitar-discovering hero, has been defeated for all time.

As a whole, "2112" reflects the postcounterculture view of a young person wishing to contribute to society despite considerable obstacles. However, numerous critical commentators have apparently assumed that Rush support the authoritarian victors of this narrative. For example, J. Kordosh—in his postinterview article on Rush's drummer-lyricist Neil Peart—wishes to connect Peart's identification with Ayn Rand's individualist architect character Howard Roark (from the novel *The Fountainhead*, 1943) with fascism. However, without explaining why individualism is fascism, Kordosh simply states: "I don't want to add that many people consider Ayn Rand to be *prima facie* fascist, but I will anyway."

The "many people" believed by Kordosh to consider Rand a fascist are probably the "new liberals" of the 1960s and '70s, who—because of their communalist, civil rights, and otherwise left-wing emphases were unable to reconcile extreme individualism with anything but extreme authoritarianism. In any case, Kordosh himself does not elaborate and, instead, lets the reader read between the lines that Rush is therefore also fascist. Of course, he also fails to elaborate on Peart's statement—several sentences later—against the political Right (and, by extension, against fascism): "I can't stand the whole concept of law-and-order and authority and everything, which is obviously the precept of right-wingism...."[31] Individualism is not fascism unless an individual or group attempts to control society without democratic process. It certainly does not *equal* fascism, and just because the controlling priests win at the end of "2112" does not mean that Rush favors this. In fact, the band has carefully argued (although perhaps not carefully enough) quite the opposite. The difficulty here may be that "2112" is under-coded, where listeners receive only a "general sense of 'understanding'" and do not interpret the specific meanings that may or may not have been intended by the composers.[32]

Neil Peart's comments, in the context of Kordosh's very harsh interview, on the similarity between Rand's *Anthem* and Rush's "2112" suggest that this may have been accidental: "The inspiration behind [the "2112" story] was. . . . It's difficult always to trace those lines because so many things tend to coalesce, and in fact it ended up being quite similar to a book called *Anthem* by the writer Ayn Rand. But I didn't realize that while I was working on it, and then eventually as the story came together, the parallels became obvious to me and I thought, 'Oh gee, I don't want to be a plagiarist here.' So I did give credit to her writings in the liner notes."[33] Peart refers to the addition of "With acknowledgement to the genius of Ayn Rand" to the liner notes of the 1976 album, but it is clear that by the time of the 1981 Kordosh interview he was mainly interested in deflecting the accusation—by one of the band's harshest critics—of any direct influence in "2112."

Reebee Garofalo, in his widely read textbook *Rockin' Out: Popular Music in the USA*, mentions Rush twice, once to suggest that the band "made a . . . considered nod toward fascism . . . with *2112*," a statement that replicates the conventional wisdom about Rush derived from the accounts of rock critics such as Kordosh.[34] However, even Rush fans—whom one would otherwise expect to be sympathetic toward the band's intended statements—are likely to interpret "2112" in such a way that Rush identifies with the theocracy of the Syrinx priests. Deena Weinstein, in her book *Heavy Metal: A Cultural Sociology*, reports that her informal survey of ticket-line Rush fans (some of whom knew all the lyrics to "2112") saw more than 70 percent of them under the impression that Rush was siding with the priests. However, unlike Kordosh's desperate attempt at lambasting Peart, the confusion in "2112" for *fans* stems from Rush's use of energetic heavy metal to depict the totalitarian priests and comparatively gentle music to depict the individualist hero. Revealingly, Weinstein—who has often used "2112" as a case study in her course on social theory—stopped making a recording available to her students (reverting to lyrics only) once this confusion became apparent.[35]

In musicological terms, Rush entered an ideologically problematic territory by making use of classical-type structural conventions—such as recurring thematic material and interrelated tonal areas—while simultaneously subverting the master narrative upon which such music is predicated. (A hero is supposed to win in the end despite all obstacles.) Narratively, the violent music at the end of "2112" defeats all other points of view; it is not the hero's music at all, but that of the story's antiheroes. In more general terms, then, "2112" expands the libertarian-individualist agenda already touched upon—lyrically and musically—in earlier Rush songs such as "Anthem" (from the album *Fly By Night*, 1975) and "Bastille Day" (from the album *Caress Of Steel*, also 1975), but now in a more negative light.[36] The work also establishes Rush's fusion of power and violence from the traditions of hard rock and heavy metal with elements such as structural complexity and large-scale cyclical construction from the tradition of progressive rock.

"Xanadu" (from *A Farewell To Kings*, 1977)

"Xanadu" is an extended work, the second track from Rush's sixth album, *A Farewell To Kings* (1977).[37] However, unlike Rush's earlier extended works (including "2112"), "Xanadu" is not formally subdivided into named subsections in the liner notes of the album.[38] The song also includes several introductory instrumental sections, comprising nearly half of its eleven-minute duration.[39] In other words, the song is rather unique, even for Rush.[40]

Lyricist Neil Peart based the song on Samuel Taylor Coleridge's poem *Kubla Khan: Or, A Vision in a Dream* (1816), with its images of a mysterious, lost paradise that—despite its incomparable beauty and its enveloping immortality—also ensnares its discoverer in an inescapable prison of madness, thus producing a lonely and bitter triumph for its occupant.[41] Indeed, the final words of Rush's song reflect this ambivalence, by transforming the previously optimistic phrase "Oh, paradise" into "Oh, *is it* paradise?" However, this particular ambivalence is not found in the original poem, so that Rush's version ends far more ambivalently than Coleridge's. The trajectory toward ambivalence is also heightened by the song's extremely long instrumental introduction and its sense of "achieving" paradise by battling nature.

The poem involves, in part, a vision of a damsel with a dulcimer. However, the Rush song entirely eschews such an element: the male protagonist is completely alone in his endeavors and evidently prefers it that way—this despite his eventual ambivalence regarding the narrative's outcome. This kind of solitary, entirely male narrative evokes the "exscriptions" (i.e., intentional omitting) of the female in 1980s heavy metal, as discussed by Robert Walser in *Running With The Devil: Power, Gender, and Madness in Heavy Metal Music* (1993). However, Rush's vision of this in "Xanadu" (and in "2112") is much closer to the celebration of male elements—power, mobility, "the road," and so on—in the music of the British heavy metal band Judas Priest (especially around 1978–84) than to the tendency, in later American heavy metal bands, to inscribe male hegemonic control over women (as in W.A.S.P.) or else depictions of a "threatening" *femme fatale* (as in Dokken, 1982–87).[42]

In the introduction of the song, Lifeson's diatonic, major-key electric guitar figurations (over an E pedal) and their accompaniment—based partly on the sounds of birds and rushing streams and partly on the use of wind chimes and temple blocks—initially evoke nature, the elements, and a "searching" quality. Indeed, the rhythmically free guitar figurations of this first introductory section (0:00–1:49) also explore the tonal area's dominant and subdominant (B major and A major), as well as occasional, hesitant "nonchord" tones. The second instrumental section (1:49–2:52) then establishes a 7/8 meter for the constructed, regularized, and insistent E-based guitar melody that appears throughout this section.

This guitar part is initially faded in, suggesting that the protagonist is "approaching." Middleton refers to "positional implications" as one of a number of "secondary significations" in a musical work. He suggests that a fade-out at the end of a song means "unendingness" or "continuous activity." In Rush's "Xanadu," there are several levels of fade-ins toward the beginning of the work, and they certainly also mean "unendingness" and "continuous activity."[43]

The insistence of the seven-note melody (and its 7/8 rhythm) is countered by interjections in the drum and bass that attempt to pull away from it, what Middleton calls an "interplay of voices."[44] Among other elements, these weaken the guitar's attempted diatonicism by mixing in G, D, and A (for example) as important secondary pitch elements. This modal mixing suggests the irony of paradise (Xanadu) being located so near to the violent, icy mountains that must be scaled in order to get there. Indeed, the repeated 7/8 guitar gesture represents the obstinance of the traveler, and the increasingly frenetic drums and the tonally thwarting bass chords represent struggles in the protagonist's narrative. Drummer-lyricist Neil Peart argues that these elements represent the "violent imagery" at the beginning of Coleridge's poem (see fig. 9.3).[45]

The third section of the introduction (2:52–3:34), in a rollicking, syncopated 4/4 meter, now features the bass and drums as coparticipants and outlines E mixolydian (with its flattened seventh scale degree, D natural). The protagonist's obstinance is now reduced to the barest minimum: a stubbornly repeated E major chord. The traveler finally arrives in Xanadu in the fourth introductory section (3:34–4:23), where Lifeson breaks through unambiguously on a joyous, diatonic guitar riff in 7/8. Although he is still playing in E major, Lifeson is now supported (rather than contradicted) by Geddy Lee's bass and Neil Peart's percussion. (A monophonic, diatonic synthesizer melody also participates in this.)

The fifth section of the introduction (4:23–4:59) reflects the grandeur and exoticism of Xanadu itself. It accomplishes this with a more moderate tempo, numerous extended chords, Eastern- or exotic-sounding gong strikes in the percussion, a pair of gently syncopated adjacent chords, and, after the lyrics begin (4:59–5:15), a carefully controlled balance in the rising versus falling arrangement of the vocal melodies. The instruments sound the pitch B in all four chords in this expository vocal section (verse 1), thus reflecting a fulfillment in Xanadu of the "dominant" obsession (paradise) that was present in the guitarist-protagonist's initial, instrumental exposition, centered on E ("2112" expresses a similar tonic-dominant motion, but on a larger

Fig. 9.3. The 7/8 guitar riff of the introduction of "Xanadu," fading in at 1:49.[46]

scale). The transition (5:15–5:21) to the following section, the chorus, involves modal mixing, with F major presented as a Phrygian clue (i.e., a chord based on the flattened second scale degree as an alternative view of E major) that Xanadu is not necessarily the paradise that it appears to be on the surface.

The chorus (5:21–5:53)—in a much faster rock beat—incorporates not only a rather tempestuous metrical and rhythmic sense, but also the modal mixing (especially E major, G major, and A major) that had earlier attempted to thwart the traveler's arrival in paradise:

> **Chorus 1 (fast, hard rock; E major, G major, A major), 5:21–5:53**
> I had heard the whispered tales of immortality, the deepest mystery.
> From an ancient book I took a clue.
> I scaled the frozen mountain tops of eastern lands unknown.
> Time and Man alone, searching for the lost—Xanadu.
> (synthesizer bridge, 5:53–6:15)

> **Verse 2 (softer, reflective rock; D with B-flat—flat-VI), 6:15–6:58**
> To stand within The Pleasure Dome decreed by Kubla Khan.
> To taste anew the fruits of life the last immortal man.
> To find the sacred river Alph. To walk the caves of ice.
> Oh, I will dine on honeydew and drink the milk of Paradise.

The lyrics are much more unsettled and ambivalent in this part of the song, where mystery, immortality, and the pursuit of paradise (recalled in past perfect, then past tense), and—in verse 2—a sense of being frozen in time in Xanadu (now in present infinitives then future tense) are articulated.[47] Lee sings this in a comparatively high falsetto, the tempo is quite fast, and the rhythms are frantic and confused sounding. This may be compared with Lee's use of his more natural (lower) vocal range for the earlier, less ambivalent, paradise-oriented exposition, which also features gently rolling rhythms (verse 1, 6:15–6:58).

The central ideological conflict of the song—of Xanadu being simultaneously a paradise and a "trap"—is explored most fully in the moderate-tempo, instrumental bridge (with its plaintively "crying out" synthesizer solo, 5:53–6:15 and 8:08–8:31) that falls between the fast chorus and the slower verse. In this section, the tonal center shifts to D, but without a voiced third in the tonic chord. A B-flat major chord (based on the flattened sixth scale degree in D) used prominently, thus signifying its characteristic, romantic-era meaning of "illusory hope."[48] The paradise seemingly embodied in Xanadu is therefore an illusion, for, once there, one cannot choose to leave it. As with the pitch B in the earlier, positive-sounding vocal exposition, the pitch D is sounded in every chord in this section (partly through an extended chord on C major). This suggests that the prior obsession on a dominant pitch, B (within E major), was unfounded. Indeed, the lyrics of chorus 1 (especially "Time and Man alone") and verse 2—which is set to the D/B-flat, "illusory hope" music—begin to convey ambivalence about the protagonist being the "last immortal man" and imply that the society of which he was once a part is now irrelevant.

However, before the chorus/verse pair repeats (with new lyrics), the third portion of the instrumental introduction reappears (6:58–7:39), thus recalling its rollicking, syncopated idiom. However, its tonal center (E mixolydian) and its faster tempo are now used as a means to return to the faster, angry-sounding E major chorus. This time it bypasses the "achievement oriented" portions of the instrumental introduction and plunges directly into the modally mixed hard rock chorus (7:39–8:08) and the subsequent "crying synthesizer" bridge (8:08–8:31) and "illusory hope" verse sections. These modifications have the effect of increasing the listener's understanding of the ambivalence experienced by the protagonist. Indeed, verse 2's "To stand within the Pleasure Dome decreed by Kubla Khan" and "To taste anew the fruits of life the last immortal man" become, in verse 3 (8:31–9:08), "*Held* within the Pleasure Dome decreed by Kubla Khan" and "To taste my bitter triumph as a *mad* immortal man." Moreover, at the end of verse 3 (his last words in the song, nearing the top of the treble clef—as in "2112"), Lee adds the ambivalent phrase, "Whoa, *is it* paradise?" (see fig. 9.4).

The song then ends instrumentally, with a repeat of the B-obsessed fifth introductory section (9:08–9:32), but this time countered by a very obtrusive synthesizer sound on a series of octave descents on the pitch E. This descending gesture parallels the deepening of the protagonist's insanity, but the simultaneous reprise of specific earlier music also reminds us of his previous obsession. Lifeson then plays a frustration-imbued solo (9:32–10:10) over the chord changes of the vocal

Fig. 9.4. Verse 3 (i.e., vocal ending) of "Xanadu," 8:31–9:08.

exposition, ending, as before, with an unsettled, Phrygian (F major chord, based on the flattened second scale degree) approach to E major (10:10–10:14). This recontextualizes the alternate (frustrating) view of Xanadu as a prison that was hinted at in the original vocal exposition.[49] It then gives way to a brief reprise (at 10:14–10:27) of the introductory 7/8 section (see fig. 9.3). This section had initially signified the traveler's obstinate desire—despite all obstacles—to arrive in Xanadu. However, in this new "paradise as prison" context, the protagonist now obsesses about leaving Xanadu, but cannot; he, like the unchanging heavens above him, is "frozen in an everlasting view."

The coda (10:27–11:04) includes descending intervals of a perfect fourth on the guitar (on the pitches E and B, in several octaves) that seem to solidify further the protagonist's descent into insanity. The band also reprises the E mixolydian modality of the third introductory section, but slows it progressively down, with chime timbres participating in the song's mixed modality "moral" that paradise is illusory.[50] The song ends with a final E-major flourish that recalls the aggressive insistence on F-sharp major at the end of "2112." However, this time we witness the anger of the protagonist himself, who realizes that he has no choice but to make the best of it.

"Cygnus X-1" (from *A Farewell to Kings*, 1977)

"Cygnus X-1: Book One—The Voyage," the concluding track on *A Farewell to Kings* (1977), is generally referred to as "Cygnus X-1."[51] It is also one of the band's most "progressive-oriented" songs, especially in terms of its frequent metrical complexities and its rather overt science-fiction subject matter. Cygnus X-1—an actual X-ray source in the constellation Cygnus—is believed to be a black hole. In the song, it is initially described in the prologue (0:00–5:01), where Rush's then producer Terry Brown provides a spoken-word passage—in his ominous British accent—that is substantially masked and altered by studio effects.[52] This includes an inordinate amount of hissing (sibilance), as though the star that is undergoing a physical transformation is also distorting the narrator's voice (0:31–0:59):

> In the constellation of Cygnus, there lurks a mysterious,
>   invisible force: the black hole of Cygnus X-1.
> Six stars of the Northern Cross in mourning for their sister's loss
>   in a final flash of glory, nevermore to grace the night.

After the star has been physically transformed into a black hole, bell-like sounds—at 1:15, clearly voicing an open fifth (E and B)—represent the newly established state of the star.[53] A repeated, ascending, rhythmic (although initially rather sporadic) bass guitar line—suggesting E minor as a tonal center—then fades in (at 1:24) as if from a vast distance (courtesy of a recording studio mixing console). The drums (at 2:12) then guitar and drums (2:24) eventually join the bass guitar on essentially the same pattern, but organized into a regular metrical alternation between 6/4 and 7/4, then 6/4 and two measures of 4/4. This rhythmic solidification—along with the original bass guitar fade-in and the addition of drums and guitar—has the effect of making the pattern's "approach" seem more concrete. Although we are not yet aware of what is approaching, we eventually find out that it is a solitary, male traveler approaching in a space ship in order to explore (as in the guitar in "2112") and/or discover (as in "Xanadu") the black hole.

As in the long introduction to "Xanadu," several more instrumental sections follow. The first (2:56–3:06) oscillates between octave As and Cs (in extremely regular 4/4 time), as if to parallel the paradoxical space-time stasis (and resultant X-ray source) of the black hole. The following section (3:06–3:21) elaborates this A/C motion with a group of three chromatically descending three-chord sequences, of which the third chord in each case makes possible either D major (via an extended F-sharp major chord) or C major (via a B-based substitute dominant chord). These pattern repetitions are also interspersed with elaborate drum fills. The cycle as a whole (stated twice) ends on C major, via an extended A chord. Thus, this section elaborates the previous alternation between A and C octaves, but now at a much more complete level, as though we are witnessing the complexities of the black hole in more detail.

The second time through, the three-part cycle bypasses the extended A chord and goes directly from C major to C-sharp minor instead. This sets up an extremely fast, chaotic, 12/8 instrumental section (3:21–3:31). (The tempo is 176 dotted quarter-notes per minute, with eighth notes consequently moving at 528 beats per minute.) This section explores further paradoxes: specifically, the G-natural versus G-sharp cross-relation inherent to C-sharp minor and E minor, and, involving the same pitches, the harsh juxtaposition of adjacent G major and G-sharp major chords. However, the band aborts this section after only two times through the pattern. The "escape" from this features a series of much slower, ascending, unison semitones (3:31–3:36), which reiterates all of the semitones voiced in the preceding chords (i.e., G to G-sharp, B to C, and D to D-sharp), plus F-sharp to G as an implied secondary dominant to the following section (see fig. 9.5).[54]

The following, rather long, half-tempo section in C minor (3:36–5:01) presents additive meters alternating between 11/8 and 12/8. It also expresses a crossrelational tonal paradox similar to the one in the previous section, but now a semitone lower. This section also repeatedly moves from C minor to F-sharp major and ends on a repeated F-sharp major chord, thus recalling the tonally similar ending of "2112," but with F-sharp in an irrational, tritonal context instead of a diatonic, dominant one (see fig. 9.6).

Geddy Lee's voice finally enters (at 5:01, or about halfway through the ten-and-a-half minute song), and we realize, as the lyrics unfold, that the individual is a futuristic astronaut-scientist searching for the black hole, Cygnus X-1. The first several vocal sections reprise much of the music of the preceding instrumental sections, including a simple

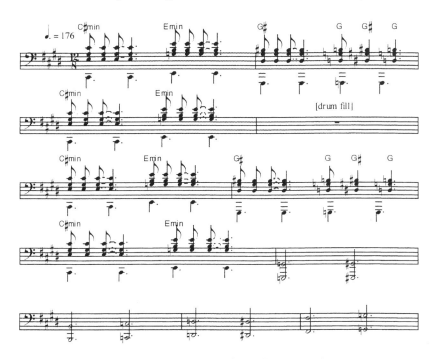

Fig. 9.5. Excerpt from "Cygnus X-1—Prologue," 3:21–3:36.

Fig. 9.6. Excerpt from "Cygnus X-1—Prologue," 3:36–5:01.

melody (over the pitches A and C, 5:01–5:14) sung using a mysterious (although natural in range) vocal quality. This is then elaborated in a hard-rock style, a piercing high-vocal timbre, and cross-relations/third relations between A major and C major (5:14–5:23).

The earlier three-part section (with all of its previous complexities, but now also with a sung text, 5:23–5:46) then presents the central ambivalence of the song, as Lee considers whether the black hole will result in his annihilation or else some kind of "astral door" to an undiscovered dimension (as in the monolith in Arthur C. Clarke's *2001: A Space Odyssey*). However, this time the underlying pattern continues to its A-based chord (instead of using C major as a pivot to C-sharp minor as before), then shifts directly to a G major chord in order to set the words "to soar." These words are "treated" artificially (via studio techniques) so as to ascend by semitone up a perfect fifth. The hero's optimistic view point at this point in the song is that the black hole *will* provide a portal to another dimension. Thus, the protagonist is undertaking a kind of "calculated risk" (see fig. 9.7).

G major—having just been elaborated by this chromatic ascent—then functions as the dominant of C major, in yet another tonal segue, to the following straightforward hard-rock narrative (5:46–7:12) of the traveler's decision to travel (on his ship, the Rocinante) into the "mystery" of the black hole.

In Greek mythology, *Rocinante* is the name of Zeus's horse. It is also the name of Don Quixote's horse and of the motor home in John Steinbeck's *Travels with Charlie*. Thus, the traditional mode of transportation

Fig. 9.7. Excerpt from "Cygnus X-1—Part I," 5:32–5:46.

for individual gods and mortals—the horse—is recontextualized (via Steinbeck's *wanderlust* and motor home) in a science-fiction context. Indeed, the brightness of C major in this part of the song underscores the hero's optimism as well as his desire for exploration and conquest and is completely consistent with that of his Rocinante precursors.

A shift to the parallel minor (C minor) at 6:28–6:45 then occurs as the lyrics refer to X-rays acting as the black hole's "siren song" and to Cygnus X-1 taking control:

> The x-ray is her siren song. My ship cannot resist her long.
> Nearer to my deadly goal, until the black hole gains control.

This section is extremely fatalistic, taking the sinister squashing of individualism of the end of "2112" and the unintended "frozenness" of the end of "Xanadu" one step further, implicating the hero *himself* in his eventual downfall. The final words here—"until the black hole takes control"—are much slower than the three phrases that precede, and are set to the multiple semitone, unison ascent of the end of one of the earlier instrumental sections. Indeed, the ascending nature of this line and the breathless anxiety of Lee's vocal style provide a sense of urgency.

The desperation continues instrumentally, first with a guitar solo (6:45–7:12) on a repeat of the chord changes of the immediately preceding C minor ("siren song") section. The mysterious octaves of the post-implosion section of the prologue then return (7:12–7:53), but C and A are replaced with C, A-flat, and B. As in the D/B-flat (flattened sixth) despair eventually present in "Xanadu," the A-flat here evokes "illusory hope." Despite the hero's initial optimism (as was also the case in "Xanadu"), he now recognizes the black hole as the trap that we already know it to be. Further instrumental complexities then follow and drive the negativism home (7:53–8:34). These features include bitonality, a chromatic descent to a new tonal area (E), alternations among measures of 4/4 and 3/4 time signatures, and a transposition of all of this up a tone (to F-sharp). The very fast, C-sharp minor, 12/8 section of the prologue (see fig. 9.5) then reappears (8:34–9:40), but this time it ends on C major and alternates with brief vocal utterances on the same music. Lee sings in an extremely high tessitura in this section—reaching as high as the A above the treble clef—as the protagonist-hero is sucked into the "unending, spiral sea" of the black hole and as his "every nerve is torn apart."

Like the priests in "2112" and paradise itself in "Xanadu," the black hole Cygnus X-1 is given the final word in this song. Ultimately, this is provided through a mysterious, soft, reflective, chord progression that reconciles C minor, E-flat minor, and two E minor chords, one with an added F-sharp (G-flat) (9:40–10:21; see fig. 9.8).

This chord progression reprises some of the ambiguity of the pitch clusters of the early parts of the song's introduction (including the pitches E, F-sharp, and A-sharp/B-flat), but also the open fifth of the star's new physical state (E/B) and several of the cross-relations (and other semitones) encountered earlier in the song (including G/G-

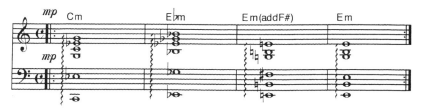

Fig. 9.8. Excerpt from "Cygnus X-1—Part I," 9:40–10:41.

sharp). This time the hero has only himself to blame, because the complexity and probable danger of the black hole were already indicated well in advance. As the pattern fades out, the hero presumably fades with it.[55] However, as unlikely as it seems, the liner notes at the end of the lyrics for this song suggest that this narrative is "to be continued."

Summary

Rush tentatively experimented with an individualist ideology and with progressive rock elements around 1974–75, including its songs "Anthem" and "Bastille Day."[56] However, it was not until the albums *2112* (1976) and *A Farewell To Kings* (1977) that the band definitively established a synthesis of its progressive hard rock style—including large-scale cyclicism and metrical constructedness—with an overtly individualist ideology and science fiction and fantasy narratives. The songs "2112," "Xanadu," and "Cygnus X-1" are perhaps extreme examples considering that the same two albums also contain a number of less complex and/or less individualistic songs, including the prodrug "A Passage to Bangkok," the "work ethic" anthem "(You Don't Get) Something for Nothing," the truth- and wisdom-oriented "A Farewell to Kings," and the anthem of diversity, "Closer to the Heart."[57] However, although casual fans are more likely to be familiar with such shorter, early Rush songs, the longer, cyclical works discussed in this article are quintessential for understanding the band's ideology, and that of its fans.

Although Rush gradually moved away from extended composition and overt libertarian individualism over its next several albums (1978–81), its later social critiques—which are considerably more succinct—were nonetheless grounded in the band's ongoing "signature" of insisting on elements of structural (especially metrical) complexity and instrumental virtuosity. These elements remained largely present, regardless of the stylistic features with which the band otherwise experimented, including mainstream hard rock, new wave and pop reggae, synth-pop, hard alternative rock, and progressive heavy metal. Furthermore, the ideological ambivalence so often expressed in Rush's extended instrumental sections of the late 1970s still functioned in the band's later music, although often in substantially moderated treatments. These included Rush's final extended work of this type,

"Hemispheres" (1978), several entirely instrumental narratives (1978 and 1981), and especially the more general social critiques posited in various shorter songs from 1978 to 1996.

Notes

1. See Edward Macan, *Rocking the Classics: English Progressive Rock and the Counterculture* (New York: Oxford University Press, 1997), 6, 12–13, 16.
2. The late-60s style had tended toward homogeneously distributed (thus, arguably more "psychedelic" and communalist) expressions across a number of instruments (as in "Light My Fire" by the Doors and "In-A-Gadda-da-Vida" by Iron Butterfly), whereas the emerging progressive style often heterogeneously distributed its soloists, giving each player one or more featured "moments." On the other hand, whereas some progressive rock bands—for example, Emerson Lake and Palmer (ELP) and Yes—often featured individual virtuosity in separate instrumental sections, other progressive rock bands—especially Genesis—preferred to explore textures of semivirtuosic ensemble playing.
3. Sales of rock albums surpassed sales of pop singles in 1969. Statistic cited in Paul Stump, *The Music's All That Matters: A History of Progressive Rock* (London: Quartet, 1998), 73.
4. Thus, I prefer to consider Pink Floyd—on the basis of its total output—a "psychedelic progressive" rock band.
5. From an interview with Bill Bruford (ca. 1996) by Paul Stump, quoted in Stump's *All That Matters*, 49.
6. My thanks to Daniel Goldmark for bringing this to my attention.
7. Jon Anderson, quoted in Jerry Lucky, *The Progressive Rock Files*, 4th ed. (Burlington, Ontario: Collector's Guide Publishing, 1998), 37; emphasis added.
8. John Covach, "Progressive Rock, 'Close to the Edge,' and the Boundaries of Style" in John Covach and Graeme M. Boone, eds., *Understanding Rock: Essays in Musical Analysis* (New York: Oxford University Press, 1997), 4.
9. Ibid., 6.
10. Jon Anderson, quoted in ibid., 7.
11. For example, Robert Walser demonstrates that elements of art music are also sometimes borrowed by heavy metal musicians. See chapter 3, "Eruptions: Heavy Metal Appropriations of Classical Virtuosity," in Robert Walser, *Running With The Devil: Power, Gender, and Madness in Heavy Metal Music* (Hanover, NH: Wesleyan University Press, 1993), 57–107.
12. Covach's more recent work suggests that he is interested in broadening the definition of progressive rock to include elements of jazz-rock fusion. See John Covach, "Jazz-Rock? Rock-Jazz? Stylistic Crossover in Late-1970s

American Progressive Rock," in Walter Everett, ed., *Expression in Pop-Rock Music: A Collection of Critical and Analytical Essays* (New York: Garland Publishing, 2000), 113–34.

13. Along these lines, I have already discussed Rush's compositional "division of labor" in chapter 1 of my Ph.D. dissertation, "Permanent Change: Individualism, Rock Sub-Genres, and the Music of Rush," University of California, Los Angeles, 2001.

14. These appropriations are discussed by Robert Walser in chapter 3 ("Eruptions: Heavy Metal Appropriations of Classical Virtuosity") of his *Running With The Devil.*

15. Individualism and progressive rock might never have emerged if the counterculture itself had not itself begun to fracture by 1968 or '69. Indeed, if the Beatles had not disbanded by 1970 and Jimi Hendrix and Jim Morrison (of the Doors) had not died in 1970 and '71, respectively, politically charged hard rock music (e.g., Jefferson Airplane and John Lennon) might have been much more prominent in the 1970s, and the genre of progressive rock might not have achieved the level of commercial success it attained in North America and the United Kingdom around 1972–78. Also, punk rock might have been interpreted as an extension of the late-1960s rather than as a reaction against progressive rock.

   The larger genre map of rock music from 1969 to 1994 would also have looked very different if the 1960s psychedelic aesthetic had continued more prominently into the 1970s. For example, Pink Floyd would have found itself competing with a larger number of psychedelic bands and might never have been as popular as it was; punk, new wave, and post-punk rock (which flourished in the late 1970s and early 1980s with the music of the Sex Pistols, the Ramones, Talking Heads, the Smiths, and other groups) might never have emerged at all; and "alternative" rock (which flourished in the early 1990s after the success of Nirvana's album *Nevermind* and Pearl Jam's album *Ten*, both 1991) would have had a much closer connection to the 1970s and '80s, with R.E.M. (1981–) becoming popular (and influential) much sooner than its mainstream breakthrough with the album *Document* (1987).

16. Libertarianism advocates individual rights, freedoms, and differences over and above political control and "sameness." The "minimal state" (or less government interference) is preferred.

17. By contrast, much of King's Crimson's early music (especially the albums *Lizard*, 1971, and *Islands*, 1972) can be seen as "psychedelic progressive rock," even though the band foregrounded virtuosity and modern jazz influences to a much greater extent than Pink Floyd did in the same period. The mid-70s incarnation of King Crimson ended in 1974 (with a live album released posthumously in 1975) and a new version of the band did not emerge until 1981, so one is left to surmise as to what influences a

continuing King Crimson might have had upon late-70s North American rock music. Certainly, the sporadic output of the group (compared to Rush's twenty-three releases over twenty-five years) has not boded well for a substantial following among fans of similar music. Indeed, my 1996 Rush fan survey suggests that King Crimson is hardly even known among Rush fans.

18. King Crimson's heavier music of the 1973–74 period actually alternates with Robert Fripp's gentler, electric guitar experiments (including music somewhat prescient of what he would later call his "Frippertronics") and with somewhat more psychedelic (and semiacoustic) music.

19. Alex Lifeson, quoted in "Music Will Not Exist In 2112," *Circus*, April 27, 1976, reprinted on the National Midnight Star website, formerly at http://syrinx.yyz.com.

20. Geddy Lee, quoted in Darcy Diamond, "Rush to Judgement," *Creem*, June 1977, 25.

21. Roy MacGregor, "To Hell with Bob Dylan: Meet Rush. They're In It for the Money," *Maclean's*, January 23, 1978, 26–27.

22. See http://www.eb.com.

23. Ibid.

24. Scott Bullock, article-interview with Neil Peart, "A Rebel and a Drummer," *Liberty*, September 1997. Quoted on the National Midnight Star website, formerly at http://syrinx.yyz.com.

25. However, the eventual outcome of this particular battle is unknown until the very end of the composition, nearly twenty minutes later.

26. Lee sings in an actual soprano tessitura, and these barely attainable pitch levels (for a male singer), combined with the important tonal inter-relationships among the work's seven sections, necessitated, among other things, transposing the entire twenty-one-minute work down a whole tone in recent live performances (and resultant recordings).

27. Bart Testa's scathing review of this album makes the connection to *Logan's Run* explicit. See *Crawdaddy*, December 1976, 73.

28. Rush's 1975 song "Anthem" refers to "wonders in the world" and "eyes gone blind."

29. This music is related to the A major music that emerged at the end of the "Discovery" section during the hero's recent excitement about sharing his discovery with others.

30. Victoria Anne Steinitz and Ellen Rachel Solomon, *Starting Out: Class and Community in the Lives of Working-Class Youth* (Philadelphia: Temple University Press, 1986).

31. J. Kordosh, "Rush: But Why Are They in Such a Hurry?" *Creem*, June 1981, 62.

32. Richard Middleton, *Studying Popular Music* (Buckingham: Open University Press, 1990), 173.

33. J. Kordosh, "Rush: But Why Are They in Such a Hurry?" 62.

34. Reebee Garofalo, *Rockin' Out: Popular Music in the USA* (Boston: Allyn and Bacon, 1997), 292. A reference earlier in the book suggests that Rush "had begun by playing Cream and Iron Butterfly covers in 1974" (289), but the band actually began in 1968, played mostly original songs by 1971–73, and recorded its first original album in 1973.

35. Deena Weinstein, *Heavy Metal: A Cultural Sociology* (New York: Lexington Books, 1991), 124–25, 295. Elsewhere in the book (263), she relates the priests' argument against individual expression to the cautions about music that are explained in Plato's *Republic*.

36. Of the five short songs on the second half of *2112*, "A Passage to Bangkok" espouses access to recreational drugs in exotic lands in Latin America, the Caribbean, and the east, "The Twilight Zone" is about Rod Serling—the creator of the classic science fiction television show who had recently died of cancer; Lifeson's "Lessons" is a Led Zeppelin-like, snappy-acoustic song about growing up (but with heavy metal power chords in the chorus); Lee's "Tears" is a mellow, semisweet song about allowing oneself to fall in love (and featuring the distinctive, sustained, late-60s keyboard instrument the mellotron); and the closing song, "Something For Nothing," is a succinct, hard rock anthem in favor of a strong work ethic.

37. Rush's fifth album, the live *All The World's A Stage*, was released in the fall of 1976.

38. Other earlier extended works by Rush include "By-Tor and The Snow Dog" (from the album *Fly By Night*, 1975) as well as "The Necromancer" and "The Fountain of Lamneth" (both from the album *Caress Of Steel*, also 1975). These works are also subdivided into sections.

39. Rush did not create an entirely instrumental narrative until "La Villa Strangiato" (on 1978's *Hemispheres*).

40. Of course, the song is also quite different from the band's earliest cover songs, its relationship-oriented hard rock songs (1974), its hard rock anthem "Working Man" (1971/74), its progressive-influenced, pseudohistorical song "Bastille Day" (1975), and its more mainstream, radio-friendly songs (e.g., "Fly By Night" and "Lakeside Park," both 1975).

41. The division of labor of Peart being credited with Rush's lyrics and Lee and Lifeson being credited with the band's music began with this album.

42. See Walser, *Running With The Devil*, especially 114–20.

43. Middleton, *Studying Popular Music*, 232.

44. Ibid., 238.

45. Interview with Neil Peart, Rush Backstage Club newsletter, October 1991.

46. As with the 7/8 introduction of "Anthem," most of the introduction of "Xanadu" is not provided in the published transcription.

47. This is similar to the grammatical trajectory from future to present to past tense in Rush's earlier song "Bastille Day" (from the album *Caress Of Steel*, 1975).

48. For example, musicologist Susan McClary discusses the idea of "illusory" or

"false" hope in relation to "flat-six" chords (especially in Schubert's Impromptu in C Minor, Op. 90, no. 1 and in the slow movement of Beethoven's String Quartet in E-flat Major, Op. 127) in her article "Pitches, Expression, Ideology: An Exercise in Mediation," *Enclitic*, Spring 1983, 76–86.

49. In Orson Welles's 1941 film *Citizen Kane*, Charles Foster Kane builds a magnificent palace for himself and his second wife. He names it Xanadu and subsequently undergoes an "ambivalence entrapment" not at all unlike the one in Rush's later narrative.

50. This is similar to the slow, ambivalent, instrumental ending of Rush's earlier song "Bastille Day" (from the album *Caress Of Steel*, 1975).

51. "Cygnus X-1 Book II—Hemispheres," the side-long title suite (a.k.a. "Hemispheres") of Rush's subsequent album, *Hemispheres* (1978), enters a rather more psychological domain than the science fiction subject matter of "Cygnus X-1" and, in fact, concerns left-brain versus right-brain thought processes. These are "anthropomorphized" in Neil Peart's lyrics about Apollonian versus Dionysian cults and the arrival of balance through a god named Cygnus.

52. Terry Brown was generally referred to as "Broon" because of the way he pronounced his own surname. Ominous narrators with British accents abound in the history of cinema, including U.S. films.

53. The underlying music of the preceding prologue features electronically generated, complex, bell-like tones and relatively arhythmic presentations of indistinct pitch clusters in a rather restrained middle-frequency range, (E, F-sharp, G-sharp, and A-sharp), thus depicting the normal state of the star before its transformation into a black hole. However, this eventually "progresses" as sporadic lower and higher G-sharps and C-sharps anticipate a change to the sounds of explosions that quickly take over the texture. These changes coincide with the spoken "final flash of glory" of the star becoming a black hole. This process involves such an extreme shift in density that the star disappears entirely from the visual spectrum.

54. Segues such as this one recall the similar transitions between sections in "2112" and "Xanadu."

55. This may be contrasted with the similarly themed, though much more psychedelic and narratively straightforward, Pink Floyd song "Set the Controls for the Heart of the Sun" (originally from *A Saucerful of Secrets*, 1968).

56. In the same period, the band experimented with multisectional and/or relatively long works, including "By-Tor and the Snow Dog," "The Necromancer," and "The Fountain of Lamneth."

57. Lee's "Cinderella Man" (based on Frank Capra's 1936 film *Mr. Deeds Goes to Town*, starring Gary Cooper) and Peart's "Madrigal" seem like filler material compared to the other four songs.

part 3

"Don't Dare Call Us 'Progressive'"

"Post-Prog" and Other Legacies

10 Somebody Is Digging My Bones

King Crimson's "Dinosaur" as (Post)Progressive Historiography

Brian Robison

At the start of his treatise *A Theory of Semiotics*, Umberto Eco defines semiotic theory formally as "a unified approach to every phenomenon of signification and/or communication" that should be "able to explain every case of sign-function in terms of underlying systems of elements mutually correlated by one or more codes."[1] He then proceeds to define semiotics more colloquially as "in principle the discipline studying everything which can be used in order to lie."[2] That is, Eco defines a sign as anything that can be taken to convey meaning, whether or not that meaning is actually true. He goes on to note the existence of nonintentional signs, expanding the definition of a "sign" to include anything that can convey meaning, whether or not the perceived meaning is actually intended.[3]

The song "Dinosaur," from King Crimson's 1995 album *THRAK*, appears to comprise an entire network of nonintentional signs, one inadvertently so cohesive and powerful that it effectively overwhelms the principal songwriter's intentional signs. Briefly put, what Adrian Belew wrote as a song about looking back on one's personal history has been widely misinterpreted as a song about looking back on the broader history of King Crimson as a band, or even the entire style category of so-called progressive or art rock.[4] This misinterpretation has occurred because, among many listeners, the broader *mis*reading carries a higher truth than the narrow, "correct" reading that Belew intended; this fact suggests that the former is consequently richer and more interesting than the latter to scholars of popular music. As I'll show, the network of nonintentional signs carries at least one intentional sign contributed by a collaborator. However, the other, more clearly nonintentional signs carry sufficient power that the widespread misreading of this song as historical commentary on progressive rock almost certainly would occur even without this addition.

The Words

Of all the cues that give rise to the misinterpretation of "Dinosaur" as historical commentary, perhaps the least ambiguous is the song's lyric content. The singing persona looks back on his youth, describing it in terms of a metaphor announced in the song's chorus: "I'm a dinosaur, somebody is digging my bones."[5] Paleozoological references include, in the first verse, "fossilized photos of my life then"; in the second verse, "doesn't take a scientist to see how / Any clever predator could have a piece of me"; and, in the bridge, "I made my fossil bed / Now I toss and turn."[6]

The historicizing intent is unmistakable; the question isn't *whether* the song offers historical commentary, but rather, *on what.* The lyricist, Adrian Belew, insists he didn't intend the song to refer to King Crimson, or any other band. "'Dinosaur,'" he explains, "had nothing to do with the term 'Dinosaur' in reference to an aging rock band. It's a personal lyric which is meant to be left open to interpretation by the listener. For me, it's a song about people digging into my past."[7]

Considered apart from the music, the words fit this claim. Throughout, Belew uses the first-person singular rather than the plural, and there are no verbal references, or even allusions, to music of any kind, rock bands, the recording industry, or earlier King Crimson songs or albums. Likewise, there are no references to Belew's early career in Nashville, or to playing as a sideman for Frank Zappa, David Bowie, and Talking Heads in the late 1970s.[8]

So, although the lyric openly invites interpretation as metaphor, it offers no verbal cues to a specific frame of reference. Given that the meaning has been "left open to interpretation by the listener," one might expect to find as many interpretations as there are listeners. Instead, interpretations have gravitated toward a common reading of the song as historical commentary. Because authenticity in American rock is still largely defined in relation to the youth market, it's likely that any performer over the age of forty would elicit an interpretation of the words "I'm a dinosaur" as autobiography. Yet rather than ascribe this message to Belew alone, as Belew himself has done, listeners have consistently interpreted it as commentary on the history of King Crimson.

The situation described above neatly illustrates many of the points made by Stanley Fish in his essay, "Is There a Text in This Class?"[9] Belew's desideratum seems to approach that "infinite plurality of meanings" that Fish's opponents such as Meyer Abrams and E. D. Hirsch fear will lead to solipsism and relativism in interpretation. Yet although Belew seeks such a plurality of meanings, the convergence of fans' interpretations demonstrates the unlikelihood of such an absolute indeterminacy, as "sentences emerge only in situations, and within those situations, the normative meaning of an utterance will always be obvious or at least accessible."[10] In the case of "Dinosaur," the situation seems more often to be "I'm listening to a song by King Crimson," rather than "I'm listening to a lyric by Adrian Belew." In particular, since "Dinosaur" did not achieve mainstream success, listeners were unlikely to encounter the song at random on radio or television. Instead, many would have known *prior* to reading or hearing the lyric that the song was by King Crimson, from the band's first full-length album in a decade. As Fish writes, "One hears an utterance within, and not as preliminary to determining, a knowledge of its purposes and concerns, and that to so hear it is already to have assigned it a shape and given it a meaning."[11] He remarks, in conclusion, "We see then that (1) Communication does occur, despite the absence of an independent and context-free system of meanings, that (2) those who participate in this communication do so confidently rather than provisionally (they are not relativists), and that (3) while their confidence has its source in a set of beliefs, those beliefs are not individual-specific or idiosyncratic but communal and conventional (they are not solipsists)."[12]

Put another way, Belew seems to have underestimated the force of King Crimson's music as a functional genre in shaping fans' perceptions. To borrow from Hans Robert Jauss, "Dinosaur," like any other song, "presupposes preliminary information and a trajectory of expectations against which to register the originality and novelty. This horizon of the expectable is constituted for the [listener] from out of a tradition or series of previously known works, and from a specific attitude, mediated by one (or more) genre and dissolved through new works.... For each work a preconstituted horizon of expectations must be ready at hand (this can also be understood as a relationship of 'rules of the game') to orient the [listener's] understanding and to enable a qualifying reception."[13]

Perhaps the most interesting aspect of what "Dinosaur" communicates is the question of how the received meaning can be so consistent even though different groups of listeners bring different communal and conventional beliefs to the table, ranging from a general acquaintance with progressive rock to a specific familiarity with the entire corpus of King Crimson. The answer may be found in the complex mixture of musical signs that "Dinosaur" comprises.

The Music

Belew may not have intended to refer to King Crimson's history, but the music of "Dinosaur" has other ideas. Table 10.1 presents an outline of the song's materials. Timbrally it comprises a broad palette of tone colors, from comparatively quiet synthesized double reeds (interlude 2) and bowed strings (intro 1, interlude 3, coda 2), to electric guitars that are variously clean and clear (interlude 1), overdriven for fuzz-tone (intro 2, verses, choruses, bridge, solo, coda 3), or even processed to mimic hypothetical dinosaur vocalizations (coda 1). A wide range of dynamic levels is incorporated, including a violent contrast of the sort that has been a trademark of King Crimson over the years: the third interlude fades to silence, which lasts for a full five seconds, before the ensemble launches into the bridge material as a foundation for guitarist Robert Fripp's solo.

The song similarly comprises a variety of contrasting rhythmic structures: these include regular bars of 4/4, either in sustained tones (intro 1) or in more rhythmic eighth notes with a conventional backbeat (intro 2, verses); more flexible additive metric groupings in the chromatic interludes, such as the alternation between 9/8 (as 3 + 2 + 2 + 2) and 6/8 (that is, 3 + 3); (interlude 1); and polymeter in the bridge,

Table 10.1. Formal Outline of "Dinosaur,"
with Time Indices of Five Recorded Performances.

		studio (1994)[1]	live (1995)[2]	live (1996)[3]	solo (1996)[4]	live (2000)[5]
intro 1 (chorus)	synth strings	0:00	0:00	0:00	—	0:01
intro 2 (chorus)	distorted guitars	0:21	0:18	0:19	0:00	0:22
verse 1	"Long ago and far away"	0:42	0:39	0:39	0:21	0:42
prechorus	"Standing in the sun"	1:02	0:59	0:58	0:40	1:02
chorus	"I'm a dinosaur"	1:12	1:10	1:08	0:50	1:12
verse 2	"Ignorance has always been"	1:33	1:31	1:27	1:11	1:32
prechorus	"Standing in the sun"	1:53	1:52	1:46	1:30	1:53
chorus	"I'm a dinosaur"	2:04	2:02	1:56	1:40	2:03
bridge	"When I look back on the past"	2:22	2:21	2:14	1:58	2:22
(prechorus)	distorted guitar	2:59	2:52	2:48	2:34	2:56
chorus	"I'm a dinosaur"	3:10	3:08	2:57	2:44	3:06
interlude 1	clean guitar chords	3:27	3:27	—	3:02	—
interlude 2	synth double-reeds with bass	3:35	3:38	—	3:12	—
interlude 3	synth strings with bass	3:54	4:02	—	3:33	—
	silence	4:41	4:55	—	4:18	3:26
(bridge)	distorted guitar solo	4:47	5:00	3:15	4:19	3:32
chorus	"I'm a dinosaur"	5:25	5:25	3:53	4:59	4:10
coda 1	dinosaur vocalizations	5:46	6:02	4:13	—	—
coda 2	synth strings	6:23	6:26	4:33	5:27	4:31
coda 3	distorted guitar tag	6:28	6:39	4:54	5:36	4:58
		6:35	6:44	4:54	5:43	5:05

1. King Crimson, *THRAK* (compact disc), Virgin 7243 8 40313 2 9.
2. King Crimson, *Deja VROOM* (digital versatile disk), Discipline Global Mobile DGM9810, and *Live in Japan* (video cassette), Discipline Global Mobile VC1.
3. King Crimson, *Cirkus: The Young Person's Guide to King Crimson Live* (compact disc), Virgin 7243 8 47431 2 3.
4. Adrian Belew, *Belenprints: The Acoustic Adrian Belew,* Volume Two (compact disc), Discipline Global Mobile DGM9802.
5. King Crimson, *Heavy ConstruKction* (compact disc), Discipline Global Mobile DGM0013.

in which vocals in 4/4 combine with an accompaniment that alternates between 7/8 (as 3 + 2 + 2) and 9/8 (as 2 + 3 + 2 + 2).

The harmonic language involves not only major and minor triads and the more common seventh chords, but also diminished and augmented triads that, particularly in the chromatic interludes, seem to share equal structural footing with the major and minor triads in the verses and choruses.[14] Tonally, the song plays out a tension between the triads of E minor and G major that frame the first phrase, although not simply as relative minor and major. Instead, for most of the song, various triads of E (major, minor, diminished) and E-flat major seem to function as one or another submediant harmony in G major or G minor; at the song's end, the final E-minor sonority threatens to invert that hierarchy. Throughout, conventional tonal cadences are avoided; instead of clearly directed motion of triadic roots by fourths or fifths, the song favors juxtapositions of third-related harmonies.[15]

Even to listeners who know little or nothing of previous music recorded under the name King Crimson, the sheer variety and intricacy of these musical materials recalls the so-called progressive rock movement of the early 1970s.[16] In particular, for many listeners, the timbre of electronically colored orchestral strings, in combination with these other features, comes across as a clear reference to the mellotron passages of classic progressive rock music by bands such as Yes, Genesis,[17] and King Crimson in the period 1969–74, even though the string chords at the outset of "Dinosaur" are *not* played on a mellotron.[18]

To listeners who do know the earlier King Crimson repertoire, the sense of historical reference is even more acute. As of 1995, when *THRAK* was released, the on-again, off-again history of King Crimson stretched back a quarter of a century, to 1969 (see table 10.2).[19] The King Crimson of the 1990s integrates musical features from its previous periods. This is true across the various songs of the album *THRAK*, but especially within the song "Dinosaur." In order to maintain a trajectory from the general to the specific, I'll describe these musical connections in relation to King Crimson's history in *reverse* chronological order.[20]

The 1994 King Crimson represents a reforming of the quartet that Fripp had disbanded in 1984, plus two additional players to form a "double trio." Eric Tamm has listed the sources of the 1981–84 band's style as "the beat(s) and instrumental format(s) of rock; world music, notably Indonesian gamelan and African percussion; high technology, notably guitar synthesizers, effects, and synth drums; and minimalism."[21]

This idiom clearly manifests art rock, but not the classic progressive rock styles of the 1970s; for new styles such as this, Edward Macan has introduced the term "postprogressive."[22] The timbre of the 1994 double trio resembles that of the 1981–84 band, thanks to the combination of Belew's voice and the instrumentation (electric guitars and

Table 10.2. An Abbreviated History of King Crimson, 1969–1996.

Under "albums," the anachronistic release dates indicate recent CD compilations of material recorded live during the period indicated. The two columns under "personnel lineups" summarize the classification schemes of Eric Tamm and Robert Fripp.

		personnel lineups	
years	albums	Tamm 1990[1]	Fripp 1999[2]
	In the Court of the Crimson King (1969)		
1969	*Epitaph* (1997)	I	one
1970	*In the Wake of Poseidon* (1970)	II	transitional I
	Lizard (1970)		transitional II
1971–72	*Islands* (1971)		two A
	Earthbound (1972)		two B
1973	*Larks' Tongues in Aspic* (1973)	III	three A
1973	*Starless and Bible Black* (1974)		
	USA (1975)		
	The Great Deceiver (1992)		
1973	*The Night Watch* (1997)		three B
1974	*Red* (1974)		three C
1974–1980		*sabbatical*	*interregnum*
1981–1984	*Discipline* (1981)		
	Beat (1982)		
	Three of a Perfect Pair (1984)		
	Absent Lovers (1997)	IV	four
1985–1993		*Guitar Craft*	*interregnum*
1994–95	*VROOOM* (1994)		
	B'boom (1995)		
	THRAK (1995)		
	THRaKaTTaK (1996)	—	five

1. Eric Tamm, *Robert Fripp: From King Crimson to Guitar Craft* (Boston: Faber and Faber, 1990), 45.
2. Robert Fripp, liner scrapbook for King Crimson, *Cirkus: The Young Person's Guide to King Crimson Live* (compact disc), Virgin 7243 8 47431 2 3.

guitar synthesizers, touch-style guitar-based instruments such as the Chapman stick, and acoustic and electronic percussion), but much of the material on *THRAK* displays a more orchestral approach to the electric guitars.[23] Conspicuously absent are the intricate "rock gamelan" textures that Eric Tamm rightly labels as the 1981–84 band's "most distinctive contribution to the rock vocabulary ... among the most impressive passages in their music are those where two, three, or all four musicians are playing rapid-fire ostinatos that interlock and counterpoint each other in a glittering pointillistic texture reminiscent of the gamelan orchestras of Indonesia."[24]

The principal riff of "Dinosaur," with its obsessive alternation between B-flat and G, may be heard as a slow-motion remnant of the minimalist strain in 1980s Crimson, but such an interpretation is by no means obvious. Instead, the more salient references to previous Crimson, both intentional and unintentional, hark back to even earlier albums, before Adrian Belew was part of the band. As summarized in table 10.2, the band formed in 1981 was the first King Crimson since 1974, when Fripp had disbanded what remained of a lineup that had originally emerged in 1973. This 1973–74 band featured a sound leaner than that of preceding Crimson, and more strikingly avant-garde improvisations; it often seemed to answer a question that Fripp posed in 1984 to summarize his lifelong interest in musical cross-fertilization: "What would Hendrix sound like playing Bartók?"[25]

Edward Macan has aptly observed that the work of the 1994 double trio "does not produce any groundbreaking innovations. Rather, the emphasis seems to be on further developing directions initially explored by the mid-1970s and 1980s incarnations of the band (the title track of *VROOOM*, in particular, suggests a 1990s reinterpretation of 'Red')."[26] Elements of the 1973–74 style to which Macan refers here are most likely the heavy power-trio timbre, the chromatic pitch vocabulary, and the blues-derived (I–I–IV–I) transposition scheme for the principal theme.

Even these connections, however, seem subtle when compared to the sheer diversity of musical materials contained in "Dinosaur," especially the chromatic interludes preceding the guitar solo. These interludes bear no obvious thematic, harmonic, rhythmic, or timbral connection to the rest of the song. Belew has commented, "The middle instrumental section ... was a separate piece I had intended for a solo record. But when I wrote it into the middle of 'Dinosaur' it fit."[27] By *fit,* Belew seems to mean that the interludes provide a suitable contrast enabling him to extend the song's total duration from roughly five minutes to six and a half, and to match the diversity of materials in the

"VROOOM" series of pieces and in "THRAK" (which the band uses as a vehicle for some of its most experimental improvisations).

In a more detailed account of the song's genesis, Belew relates, "One morning in Woodstock, New York, during the first rehearsals of the nineties King Crimson, Robert Fripp excitedly showed me five chords he had written which had a tense quality to them. He said he hoped we could create out of them the Crimson equivalent of 'I am [the] Walrus.'"[28]

Other than a generally ominous tone, the most immediately identifiable connections between "I am the Walrus" and "Dinosaur" are the close match of tempo (84 and 90 beats per minute, respectively) and the rocking contour of alternating eighth notes in the two songs' introductions (in "I am the Walrus," the alternation between right-hand fingers and thumb on electric piano, and in "Dinosaur," the alternation between B-flat and G). Thus, listeners are not so far off the mark in hearing references to earlier music: Belew may not have been trying to refer to the history of progressive rock, but he was consciously referring to a song from its *pre*history.

Belew's account continues:

> After I added a few more chord changes to accommodate the melody I had in mind, I was stumped. Weeks later I was still musing over this song when King Crimson traveled to Argentina for a month of writing, rehearsing, and live performances. During the month I continued to work on the song (and others), eventually adding a bridge which reminded me of a part of *The Rite of Spring*. I noticed much of our new instrumental material, such as "VROOOM" and "THRAK," had become epic in size; seven minutes or so in length. I felt this song had to be an epic pop song. I had written a rubato piece meant to be played by a string trio. When I added the rubato piece to the middle of the song, "Dinosaur" was complete. With the additions created by the rest of the band it's become my favorite Crimson song.[29]

Prior to the 1973–74 band, the years 1971–72 witnessed a series of transitional rosters and less noteworthy albums, to which "Dinosaur" contains no clear references, either intentional or unintentional. Thus, the musical contrasts of Belew's interludes inadvertently reach back *past* the 1971–72 incarnation of Crimson, to the period 1969–70, from the debut album *In the Court of the Crimson King* to *Lizard.* These represent the portion of King Crimson's output closest to the mainstream notion of progressive rock, marked by extended suites, a striking variety of musical materials, particularly in contrasts of tempo and dynamic levels within the same song, and symphonic colorations courtesy of the mellotron. Even though the band's original incarnation lasted only a year, Edward Macan notes that "King Crimson's first album, *In the Court of the Crimson King* (released October 1969), had an especially powerful impact on the nascent progressive rock movement, and just may be the most influential progressive rock album ever released."[30] In short, even though Belew intended no such reference to the earliest work of King Crimson, by assembling such disparate musical materials that prominently contrast timbres characteristic of rock and symphonic music, he inevitably recalls the glory days of progressive rock.

So far, all of the musical references in "Dinosaur" consist of inadvertent allusions to the general style of earlier King Crimson rather than outright quotations. There is, however, one nearly direct paraphrase: the guitar riff from the chorus, iterating the minor third B-flat–G in even eighth notes, recalls another repeated minor third B-flat–G in even eighth notes within the song "Cirkus," which is the opening cut on King Crimson's 1970 album *Lizard.*[31]

On this two-pitch riff, it's noteworthy that, as Belew relates, "['Dinosaur'] began with Robert showing me a sequence of five chords he had written. I added more and more changes to accommodate the melody I was writing and ended up with an epic!"[32] This "sequence of five chords" is almost certainly that underlying the guitar riff, implying that Fripp may well have planned the B-flat–G riff from the start.[33] If so, this reference entails a healthy dose of irony, because Fripp has frequently invoked the "dinosaur" metaphor to describe the rock music industry, and always with a decidedly pejorative tone. For example, discussing his decision to break up King Crimson III in 1974, he has said, "The band ceased to exist in September 1974, which was when all English bands in that genre should have ceased to exist. But since the rock'n'roll dinosaur likes anything which has gone before, most of them are still churning away, repeating what they did years ago without going off in any new direction."[34]

Eric Tamm describes how, in the late 1970s, "Fripp railed against what he called the music industry's 'dinosaurs'—cold-blooded, reptilian corporate entities of immense size and dangerously little intelligence. As an alternative way of presenting music to the public, he proposed the 'small, mobile, intelligent unit'—a phrase which became the Frippism *par excellence* of the late 1970s."[35]

Hence, Fripp's contribution of the "Cirkus" paraphrase represents a wry touch of self-persiflage, characteristic not merely of his bone-dry wit (e.g., "Tuning a mellotron doesn't"), but also of his often bewildering, mercurial persona as reluctant mentor to Guitar Craft.[36]

Interpretation

The musical connections that I've described powerfully reinforce the impression that "Dinosaur" refers to the band King Crimson and to the classic progressive style, even though Adrian Belew's tenure with the band dates from 1981, not 1969.[37] On many levels, to many listeners,[38] the words and music of "Dinosaur" combine to suggest a richer hearing of the song, as wry commentary on the band's position in rock past and present, and on 1970s so-called progressive rock from the perspective of the 1990s. This interpretation shows up in print in Bradley Bombarger's review of the album *THRAK*, in which he confidently writes, "A future Crimson manifesto can be gleaned from the barbed hooks and ominous textures of the album's third track, 'Dinosaur.' On the bridge, Belew pre-empts questions of continued relevance with a self-deprecating exposition on the fate of the aging but still evolving art rocker."[39]

So, despite Belew's intentions, "Dinosaur" is taken to acknowledge the band's status as an emblem of progressive rock (a style now generally regarded as, at best, irrelevant, if not actually extinct), even though the song doesn't replicate the sound of classic progressive rock. In this regard, the dinosaur metaphor necessarily entails some irony, in that over the years King Crimson progressively became less and less characteristic of the classic progressive rock style that the band's original incarnation helped to define; even in 1973, its status as an icon of progressive rock was already problematic.[40]

It's also worth noting that many features of progressive and postprogressive rock crop up in the so-called alternative music scene of the 1990s. On the whole, it seems to be the case that progressive rock was a predecessor of alternative rock rather than a direct influence. That is, over the years, mainstream rock has tended to preserve certain characteristics (such as harmonic and rhythmic regularity); accordingly, certain traits marked as "other" (such as harmonic and rhythmic irregularity) tend to recur as reactions against the norm. In this regard, popular music over the decades may be no less cyclical than art music over the centuries.

On the other hand, in spite of mainstream rock journalism's attempt to erase progressive rock from the popular consciousness, it does show up in surprising places. Among recent artists who have cited one or another influence from King Crimson are guitarist Vernon Reid (formerly of the heavy metal and funk band Living Colour) and the late Kurt Cobain, one of the key figures in the grunge rock of the 1990s.[41] Additionally, the mellotron, an analog dinosaur in the age of digital synthesizers, has begun to show up on songs such as Juliana Hatfield's "My Darling," and the mellotron's predecessor, the Chamberlain, is featured throughout Fiona Apple's 1996 album *Tidal*.[42]

Conclusion

A quarter century after progressive rock's heyday, "Dinosaur" seems to reflect on early progressive rock's burial under successive strata of shifting popular and critical tastes, fossilization in CD reissues and "classic rock" radio formats, and recent excavation by scholars to dust it off and analyze, theorize, historicize, and recontextualize it.

The project of burying progressive rock began long before the arrival of its punk and new wave successors. Many mainstream critics and journalists regarded progressive rock as pretentious, found its popular success appalling, and were only too eager to declare it dead and gone. Note, for example, from the start of a record review by Alan Niester in *Rolling Stone*, who writes, "Remember art rock? Well, it still lives. Every year or so Robert Fripp claws his way from a graveyard of past musical fads, emerging like something out of a *Weird Tales* comic book, to snivel in an educated English accent that classicism in rock music lives on."[43]

Niester wrote these words in 1973—not after the decline and fall of progressive rock, but during the peak of its artistic and commercial success.[44] So, when punk and new wave took center stage in the late 1970s, such critics were quick to posit a complete break, though scholars such as John Covach have recently highlighted connections between the supposedly ancient and modern practices.[45]

Digital fossilization of classic progressive rock has preserved enough of the beast to imagine a reconstruction of its features, in spite of the attempts to bury it. Compact disc reissues have made an enormous archive of music available—of course, not from any altruistic motives on the part of record companies, but because of the easy money to be gained by selling aging baby boomers their favorite albums all over again. And classic progressive rock, although not the bread and butter of classic-rock radio formats, fits neatly into the 1967–1975 "golden age" of rock that Allan Moore has identified so that the hits of 1970s progressive rock (such as Yes's "Roundabout") can still be heard on broadcast.[46]

Increasingly of late, these fossil records are being excavated and displayed. If progressive rock has suffered disproportionately from the historic dearth of musically trained scholars who study rock, it stands to benefit disproportionately from the recent increase of interest and activity in the study of rock by academic musicologists.[47] Thanks to its borrowings from classical European idioms, progressive rock is in many respects more easily analyzed by conventional means (and hence validated among musicologists) than many other rock styles or genres.[48]

My consideration of "Dinosaur" in the context of King Crimson's previous output and the style category of progressive rock reveals significant overtones of irony in the song, both as Belew (and Fripp) created it and as their fans have received it. The imbalances and instabilities among intentional and unintentional signs in turn call our attention to the highly questionable project of declaring any historical style of popular music (1950s Nashville, 1960s psychedelia, 1970s disco) "alive" or "dead": who gets to decide; and by what criteria; and for what motives? As Allan Moore has noted, from a musical perspective, all too many rock "styles" have been, at best, musically underdetermined, and at worst, defined by institutions rather than musical features.[49] As a result, attempts to delimit a given musical style must often fall back on chronological boundaries, rendering any pronouncement of death tautological (e.g., "In 1997, progressive rock, as practiced between 1967 and 1977, is dead," or, "In 1997, grunge rock, as practiced between 1990 and 1996, is dead"). And then there's the troublesome business of trying to define the term *dead*: not currently produced? Not currently in the mainstream? Or perhaps some intermediate criterion: not currently selling *X*-thousand copies? "Dinosaur" thus poses a challenge to scholars of popular music: To what extent are we engaged in living, breathing historiography, and to what extent do we sometimes unwittingly fossilize the conventional biases of mainstream journalism, or mainstream musicology?

Just as the song "Dinosaur" can take on a richer meaning if we hear it in a way that Adrian Belew did not intend, I believe that the term *postprogressive* can take on a richer meaning if we read it in a way that Edward Macan did not intend. Whereas Macan introduces the word to signify "after progressive" (that is, chronologically occurring *after* the classic "progressive" rock style), I think it offers much more to popular-music scholars if we appropriate it to signify "after *progress*" (that is, having done with the metanarrative of forward historical development). Teleological models too often blind historians to interesting deviations that don't support their ideas of evolutionary development, resulting in regrettable omissions or misrepresentations. This has been the case, to varying degrees, in several treatments of progressive and postprogressive rock in the literature on popular music.[50] We could better understand these and many other idioms by adopting an increased awareness of how familiar, intuitively appealing ideas, such as the alleged life and death of musical styles, even when we apply such ideas with the best of intentions, can be used in order to lie.

Notes

An earlier version of this article was presented at the 1997 national meeting of the United States Chapter of the International Association for the Study of Popular

Music. Here I would like to thank Kevin Holm-Hudson for insightful comments and editorial guidance in bringing this essay to its present form; Tim Hughes and Theo Cateforis for perceptive responses to the conference presentation of this material; and Marty Hatch, Greg Karl, and John Covach for careful readings of a previous version of the manuscript.

1. Umberto Eco, *A Theory of Semiotics* (Bloomington: Indiana University Press, 1976), 3.

2. Ibid., 7.

3. Ibid., 17–19.

4. Strictly speaking, "progressive" rock represents a subset of styles within the broader category of "art" rock, but many writers use the terms interchangeably. Examples of art rock that typically aren't labeled as "progressive" include the music of Captain Beefheart, David Bowie, Brian Eno, Kraftwerk, Mike Oldfield, Talking Heads, Tangerine Dream, Vangelis, and Frank Zappa. For a general survey of art rock styles, see John Rockwell, "The Emergence of Art Rock," Anthony DeCurtis and James Henke, eds., *The Rolling Stone Illustrated History of Rock and Roll* (New York: Random House, 1992), 492–99. For a survey of the various substyles typically taken together under the rubric of progressive rock, see Allan Moore, "Progressive Styles and Issues," in *Rock: The Primary Text* (Philadelphia: Open University Press, 1993), 56–103; and Edward Macan, "The Progressive Rock Style: The Music" and "Related Styles," in *Rocking the Classics: English Progressive Rock and the Counterculture* (New York: Oxford University Press, 1997), 30–56 and 126–43.

5. Here I discount as perverse any nonmetaphorical readings of the lyric content, such as any that imagines being addressed by an articulate *Tyrannosaurus rex*, or which ascribes a delusional state to Belew, such that he believes himself to be a *T. rex*, or that imagines that a perfectly sane Belew has constructed a singing persona who is or believes himself to be a *T. rex*, and so on.

6. King Crimson, *THRAK*, Virgin compact disc 7243 8 40313 2 9 (1995). The term "THRAK" seems to have arisen as an onomatopoeiac label for polymetric combinations of percussive chords, as exemplified in this album's title track, which counterposes patterns in 5/8 and 7/8. See Eric Tamm's description of a 1986 precursor, in *Robert Fripp: From King Crimson to Guitar Craft* (Boston: Faber and Faber, 1990), 187.

7. Adrian Belew, "Adrian Belew Answers: Part Three," *Elephant Talk* 359 (March 9, 1997). *Elephant Talk* is an online newsletter devoted to King Crimson and related topics, moderated by Toby Howard; as of October 2000, it can be found at the website http://www.elephant-talk.com, maintained by Daniel Kirkdorffer. This three-part question-and-answer session with Belew can be found by searching the *Elephant Talk* archive, using the keywords "Belew Answers."

8. In the context of Belew's acoustic solo album *Belewprints: The Acoustic Adrian Belew, Volume Two* (Discipline Global Mobile DGM9802), his rendition of "Dinosaur" comes across as just such a personal statement. Without the King Crimson imprimatur—and, more importantly, without the dense King Crimson timbre—the song projects a far more intimate, less *collective* character.

9. Stanley Fish, "Is There a Text in This Class?" in *Is There a Text in This Class?* (Cambridge: Harvard University Press, 1980), 303–21.

10. Ibid., 307.

11. Ibid., 310.

12. Ibid., 321.

13. Hans Robert Jauss, *Toward an Aesthetic of Reception*, trans. by Timothy Bahti (Minneapolis: University of Minnesota Press, 1982), 79. Although Jauss is concerned with broader questions of a work's intertextual relation to genre rather than putatively intratextual constructions of meaning, his formulation seems entirely appropriate, for reasons that I hope my musical analysis will make clear.

14. That is, although the augmented triads can be heard locally as altered dominants, their unconventional resolutions complicate the project of extending such an interpretation over more than one or two measures.

15. This complex of third-related harmonies somewhat resembles the hexatonic systems of pitch organization, described by Richard L. Cohn, "Maximally smooth cycles, hexatonic systems, and the analysis of late-Romantic triadic progressions," *Music Analysis* 15, no. 1 (1996): 9–40.

16. When I first heard "Dinosaur" in the fall of 1996, I belonged to this category of listeners. At that time, my only prior knowledge of King Crimson consisted of having heard "In the Court of the Crimson King" on album-oriented rock radio in the 1970s, and having seen a brief video excerpt of "Larks' Tongues in Aspic, Part One" in September 1996.

17. One must distinguish here between the classic "prog-rock" that Yes and Genesis produced in the 1970s (on Yes albums such as *Fragile* and *Close to the Edge*, and on Genesis albums such as *Nursery Cryme* and *Foxtrot*) and the more mainstream rock these bands produced in the 1980s (on Yes albums such as *90125* and *Big Generator*, and on Genesis albums such as *Abacab* and *Invisible Touch*). For a more detailed discussion, see John Covach's "Progressive Rock, 'Close to the Edge,' and the Boundaries of Style," in John Covach and Graeme M. Boone, eds., *Understanding Rock: Essays in Musical Analysis* (New York: Oxford University Press, 1997), 4–5, and Edward Macan, *Rocking*, 191–95.

    It should also be noted that although King Crimson was widely perceived as an influential progressive-rock band, its musicians perceived themselves as operating *outside* that style. Macan quotes percussionist Bill Bruford: "[There was] no sense of alliance or cooperation in a musical movement between the chief players. In 1972–74, for example, no self-respecting member of King Crimson would have been seen dead in a musical movement that contained Genesis"—and this in reference to a time *before* Genesis turned to a more commercial style (Macan, *Rocking*, 25).

18. Many listeners (myself included) have instantly assumed that the bowed-string chords at the outset of "Dinosaur" are those of a mellotron. This assumption derives partly from an inexact memory of the mellotron orchestral-strings timbre, and partly from a predisposition generated by the liner notes of the *THRAK* jewel box, which (directly under the disc itself) credit Robert Fripp with "Guitar, soundscapes, mellotron."

   However, in the *Live in Japan* video (Discipline Global Mobile VC1), Belew can be seen triggering the bowed strings with his guitar, and in response to a fan's question online, he identifies the sound source as a patch he wrote for the Roland GR-1 guitar synthesizer ("Adrian Belew Answers: Part Two," *Elephant talk* 357 (March 6, 1997). Played side by side, the difference in timbres is hard to mistake, and the breaks in common tones from chord to chord hint at the use of a guitar as the controlling device, rather than a keyboard. (For clear comparison, prominent mellotron parts can be found at or near the beginnings of "Epitaph" and "In the Court of the Crimson King" on *In the Court of the Crimson King*, and in the introduction to "Starless" on *Red*.)

   Yet so powerful is the desire to hear the string sounds in "Dinosaur" as a mellotron that it can overwhelm even direct visual evidence to the contrary. In an online review of King Crimson's performance at Town Hall, New York City, June 3, 1995, Mitch Goldman writes that " 'Dinosaur' featured Belew's synthesized guitar playing; he duplicated the mellotron parts that Fripp plays on the *THRAK* LP." As of October 2000, this review can be found at http://ezone.org/ez/e4/articles/goldman/crimson.html.

19. King Crimson's lineup of personnel has changed over the years, sometimes drastically, with Fripp's participation the only constant. These various rosters have been classified somewhat differently by Eric Tamm and Robert Fripp, as shown in the last two columns of table 10.2. Rather than refer to the various incarnations by either Tamm's or Fripp's classification scheme, I'll always specify the active years of the lineup under discussion.

20. Although it's possible that someone could come to "Dinosaur" knowing *only* King Crimson's music of the 1970s, this seems a freakishly uncommon situation. Instead, it's far more likely that anyone who knows their 1970s music would also be aware of the band's 1980s incarnation. On the other hand, several of my friends who admire the 1980s King Crimson were surprised to learn that any version of the band existed prior to 1981. And, as I'll presently show, the most specific cue to cognoscenti refers to a track on one of the band's early albums rather than a later one.

21. Tamm, *Robert Fripp*, 137–38.

22. Macan, *Rocking*, 206–11.
23. That is, instead of multiplying the number of interlocking parts in the manner of the 1980s band, the double trio features more doubling of instruments on a part, frequently exploiting the extended range of pitches available on the Chapman stick and the Warr guitar (guitar-like instruments specifically designed for touch-style playing—that is, a style in which the player vibrates the strings by the force of tapping them against the fingerboard, rather than by plucking them with a guitar pick). The sextet can be heard playing almost literally as a double trio on the tracks "VROOOM" and "VROOOM VROOOM," thanks to the simple expedient of manipulating the balance between left and right channels during stereophonic playback. This procedure highlights the extent to which the same instrumental part is shared by two players, in contrast to portions of "Dinosaur," in which the same procedure may pan the same performer mixed left and right (such as Belew's vocal), or reveal that the two guitars are playing two different parts.
24. Tamm, *Robert Fripp*, 139. Through his teaching in Guitar Craft, Fripp continued to explore guitar counterpoints after he broke up King Crimson in 1984; such passages can be found in his work as recently as 1991, in the songs "Sunday All Over the World," "Transient Joy," and "Storm Angel." These tracks appear on the album *Kneeling at the Shrine* (Editions EG compact disc EEG 2101–2), which presents the collaboration of Fripp with his wife Toyah Willcox (singing), Paul Beavis (drumming), and Guitar Craft alumnus Trey Gunn (playing the Chapman stick), the ensemble recording under the name Sunday All Over The World.

    Fripp's temporary abandonment of "rock gamelan" is prefigured on the 1993 album *The Bridge Between* (Discipline compact disc DR 9303 2), which documents performances by another incidental project, the Robert Fripp String Quintet. Here, Fripp again collaborates with Trey Gunn, this time with three other Guitar Craft alumni. Although Fripp can be heard participating in typically intricate "Crafty" textures, these occur in tracks *not* composed by Fripp: "Bicycling to Afghanistan" (Curt Golden), "Kannon Power" (Hideyo Moriya), and "Blockhead" (Paul Richards).

    The latest line-up of King Crimson, as of 2001, is again a quartet, consisting of Fripp and Belew (who were in the 1981–84 formation) plus Trey Gunn (touch guitar and Ashbury bass) and Pat Mastelotto (electronic percussion). This new version of the group resulted from a series of improvisational permutations of the group described by Fripp as "ProjeKCts." To date the 2000–2001 quartet has released two recordings: *The ConstruKCtion of Light* (Virgin compact disc 7243 8 49261 2 0, 2000) and *Heavy ConstruKCtion* (Discipline Global Mobile compact disc DGM0013, 2000), a live recording from the *ConstruKCtion* quartet's May–July 2000 European tour.

I should stress that not all of *THRAK* sounds utterly unlike 1980s Crimson—in particular, the ballads "Walking on Air" and "One Time" clearly recall "Matte Kudesai" and "Two Hands." Nor has Fripp abandoned the 1980s rock gamelan compositions; to the contrary, their live performances regularly include "Frame by Frame," "Three of a Perfect Pair," and "Elephant Talk." What is striking is that none of the new compositions in 1994 incorporates rapidly interlocking textures. The nearest approximation is the 5/8 versus 7/8 of "THRAK," and this seems to represent a holdover from Guitar Craft (see note 6 above).

25. Robert Fripp, quoted in Tamm, *Robert Fripp*, 31.

26. Macan, *Rocking*, 210. The connection between "Red" and "VROOOM" is made musically explicit by the mechanically repeated eighth-note chords that appear in "VROOOM VROOOM." A musical bridge between "Red" and "VROOOM" can be found in the track "Breathless" on Fripp's 1979 solo album *Exposure* (Editions EG compact disc EGCD 41).

27. Adrian Belew, "Adrian Belew Answers: Part Two," *Elephant Talk* 357 (March 6, 1997). Interestingly, the interlude section is omitted from more recent performances of "Dinosaur"—as is evident from a 1996 performance on the live compilation *Cirkus: The Young Person's Guide to King Crimson Live* (Virgin compact disc 7243 8 47431 2 3, 1999) and from a June 2001 performance on *Heavy ConstruKCtion*. It may be that the overtly "chamber music" qualities of the instrumental section prompted its omission, as part of King Crimson's shedding of its "progressive rock" image.

28. Adrian Belew, liner notes to *Belewprints*. Belew uses almost the same words to describe this connection in response to a question online: "When I first began working on 'Dinosaur,' Robert mentioned that he would like to see the Krimson [*sic*] equivalent of 'I am [the] Walrus.' Though the two songs don't sound alike, I was thinking in those terms as I continued to work on 'Dinosaur.'" ("Adrian Belew Answers: Part Two," *Elephant Talk* 357 (March 6, 1997).

In a much-quoted remark, Robert Fripp has commented on the importance of the Beatles' *Sergeant Pepper's Lonely Hearts Club Band* (1967), especially the song "A Day in the Life," as a catalyst for the formation of King Crimson. Influences of other songs or albums are less often noted. In addition to serving as a model for "Dinosaur," one may trace to the coda of "I Am the Walrus" Fripp's interest in perpetual contrary motion between outer voices, such as occurs in portions of "Larks' Tongues in Aspic, Part One" (1973; see Gregory Karl's essay in this volume) and in "VROOOM VROOOM" (1994).

29. Adrian Belew, liner notes to *Belewprints*.

30. Edward Macan, *Rocking*, 23.

31. This theme can be heard several times in "Cirkus," at time indices 0:42–0:54, 1:29–1:55, 3:53–4:18, and 4:52–5:18. Belew, in the response

quoted earlier, states specifically that he had *not* been listening to early King Crimson at the time "Dinosaur" was created. Fripp had remastered *Lizard* for compact disc format in 1989—hence, when the band wrote "Dinosaur" in 1994, the material from the prior album was, at most, only five years distant in Fripp's memory, rather than twenty-four. The distilled, abstract character of the "Dinosaur" riff seems to conform to motives of Fripp's compositions since Guitar Craft, especially as heard in the onomatopoeically titled tracks "VROOOM," "VROOOM VROOOM," and "THRAK."

32. Adrian Belew, "Adrian Belew Answers: Part Two," *Elephant Talk* 357 (March 6, 1997).

33. Kevin Holm-Hudson tells me that Fripp has claimed as much, and that he "has recently indicated (on his diary at the DGM web site) that the B-flat to G guitar riff is indeed a reference to *Lizard*. (Whether he intended it to be so at the time or whether he is only now conceding that it could be a reference, responding to fans' (mis)interpretations, is something I suppose we shall never know; Fripp is notorious for revising his own history.)" Personal communication with the author, September 29, 1999.

   DGM is Discipline Global Mobile, Fripp's record company; unfortunately, as of October 2000, the DGM website (http://www.discipline. co.uk) doesn't offer a searchable archive in which to locate the appropriate entry from Fripp's online diary.

34. Fripp, quoted in Macan, *Rocking*, 206.

35. Tamm, *Robert Fripp*, 9.

36. See Tamm's account of his experience in Guitar Craft, *Robert Fripp*, 150–95. Fripp's inscrutable behavior and cultivation of skepticism toward himself as a leader recalls similar tactics employed by George Ivanovitch Gurdjieff toward his students: in Tamm's useful summary, "layers of acting, multiple personas, irony, sarcasm, ambiguity" (93).

37. Belew's art-rock credentials prior to King Crimson include touring with Frank Zappa, David Bowie, and Talking Heads; note that these artists are *not* typically associated with classic "prog-rock styles," and are thus less apt to be characterized in the popular press as "dinosaurs." Hence, for listeners at all familiar with King Crimson's personnel changes over the years, it's more natural to interpret the claim "I'm a dinosaur" as speaking for the band, rather than for Belew alone.

38. Note that in the online comment cited earlier, Belew explicitly states that the song "had nothing to do with the term 'dinosaur' in reference to an aging rock band," even though the immediate question doesn't even broach the subject. This mismatch implies that Belew is responding to a general *line* of questioning that he has faced before, based on the misinterpretation of the song as I've described it.

39. Bradley Bombarger, review of *THRAK, Rolling Stone*, June 29, 1995, 43.

40. As David Fricke has commented on the 1973–74 band, "At its most daring, King Crimson had more in common with jazz adventurers like the electric Miles Davis or the Art Ensemble of Chicago than it ever did with nominal art-rock peers like Yes and Genesis." Fricke, "Return of the Crimson King," *Rolling Stone*, April 29, 1993, 20.

41. Ibid. "Fripp notes with pride that guitarist Vernon Reid of Living Colour is an avowed fan of [the 1973] lineup . . . Reid told Fripp that one of his favorite Crimson tracks was 'The Great Deceiver,' from the '74 LP *Starless and Bible Black*." Bill Bruford refers to Cobain in an interview by Andras Toth for the Hungarian newspaper *Magyar narancs* (http://hix/mit/edu/ narancs): "I think some of the music is now probably a bit dated, but for example if you play 'Red,' it feels extremely fresh like it was written tomorrow, and it seems to resonate with the time. It was written in 1974, but it was taken on-board by some of the grunge people, Kurt Cobain mentioned it in public, it seems to be a very influential piece to him." This and other interviews with King Crimson personnel can be found at http://www.elephant-talk.com by following the links for "interviews."

42. Juliana Hatfield, *Only Everything*, Atlantic 92540–2 (1995); Fiona Apple, *Tidal*, Sony OK 67439 (1996). Hatfield's use of the mellotron in "My Darling" is one of several anachronistic coloristic touches on *Only Everything*, along with Wurlitzer electric piano on "Universal Heart-beat," theremin on "Dumb Fun," and Hohner clavinet on "Outsider." The Chamberlain appears on every track from *Tidal* except "Never is a Promise," which uses a real string quartet.

43. Alan Niester, review of *Larks' Tongues in Aspic, Rolling Stone*, August 31, 1973, 82.

44. See also Edward Macan, "The Critical Reception of Progressive Rock," in *Rocking*, 167–78.

45. See Covach, "Progressive Rock, 'Close to the Edge,' and the Boundaries of Style."

46. Moore, *Rock: The Primary Text*, 29.

47. At the Cross(over) Relations Conference held at the Eastman School of Music in September 1996, out of fifty-two papers read, thirteen were gathered under the rubric "Mini-conference on progressive rock"—a proportion of one in four. Compare this with only *four* papers on African-American composers and performers (Rich Will on Jimi Hendrix, Tim Hughes on Stevie Wonder, Mitchell Morris on Barry White, and Richard Rischar on vocal ornamentation by artists such as Whitney Houston, Mariah Carey, and Boyz II Men). During the session comprising the first three of these four, conference coorganizer Robert Fink revealed that these were the *only* papers on African-American topics proposed in response to the conference's

call for papers; so, for the total pool of proposals submitted, the proportion would be even lower than 8 percent.

48. See Susan McClary and Robert Walser, "Start Making sense! Musicology Wrestles with Rock," in Simon Frith and Andrew Goodwin, eds. *On Record* (New York: Pantheon Books, 1990), 277–92; John Covach, "We Won't Get Fooled Again: Rock Music and Musical Analysis," in David Schwarz, Anahid Kassabian, and Lawrence Siegel, eds., *Keeping Score: Music, Disciplinarity, Culture* (Charlottesville: University Press of Virginia, 1997), 75–89, also published in *In Theory Only* 13, nos. 1–4 (1997): 117–41; and Don Michael Randel, "The canons in the musicological tool-box," in Katherine Bergeron and Philip V. Bohlman, eds., *Disciplining Music: Musicology and its Canons* (Chicago: University of Chicago Press, 1992), 10–22.

49. Moore, *Rock: The Primary Text*, 58.

50. Historiographic attitudes in recent texts range from a single sympathetic paragraph in Paul Friedlander's *Rock and Roll: A Social History* (Boulder: Westview, 1996), 244, through peremptory dismissal via a single unsympathetic paragraph in Michael Campbell's *And the Beat Goes On: An Introduction to Popular Music in America, 1840 to Today* (New York: Schirmer Books, 1996), 282; to the extensive dismissal in John Rockwell's "The Emergence of Art Rock." These treatments may be contrasted with chapter-length discussions in Joe Stuessy, *Rock and Roll: Its History and Stylistic Development* (Englewood Cliffs, N.J.: Prentice-Hall, 1994) and in Moore, *Rock: The Primary Text* with Macan's book-length study, *Rocking the Classics*; and with the ongoing work of John Covach.

11 How Alternative Turned Progressive

The Strange Case of Math Rock

Theo Cateforis

This chapter considers progressive rock and its relationship with the "alternative rock" music culture of the 1990s.[1] At first glance, this might seem akin to mixing oil and water. In the 1990s, after all, alternative rock bands like Nirvana and Soundgarden deliberately bypassed the complexity of the typical progressive rock ensemble in favor of the simple, direct power of 1970s hard rock and punk guitar riffs. Similarly, where progressive rock lyricists and singers traditionally had looked outwards to fantastical and mythological topics, alternative rock vocalists like Pearl Jam's Eddie Vedder focussed inward, toward expressions of personal anguish. However, as journalist Neil Strauss has noted in a memorable 1997 *New York Times* article, these stylistic traits speak for only the most specified and narrow definition of alternative rock—the version favored by FM radio playlists and *Rolling Stone* features.[2] Strauss points out that contemporaneous with the Pearl Jam "mainstream" variety of alternative rock there existed in the 1990s a large, stylistically eclectic collection of comparatively obscure alternative rock artists spread across dozens of subgenres—among them "orchestrated pop," "noize," "analogue pop," "drone rock," "velvet introspection" etc.—with ties to influences running the gamut from the Beach Boys and the Velvet Underground to minimalism and the avant-garde. Strauss does not intend his list to be authoritative, but his point is well taken: alternative rock of the 1990s was not simply synonymous with the wave of grunge bands that Nirvana and Soundgarden helped spawn. The larger definition of 1990s alternative includes all manner of influences—even progressive—as part of its fold.

My focus centers around a descriptive "progressive" alternative rock category not found among Strauss's list but nonetheless familiar to most fans who have waded through any significant amount of 1990s rock critic journalistic lingo: *math rock*. Like many other well-traveled alternative subgenres, such as "slocore" (bands who play painfully slow songs) or "lo-fi" (bands who revel in the tape hiss of four-track home recordings), the clues to math rock's basic meanings are found in its name. Math rock bands are those whose songs suggest some parallels between mathematical abstraction and forms of musical complexity. Such a connection, as we will see, is more figurative than literal—most mathematicians would struggle to find any connection between their discipline and the music of a math rock band. But then again, the term *math rock* did not originate in mathematics. While its precise roots are unknown, math rock can be dated at least as far back as the late 1980s when it was first applied to a small number of mid-Atlantic and mid-Western American "college town" bands such as Butterglove, Breadwinner, Honor Role, Slint, and Bitch Magnet, steeped in the punk and underground rock scenes of cities such as Richmond, Virginia and Louisville, Kentucky.[3] While the collected recorded output of these bands amounts to little more than a handful of EPs and albums on tiny independent labels, they initiated a novel brand of heavy, guitar-based rock that combined the rhythmic power of thrash metal bands, such as Metallica, with the nuanced, interwoven ostinato patterns of mid-1970s and early-1980s King Crimson. Math rock continued to spread in the 1990s with the releases of artists such as Craw, Shellac, Don Caballero, Drive Like Jehu, Helmet, Pitchblende, Shudder to Think, Uzeda, and many more.

Math rock can be distilled to a few main features. The most prominent of these is the extensive use of asymmetrical or "odd" time signatures and shifting mixed meters. This gesture could be considered "mathematical" in as much as it dispenses with the evenly divided rhythmic pulse common to the largest majority of rock music and elevates the numerical accents of the music's odd metrical patterns to a position of prime importance. For fanatical listeners and music analysts alike, the experience of a math rock song can often turn into a counting exercise, as one tries to follow the twisting metrical constructions. But math rock's name also seems to derive from a more symbolic understanding of mathematics as a discipline of logic, abstraction, and precision. Math rock guitarists rarely play chord progressions, leaving behind the teleological implications of tonal harmony in favor of stark shifts between contrasting scalar and harmonic patterns. Likewise, most math rock bands dispense with traditional verse/chorus forms, often deploying lyrics composed of seemingly random metaphoric tableaux and static imagery lacking in any strong narrative impulse. Some math rock bands such as Don Caballero eschew vocals entirely, building their songs out of modular instrumental sections.

Math rock's musical complexities, like those of progressive rock, present numerous opportunities for musical analysis. Yet these features should not obscure the music's specific cultural significances. Math rock, for example, seems notable for the degree to which it makes difficult the act of ritualized dance, negating one of popular music's most enduring social forces. While much math rock consists of upbeat tempos, the music generally lacks a repetitive rhythmic character, such as one might find in the shape of a backbeat, one-drop, four-to-the-floor or syncopated Latin groove. Listeners, it would seem, are offered few points of bodily identification. In the absence of a steady, divisible pulse, math rock has instead been depicted as "sharp," "jagged," and "angular" music. These descriptions, of course, can be applied to conceptions of the body. But the visions they conjure resemble more the distorted bodies of a cubist Pablo Picasso painting than the smooth sway of bodies on a dance floor. As we will see, there are other ways as well in which math rock's musical impulses relate to the body. But before we address such issues, it will be helpful to consider in greater depth some of the features that distinguish math rock as a musical practice. We thus begin with the analysis of a prototypical math rock song, the instrumental "Stupid Puma," off of one of the genre's better-known albums, Don Caballero's 1995 release *Don Caballero 2*.

Math Rock: Analyzing Complexity

> Don Caballero is Instrumental
> Don Caballero is Rock Not Jazz
> Don Caballero is Free of Solos[4]

This statement, which was included on promotional copies of *Don Caballero 2*, is the closest that one could hope to come in defining a succinct math rock manifesto. As these few pithy sentences indicate, math rock frowns upon virtuosity for the sake of showmanship. In this respect math rock departs from the typical 1970s progressive rock or 1980s heavy metal band. While math rock songs may be technically imposing and demonstrate the players' dexterity, at no point are they virtuosic in the sense that many would understand that term. The song's unified complexity collapses the distinction between figure and ground. As the fanzine *Tuba Frenzy* summarized in a discussion of math rock, "[for a virtuosic heavy metal guitarist like Yngwie Malmsteen] the music serves as a cushion on which to show off. To show people that he can play, to demonstrate his physical dexterity on a piece of wood, [whereas a math rock] band like Breadwinner—they're not playing fast for any other reason then [*sic*] the bridge needs to be fast to work well as it segues from the chorus or whatever."[5] Math rock is music of precise, rigid control and dazzling musical communication, but at the genre's center there exists no overt subject. The Dionysian heroic lead is cast aside, leaving only the music's skeletal framework of riffs and patterns. In the end, math rock's intense self-discipline and self-denial resembles most of all a form of musical asceticism.

    "Stupid Puma" exemplifies the importance of "the riff" as part of math rock's stringent musical style. At nearly four and a half minutes in duration, "Stupid Puma" is one of the album's shorter songs. Still, its form is dense—the song divides into roughly seven discrete sections, each of which revolves around a single looped guitar riff. These riffs give the song a grounded, repetitive framework. Table 11.1 outlines the form of "Stupid Puma" as divided through these guitar riffs. This outline traces the song's general form along two specific parameters: shifts between different meters and between different harmonic areas or motivic ideas. As the diagram shows, there is a remarkable fluidity to the song's overall metric shape. Only near the song's conclusion does the meter hold over from one section to the other.

While I have assigned distinct meters to each of the looped riffs in table 11.1, it is important to point out that the patterns *within* these meters are not immutable. Often these loops have an ambiguous quality that invites multiple readings. The opening 5/8 riff (section A; see figure 11.1) for example, which begins with guitar alone, initially sounds *not* as if it phrased in a 3 + 2 eighth-note grouping (as notated in table 11.1), but in a 2 + 3 pattern. The riff initially begins on the second eighth note and divides into a B–F-sharp interval that then swoops down to C–F-sharp—G, which we hear as an adjoining phrase. But when the rhythm section enters, their accents shift the pattern over one eighth-note to create the 3 + 2 grouping notated in the example. We now hear G as the downbeat, and the lower F-sharp serves as a slurred pickup.

Table 11.1. "Stupid Puma" Outline.

Section	Length	Meter	Key Area
A	16 repetitions	5/8	E minor
B	8 repetitions	11/8 [3/4 & 5/8]	G♯ phrygian
C	interlude (4 bars)	3/4 5/4 3/4 4/4	AM7 chord
B	4 repetitions	11/8 [3/4 & 5/8]	G♯ phrygian
D	8 repetitions	12/8 [5/8 & 7/8]	C–F♯ tritone
E	8 repetitions	7/8	A phrygian
A	108 repetitions	5/8	C–F♯ tritone
F	16 repetitions	6/8	A♯–E, A–D♯ tritones
G1	16 repetitions	6/8	G major, with tritones
		Pause	
G2	8 repetitions	5/8	G major, with tritones
		Pause	
G2	8 repetitions	5/8	G major, with tritones
		Tag	

Fig. 11.1 Section A.

Further ambiguities arise in section B (see fig. 11.2) when the meter changes to 11/8. I have notated the pattern in two phrases of 6/8 + 5/8, but drummer Damon Che's articulations complicate this reading. Because Che accents this pattern with five solid quarter-note beats on the open high hat, one is likely to hear the pattern as a 4/4 meter with an added 3/8 bar, or as a 3/4 pattern with an added measure of 5/8. The latter of these two makes more sense because such a division preserves the guitar loop's internal G-sharp–D-sharp–G-sharp–A–C-sharp–(A) repetition. Overall, such "slippery" relationships add dramatically to the complexity of the song's surface texture.

From a stylistic standpoint, section B demonstrates one of math rock's strongest affinities—with the power riffing of heavy metal. The guitarists jettison the relatively clean tone color of section A in favor of a distorted sound played with slashing power chords. In addition, the riff's implied phrygian scale assumes a melodic shape that could be considered almost a cliché of the late 1980s/early 1990s heavy metal guitar lingo popularized by bands like Metallica. As Don Caballero guitarist Ian Williams explained to me, though, their heavy metal allusions are never entirely "straight." The band flaunts their metal riffs, aware that they are clichés. The endeavor is thus partly ironic. While math rock may adopt some of heavy metal's timbre and harmonic language, there is a looseness, even a knowing "sloppiness," to much of the music that a heavy metal band would find intolerable. One hears this in section C (see fig. 11.3). This section essentially is an interlude driven by four brief A major 7 chords, which divide the passage

Fig. 11.2. Section B.

Fig. 11.3. Section C.

approximately into four measures of 3/4, 5/4, 3/4, 4/4. The meter, though, is not exact. Che plays an awkward, unexpected drum fill on the fifth beat of the 5/4 measure that momentarily jerks the pulse, creating a hesitation. His fill draws the song out of its pulse, and makes the identification of the 5/4 meter fuzzy at best. For all of math rock's precision, many times it is not exact. A heavy metal band typically would "clean up" such rough spots. Don Caballero, however, are not a heavy metal band—their music reflects more the gritty realism of punk and alternative. As such, few fans would confuse a math rock song such as "Stupid Puma" as belonging within the realm of heavy metal.

On the whole, "Stupid Puma" enjoys a more profound link not with heavy metal, but with ideas of minimalist musical performance, particularly those of Steve Reich's early 1970s compositions such as *Drumming* and King Crimson's early 1980s albums *Discipline* and *Beat*. This connection especially leaps out at the listener in the song's sprawling middle section, which lasts nearly two minutes and spans 108 repetitions of the song's opening riff. The repetitions in this section of "Stupid Puma" are not merely persistent, but are subjected to what sounds like a series of processual changes. Much as Reich shifts the accent patterns in his minimalist pieces to create a dynamic, rippling surface effect, so Don Caballero's guitarists use offbeat chordal accents to highlight the riff's ambiguous nature, thus emphasizing a quality which had been subtly implied in the song's opening measures. But unlike Reich, Don Caballero do not employ any large formal or processual designs in the middle section of "Stupid Puma." They simply juxtapose two different chordal accents in the guitar to create their variety. The first chordal accent, stressed on the third eighth-note, F-sharp, splits the pattern into a 2 + 3 division (this is notated as section A, variation 1; see fig. 11.4). The second chordal accent, however, stressed on the fourth eighth note, C, splits the

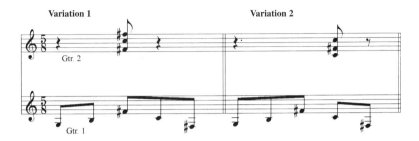

Fig. 11.4. Section A, Variations 1 and 2.

pattern into a 3 + 2 division (this is notated as section A, variation 2; see fig. 11.4). These two accents receive equal time as the band plays each one four times before alternating and playing four repetitions of the other. These accents start to merge slightly as the guitarists place a short pickup emphasis on the third eighth-note as it leans into the louder fourth eighth-note accent. Eventually they throw the entire pattern off course when they emphasize the second eighth-note, B, for four repetitions, creating a new temporary downbeat. The primary 3 + 2 accent pattern soon resumes, though, and the band moves into a new set of timbral variations. The guitarists play the riff as harmonics, and drummer Damon Che explores the lighter sounds of rim clicks before moving to the sustained buzz of a ragged snare drum roll.

As the lengthy middle section gradually unfurls, it also becomes more and more apparent just how central the interval of the tritone is to the song's general harmonic character. Not only is the interval C–F-sharp embedded in the riff's 5/8 center, but it also is the interval around which the middle section's two main guitar chord accents are centered. It is featured as well as part of the main riff in section D (see fig. 11.5). It is little surprise that the tritone should hold a fasci-

Fig. 11.5. Section D.

nation not only for Don Caballero, but for math rock bands in general. With its decentered shape, spanning the length of three whole tones, the tritone provides the ideal "abstract" sound. It is a perfect complement to math rock's "abstract" meters. By the song's end, "Stupid Puma" has become saturated with tritone colorings beyond the initial F-sharp–C interval. Section F uses chord punctuations with alternating A-sharp–E and A–D-sharp tritones, and section G's various manifestations revolve around a C-sharp–G chord that overrides the apparent g major scale implied by the guitar's descending B–A–G line (see figs. 11.6–11.8). In math rock songs such as "Stupid Puma," where the idea of modal or harmonic key areas are at times rendered obsolete, the tritone serves as an ideal harmonic substitute.

Fig. 11.6. Section F, Variations 1 and 2.

Fig. 11.7. Section G.

Fig. 11.8. Section G2.

Math Rock, Mathematics, and the Body

Based on this analysis of "Stupid Puma," a mathematician could easily argue that there is painfully little about such a song that could be considered mathematical. I have demonstrated the many ways in which one may "count out" the song's content, but this leaves us, at best, at the level of rudimentary arithmetic. Does the connection between math rock and mathematics run any deeper? In order to attempt an answer, I want to frame my analysis in terms of what it represents: a transcription. A transcription approaches a song like "Stupid Puma" as an oral, temporally sounding phenomenon and asks of it, "What is really going on in the music?"[6] Transcription, as such, is a partial response to the problem of how one can best freeze sound and represent it through notation. In this respect it is similar in function, if not result, to the act of mathematical problem solving. Both a transcription and a mathematical problem seek a solution.

I can best explain how my experience transcribing math rock and Don Caballero's "Stupid Puma" might be related to mathematical problem solving through an analogy. In his book *Emblems of Mind*, a study of the links between music and mathematics, the music critic Edward Rothstein explains the "beauty" of mathematics by recounting a famed fable about the mathematical prodigy Carl Friedrich Gauss. When Gauss was ten, his class at school was given a long addition problem to solve. "They were asked to add the numbers from 1 to 100 (or some similar series). Gauss thought a moment, then wrote down the answer: 5,050. The trick of such a calculation had been known, of course, but not to the young Gauss. Nevertheless, he recognized that if you take the first and last numbers in the series (1 and 100) and add them that you get 101. If you take the second and second to last, you also get 101, and so forth until you add 50 to 51. There were fifty such pairs of numbers. Hence the answer was 50 x 101."[7] One could have solved the problem simply by adding all the numbers together, but the "beauty" of Gauss's solution, Rothstein suggests, is that his method recognizes a pattern, and then employs the pattern to understand the working of a series. Gauss takes what, on the surface, appears to be a complex, or at least laborious, task and through the logic of abstraction shows the pattern capable of solving the problem. The simplicity of the pattern in the face of the problem's enormity is what makes the mathematical solution "beautiful."

The process and goal of transcription in analyzing a math rock song like "Stupid Puma" approximates Rothstein's descriptive aesthetic of mathematical "beauty." A math rock song presents the music analyst with a "problem." The song's shifting meters and complex rhythms give the illusion of a high surface density and musical complexity. As any introductory music class instructor can testify, it is difficult enough for many "untrained" listeners to locate the beat and measures in as simple a meter as 4/4. Math rock only intensifies the problem. If the listener does not recognize the patterns that dictate the song's many meters, then the prospect of counting through that song can indeed seem daunting—not unlike having actually to add all of the numbers to find the solution to Gauss's mathematical problem. But when one finally locates the patterns that provide the song with a unifying logic, then the solution seems "beautiful" in its simplicity. Through the manipulation of a handful of patterns, the song's mystifying complexity has seemingly disappeared. For math rock fans who engage the music on this level, their listening experience undoubtedly becomes a strong form of empowerment. They have solved a metrical puzzle.

Because my own experience of analyzing math rock involved locating and counting out these intensified riffs and patterns, I presumed that for most math rock groups the act of "keeping time" was a matter of prime importance. But according to Ian Williams, he and his fellow band members arrived at their riffs and patterns not by consciously "counting out" their music's complex metrical grids, but more by instinct. Even though a music analyst might hear that a song's meters were in 5 or 7 or some asymmetrical combination, this did not necessarily mean that it was the band's *intention* to play in that specific meter.[8] Most math rock guitarists, Williams claimed, were most likely simply imitating a style and sound. Williams described Don Caballero's compositional process as one where he would bring in the riffs for new band material, play them, and then, if necessary, count them out to aid in the learning process. The crucial point is that he would arrive at a pattern first, but would assign it a meter only at a later juncture. Like many rock musicians, then, math rock players do not want the compositional process to become premeditated. They value the spontaneity of discovery. And in this respect, the complexity of the meter in math rock is best understood as a descriptive, not prescriptive, trait.

To summarize the complexity of "counting" in math rock, a disjunction must be recognized between my analysis and the way that the music is conceived. When I give a label to complexity in my math rock analysis, I must locate the patterns, and to do this I must count them out. I will, of necessity, focus my attention squarely on the music's meter. However, the math rock musicians do not worry themselves with the type of "brute force solution" that I must employ to understand this complexity.[9] They work through the mathematical problem backward, beginning with the answer key, and filling in the solution (the meter) only to make sense of the answer. While these two conceptions of math rock are not the same, both math rock's creation and reception nonetheless focus around the riff. Because math rock's asymmetrical patterns represent the style's structural core, they assume a heightened significance. Math rock is, if nothing else, about the riff or the pattern. Math rock confronts the problem of composition and arrives at a brazenly abstract solution. The vagaries of verse/chorus or lyric narrative structures are dispensed with. The math rock musicians intensify their gazes upon the riff until it becomes the music's overwhelming essence.

Math rock's rigorous musical approach is reflected in the music's critical reception. Journalists and fans alike constantly describe math rock invoking the imagery of machines, architecture, surgery, and the military. These disparate areas are linked together by their emphases on precision and discipline. Consider the following excerpts, lifted from reviews of math rock records and artists:

- (on machinery:) "guitars that methodically churn like threshers through a wheat field, underpinned by coldly relentless lunge-lurch rhythms"[10]
- (on architecture:) "powerful drumming undergirds a complicated lattice of harmonically puzzling, contrapuntal guitar lines and thick, propulsive basslines"[11]
- (on surgery:) "[the songs resemble] sharp and succinct methods of acupuncture treatment"[12]

- (on the military:) "[Helmet] formulated a metal-bore sound so clean, crisp and martial that some wags adopted Teutonic accents when discussing 'das precision rock sound.'"[13]

As distinctive as this discourse may be, it did not originate with math rock. Such terms were already part of the discourse attending Metallica's popularity in the mid-1980s. Consider, for example, Simon Reynolds's review of Metallica's influential 1988 math-metal album *And Justice For All*. . . . Reynolds's description, which paints a world where the smooth lines, curves, frailities, and imperfections of the human body have been replaced by sharp angles, vectors and surgical incisions, could be taken as a virtual primer of the type of thorough-going interpretive language that has accompanied math rock through the 1990s:

> Musically the key word is hygiene. This is completely sublimated rock, on a quest of a purity of form, light years beyond raunch or blues rock. Metallica turn heavy metal's melodrama into algebra. This isn't thrash, but thresh: mechanized mayhem. There's no blur, no mess, not even at peak velocity, but a rigorous grid of incisions and contusions. Everything depends on utter punctuality and supreme surgical finesse. It's probably the most incisive music I've ever heard, in the literal sense of the word.
>
> Metallica are austere, but they're also generous. Their songs are epic constructions, that use up and discard hundreds of riffs that other bands would give their eye teeth for. At its best, there's a concentrated complexity that suggests the almost stellar beauty that mathematicians claim is to be found in the higher reaches of pure maths. The tempo shifts, gear changes, lapses, decelerations and abrupt halts, play unnerving games with your sense of time. Nothing flows, everything is severed from itself.[14]

By employing the language of machinery ("gear changes," "decelerations," "abrupt halts") to describe the human practice of making music, Reynolds in effect infers a metaphorical equation that posits that the acts of "people" are equivalent with those of "machines." The music's asymmetries invite such comparisons. As Ian Williams explained to me, he believes that math rock's odd time signatures give the music an "impersonal" or even "nonhuman" quality.[15] Because the human body itself is symmetrical—two arms, two legs, and so on— Williams suggests that we naturally navigate ourselves to the motions of symmetrical rhythms and metrical patterns. Math rock forces the body to make sense of the music via alternate methods (through comparisons to machines, for example). In this respect Williams echoes the arguments of sociolinguist George Lakoff and philosopher Mark Johnson, who have posited that such metaphoric comparisons are not merely fanciful or decorative, but basic conceptual tools.[16] Metaphors stem from our bodily experience of our surrounding environment. As such, they allow us a means to understand music's otherwise fleeting, temporal properties. Whether we couch the music in metaphors of machines of geometrical figures, these constructions ground the music in an experiential realm.

Math rock's most pervasive metaphor—which implies that "people are machines"—is rooted deeply in the history of human experience. As far back as the seventeenth century, philosophers such as René Descartes adopted the mechanics of the clock as a metaphorical map by which one could understand the inner workings of the human physique.[17] Over the centuries this metaphor has changed to match advancements in society and technology. Yet regardless of whether the human body has been compared to the component parts of a motor engine or the human mind to the structure of a computer, the equation has provided a forceful means for understanding human experience. In the case of math rock, the metaphor has offered a point of reference both for those who would praise and criticize the music. Either math rock musicians are honored for their ability to mimic the precision of machinery or they leave cold those who hear the music as devoid of a subjective or "human" center. Either way, the reactions are rarely neutral.

Concluding Thoughts: For Whom the Music Sounds

This chapter gives an overview of the alternative genre math rock, and suggests some ways of understanding its progressive characteristics. Although I have focused on math rock's supposed "mathematical" parameters, such as its asymmetrical meters, I do not want to leave the reader with the impression that these qualities constitute math rock's complete generic domain. Math rock albums have been colored by many other influences, ranging from world music to avant-garde jazz. Also, despite the significant role that abstraction plays in math rock, one can point to many songs—such as those on Slint's influential *Spiderland*, for example—that contain obvious narrative lyric structures.

As with most genres, math rock's meaning is flexible; its scope changes according to the tastes of its audiences and practitioners. This was made apparent to me when I posted to an Internet music listserv the question of what the term *math rock* might mean, and asked if people could offer examples of math rock bands. In answer to my query, a few people responded that they had thought that math rock referred not only to the bands that I have mentioned in this chapter, but also to other recent "indie" artists such as Tortoise, The Sea and Cake, Rachel's, and June of 44, among others. All of these bands are aligned by an experimental attitude, and a desire to expand popular music's language through the addition of such elements as jazz, classical music, and electronics. Sonically they share very little with a band such as Don Caballero. Their textures are much lighter, the instrumentation more varied, the mathematical component of "counting" less prominently used, and their timbres largely devoid of the powerful guitar crunch so essential to the math rock described in this chapter. Apparently the *math rock* label has gravitated toward these bands because their nonrock influences make the music somehow more "difficult to understand."[18] In this formulation math rock is equated not with a particular style, but with the idea of complexity itself. Much as mathematics is often seen in Western culture as a generic symbol of complexity, so math rock has become a free-floating "complex" signifier. Math rock has come, through its dissemination, to signify complexity of virtually any stripe on the underground music scene.

If the term *math rock* has come increasingly to simply mean "difficult" music, then its wide acceptance as a communicative genre is evidence of an audience constituency not bound by any strict stylistic or subcultural fences. In this respect the initial emergence of math rock in the early 1990s marks one of the major points where the insular stylistic allegiances once so crucial to alternative music in the 1980s began to fall by the wayside. It is important to remember that in the 1980s the majority of alternative listeners defined themselves *against* heavy metal, hard rock, and progressive rock. Complexity of the type that would surface later in math rock bands was not valued, but abhorred. Near the decade's end, though, the 1970s classic hard rock and metal canon considered anathema to most alternative audiences suddenly began to gain a new cachet. Led Zeppelin, for example, who during their time had been dismissed as emblems of overindulgence, began receiving in the late 1980s lavish, glowing critical reappraisals.[19] Most significantly, in 1990 Joe Carducci published his wildly polemical tome *Rock and the Pop Narcotic*, in which he extolled the virtues of 1970s hard rock music side by side with those of punk groups like Black Flag.[20] What made this so astonishing was that Carducci was not a rock critic; he was a punk insider who had cut his teeth working for SST records, the most prolific 1980s American underground record label. Carducci's influential book blurred the lines between alternative rock and the pantheon of classic rock and metal canons. By the mid-1990s, it had become virtually de rigueur for alternative and indie artists to embrace a multitude of previously forsaken styles. Alternative had become a world where "the Velvet Underground and AC/DC can peacefully coexist on one record shelf."[21]

Math rock today stands on the broken rubble of the glaring audience dichotomies that once helped define 1980s alternative music. In this new light math rock has become emblematic of a generation of young, educated, and musically inquisitive middle-class listeners. They are much like the musicians that Cotten Seiler describes in his ethnography of the Louisville, Kentucky "independent" scene, which in the late 1980s and early 1990s was home to such important math rock bands as Slint and Rodan. As Seiler describes, the musicians in these and other bands seemed consciously aware of their positions as "artists" and valued the ability to forge new artistic inroads, however "difficult" they might be. Classical, jazz, punk, and the avant-garde alike were open for exploration. Encouraged by such record labels as Touch and Go and Drag City, Louisville's alternative bands drifted away from the scene's punk sources and, as Seiler suggests, their music became the stuff of "bedroom contemplation."[22] That math rock should thrive in such an environment, though, ultimately provides us with one of the genre's most ironic disjunctions. The music is so visceral in its musical textures that its harsh, propulsive rhythms practically demand some form of active (even if mechanical) motion. Yet math rock's audience, for the largest part, seems to have confined themselves to their bedrooms to contemplate the music's mesmerizing complexities.

Notes

1. For his contributions to this chapter I am indebted most of all to Ian Williams of Don Caballero. Richard Nance and the other members of the "Mark Eitzel—Firefly" listserv provided valuable insights as well. Lastly, special thanks are due to David Hurtgen for his help with the transcriptions, and to Shawn Singh, who helped with the musical examples.
2. Neil Strauss, "Forget Pearl Jam. Alternative Rock Lives," *New York Times*, March 2, 1997, sec. H, p. 34.
3. Ian Williams, interview, December 11, 1999. Butterglove and Breadwinner both formed in Richmond, Virginia. Slint formed in Louisville, Kentucky, and Bitch Magnet formed at Oberlin College in Ohio before moving to Chapel Hill, North Carolina.
4. This statement is taken from the promotional CD copy of *Don Caballero 2* and is not included on the actual commercial release.
5. A. C. Lee, "Straight Outta Context: A Dialogue with Polvo's Dave Brylawski," *Tuba Frenzy* 3 (1996), 53.
6. Peter Winkler, "Writing Ghost Notes: The Poetics and Politics of Transcription," in David Schwarz, Anahid Kassabian, and Lawrence Siegel, eds., *Keeping Score: Music, Disciplinarity, Culture* (Charlottesville: University of Virginia Press, 1997), 169–203.
7. Edward Rothstein, *Emblems of Mind: The Inner Life of Music and Mathematics* (New York: Avon Books, 1995), 143.
8. This was confirmed for me not only by Ian Williams, but also in a personal correspondence (May 13, 1999) with Richard Nance, the drummer for a 1980s 'proto' math-rock band, The Dust-Devils. Nance claimed that his New York–based band, which often drew comparisons to Sonic Youth, had written songs in 7 and 9, but that they never bothered, as a group, "to count it out."
9. Rothstein refers to a "brute force solution" in *Emblems of Mind*, 141, as a solution to a mathematical problem that recognizes no shortcut, but rather attempts to prove its answer through a lengthy chain of steps and exact measurements.
10. Greg Kot, "Tar," in Ira Robbins, ed., *The Trouser Press Guide To '90s Rock* (New York: Fireside, 1997), 725.
11. Peter Margasak, "Slint," in ibid., 661.

12. Tim Ross, "Don Caballero—2, Review," *Tuba Frenzy*, 69.

13. David Sprague, "Helmet," in Robbins, ed., *Trouser Press*, 342.

14. Simon Reynolds, *Blissed Out: The Raptures of Rock* (London: Serpent's Tail, 1990), 165.

15. Ian Williams, personal correspondence, October 16, 2000.

16. George Lakoff and Mark Johnson, *Philosophy in the Flesh: The Embodied Mind and its Challenge to Western Thought* (New York: Basic Books, 1999).

17. On the history of the metaphor equating "man" and "machine," see Andrew Kimbrell, *The Human Body Shop: The Engineering and Marketing of Life* (San Francisco: HarperCollins, 1993) and Anson Rabinbach, *The Human Motor* (Berkeley and Los Angeles: University of California Press, 1990).

18. In my December 11, 1999, interview with Ian Williams he concurred that math rock indeed had accrued this broad generic domain.

19. See Joe Gore and Andrew Goodwin, "Your Time Is Gonna Come: Talking about Led Zeppelin," *One Two Three Four* no. 4 (1987): 4–11.

20. Joe Carducci, *Rock and the Pop Narcotic: Testament for the Electric Church*, 2nd ed. (Los Angeles: 2.13.61, 1994).

21. David Daley, "Veruca Salt: Hell's Belles," *Alternative Press* 11, no. 108 (1997): 58.

22. Cotton Seiler, "Something in the Water: Independent Rock Music in Louisville, Kentucky," M.A. thesis, University of Kansas, 1998, 56.

Notes on Contributors

Durrell S. Bowman's dissertation, "Permanent Change: Culture, Ideology, Genre, and the Music of the Rock Band Rush" (UCLA, 2001), involves musical-cultural interpretations of the Toronto band's "progressive hard rock." He has taught three courses (on film music, the music for film noir and Hitchcock suspense-thrillers, and music appreciation) and has also presented a number of conference papers. His media-enriched review-article about *South Park: Bigger, Longer and Uncut* and his article on "art rock" (for the *Encyclopaedia Britannica*) were both published online in late 1999. He is planning for an academic career in musicology but is also developing a web-based, media-enriched learning program and is active as a semiprofessional choral tenor. He used to sing lead vocals and play keyboards in a rock cover band.

Theo Cateforis is a visiting instructor of music at the College of William and Mary. He received his Ph.D. in music history from the State University of New York at Stony Brook. His publications have appeared in *The Journal of Popular Music Studies* and the book *Musics of Multicultural America*.

John S. Cotner is completing a Ph.D. in music theory at the University of Wisconsin-Madison. His dissertation, provisionally titled "Archetypes of Progressive Rock circa 1966–1973," deconstructs aesthetic and ideological codes in 1960s and 1970s rock, and offers alternative approaches to the analysis of recorded musical works by Jimi Hendrix, Pink Floyd, the Beatles, and King Crimson. His recent article "Music Theory and Progressive Rock Style Analysis" appears in the book *Reflections on American Music,* volume 17 of *Monographs and Bibliographies in American Music* published by the College Music Society. He received Bachelors and Masters degrees in theory and composition from the University of Arizona, and has taught there, at the University of Wisconsin, and at Madison Area Technical College. His research interests include postromantic extended tonality, musical semiotics, and aesthetics.

Kevin Holm-Hudson is an assistant professor of music theory at the University of Kentucky. He has also taught music theory at Syracuse University, the University of Illinois, and at Northwestern University. His research interests include American twentieth-century experimental music and analysis of popular music; he has presented papers on these topics for the Society for Music Theory, the (Sonneck) Society for American Music, and the International Association for the Study of Popular Music. He is also the author of articles published in *Leonardo Music Journal, National Association of Schools of Music Proceedings,* and *Popular Music and Society.*

Gregory Karl holds a Ph.D. in musicology from the University of Cincinnati. He has taught at the University of Virginia, worked in the orchestra libraries of the Cincinnati Orchestra and Boston Symphony, and is a partner in Measure for Measure, a music copying, library, and preparation service based in New York. His research interests include the music of Prokofiev and Shostakovich and narrative elements of musical structure. He has published articles in *The Journal of Musicological Research, Music Theory Spectrum, GAMUT,* and *Music Research Forum,* and is the author, with Jenefer Robinson, of "Shostakovich's Tenth Symphony and the Musical Expression of Cognitively Complex Emotions" in *Music and Meaning.*

Brian Robison is a composer, singer, instrumentalist, and conductor. He has taught in the Department of Music at Cornell University, where he completed his doctorate, and in the School of Music at Ithaca College; he has also served as assistant director of the United States Office of Répertoire International de Littérature Musicale. As a composer, he has received awards from the Pennsylvania State University, the American Conservatory at Fontainebleau, and Cornell University, and commissions from the Bucket Consort, the Paterson Duo, and the American Composers Orchestra. In addition to progressive rock, he has written on Brazilian popular music, applications of fuzzy-set theory in music analysis, and the music of Harrison Birtwistle. As a teenager, Brian first encountered the octatonic collection in a column in *Guitar Player* magazine.

Jennifer Rycenga writes on the intersection of politics, sexuality, music and religious experience. She has published articles on lesbian experience and music in *Queering the Pitch* (edited by Philip Brett, Elizabeth

Wood, and Gary Thomas, Routledge 1994) and *Keeping Score* (edited by David Schwartz, Anahid Kassabian and Lawrence Siegel, University of Virginia 1997). She is coeditor, with Marguerite Waller, of *Frontline Feminisms: Women, War and Resistance* (Garland, 2000), which includes her article on the black abolitionist feminist Maria Stewart. Rycenga is an associate professor of comparative religious studies at San José State University.

John J. Sheinbaum has taught at Cornell University and the University of Rochester, and is currently an assistant professor of musicology at the Lamont School of Music of the University of Denver. His primary research interests include Western art music of the nineteenth and early twentieth centuries, popular music, and historiography. He is completing a dissertation at Cornell University on cultural readings of orchestration and form in Mahler's symphonies.

Dirk von der Horst is adjunct lecturer of Liberal Studies at Southeastern University, Washington D.C. He holds a Master of Theological Studies from Garrett-Evangelical Theological Seminary and a Master of Arts in critical and comparative studies in music from the University of Virginia. His research interests lie primarily in the intersections of religion, music, and sexual politics. He is currently preparing an essay on Antonio Cesti's *Orontea* for publication.

Deena Weinstein is an internationally known specialist in rock music studies. Her books include *Heavy Metal: The Music and Its Culture* and *Postmodern(ized) Simmel* (Routledge, 1993). She has also published eighteen book chapters and forty articles in professional journals on topics ranging from sociology of rock music to postmodernist theory. She is a professor of sociology at DePaul University and is also a long-time rock critic for various magazines.

Index